SCHOOLS
and DELINQUENCY

Kenneth Polk

University of Oregon

Walter E. Schafer

University of Oregon

PRENTICE-HALL, INC., ENGLEWOOD CLIFFS, NEW JERSEY

Prentice-Hall Sociology Series

Neil J. Smelser, *Editor*

Chapters V and VI are based on research supported by Grant No. 65041 from the President's Committee on Juvenile Delinquency and Youth Crime, Office of Juvenile Delinquency and Youth Development, U. S. Department of Health, Education, and Welfare. Chapters VIII, IX, and X are based on research supported by Public Health Service Grant No. MH14806, National Institute of Mental Health (Center for Studies of Crime and Delinquency).

Selections from: *The Educational Decision-Makers* by A. V. Cicourel and J. I. Kitsuse, © 1963, by permission of The Bobbs-Merrill Company; *Social Relations in a Secondary School* by D. H. Hargreaves, © 1968, by permission of Routledge & Kegan Paul Ltd.; *The Other Side: Perspectives on Deviance*, H. S. Becker, ed, © 1964, *The Outsiders: Studies in the Sociology of Deviance* by H. S. Becker, © 1963, *Behavioral Science for Social Workers*, E. J. Thomas, ed. © 1967, and *The Adolescent Society* by J. S. Coleman, © 1961, by permission of The Macmillan Company.

Photographs on pages 1, 31, 143, 164, 181, and 239 by Bill Agee.

© 1972 by Prentice-Hall, Inc., *Englewood Cliffs, New Jersey*

ISBN: P 0–13–792986-2
       C 0–13–792994-3

Library of Congress Catalog Card Number 73–39744

10 9 8 7 6 5 4 3 2 1

Printed in the United States of America

Prentice-Hall International, Inc., LONDON
Prentice-Hall of Australia, Pty. Ltd., SYDNEY
Prentice-Hall of Canada, Ltd., TORONTO
Prentice-Hall of India Private Limited, NEW DELHI
Prentice-Hall of Japan, Inc., TOKYO

CONTENTS

iii

PREFACE

No one can claim that schools as organizations or those who work within them have an easy assignment. But neither can any informed person ignore the fact that schools are falling far short of their potential for educating our youth. Only in recent years has the enormity of educational failure been fully recognized. The rising rates of juvenile delinquency and adolescent alienation are causing increasing alarm. Perplexed and troubled, parents, the public, and professionals who work with adolescents are searching for answers and solutions.

We propose that educational failure—by schools as well as by students—is directly related to delinquency. Thus, this book, intended for students and scholars of sociology and of education, for educational policy makers and practitioners, and for those who work with deviant youth in other settings, examines three propositions. First, juvenile delinquency is partly caused by adverse school experiences. Second, those adverse experiences—academic failure, misbehavior, psychological or physical withdrawal—are partly caused by forces inherent in the structure and practices of the school itself. Third, schools can be much more effective in preventing and reducing delinquency than they are at the present. The book is not intended to provide the last word on the educational sources of delinquency, nor to describe or evaluate all the different kinds of effort to bolster the influence of the school in offsetting adolescent crime. Rather, it seeks to set forth a conceptual framework for better understanding the overt and covert causal linkages between the school and delinquency, to offer supportive evidence, and to point out the implications of our analysis for theories of delinquency and of educational practice.

The book is a joint effort—the result of collaborative discussions, teaching, and writing with other students and colleagues. While nearly all the chapters are self-contained (many have been published elsewhere), each has been developed within our intellectual framework. And each chapter's connection to that framework will be apparent.

Different parts of the work have resulted from support by the Center for Research on Social Organization and the School of Social Work of the University of Michigan, the Office of Scientific and Scholarly Research of the University of Oregon, the National Institute of Mental Health, the President's Commission on Law Enforcement and Administration of Justice, and the Youth Development and Delinquency Prevention Administration (formerly the Office of Youth Development and Juvenile Delinquency). We gratefully acknowledge the support of each of these agencies throughout the past several years.

In addition to the co-authors of several of the chapters, many persons have contributed directly and indirectly to the book: Jayne Cooper, Troy Duster, Gary Hamilton, Helen Hasenfeld, Robert Hsieh, Solomon Kobrin, Frank Maple, Arthur Pearl, Albert J. Reiss, Jr., Rosemary Sarri, Charlene Simpson, Robert Thompson, Robert Vinter, and Stuart Wilson. We also acknowledge the able editorial assistance of David Robinson and Joan Lee of Prentice-Hall. Many of our students during the past several years at the University have contributed more than they can know through their stimulation, probing inquiry, and creative reactions to our ideas. To them we owe our thanks.

Finally, we owe a great deal to our families—Joan, Ben, Sarah, Susan and Eunice, Kimberly and Kristin—for their patience and encouragement, not only as we worked on this book, but throughout the past several years of study and work.

1
perspectives on the school experience and delinquency

schools
+
delinquency

This book examines the proposition that school experience may function as an important determinant in the generation and maintenance of delinquent careers. We call attention to the possibility that the organizational logic and ideology of our schools virtually assures that there will be delinquency. Our operating premise is that within the procedures we have adopted for educating children lie assumptions about the abilities and conduct of young people and how they should be educated. These assumptions, we argue, themselves create categories of children, such as *bright, culturally deprived, dull, troublesome,* and so on. Such categories are responded to by the *individual actors* (students, teachers, principals and also by *organizational mechanisms* (especially the tracking system) whereby the school as an organization relates to the child. The resulting individual and organizational categories are of fundamental importance in establishing the legitimate and illegitimate adolescent identities that can be identified in delinquent behavior.

This book is somewhat different from others concerned with problems of educational adjustment and deviance. Certainly the focus here is different from those which see delinquency as flowing from one or another set of individual-centered problems, such as might be expected in classic psychiatric or counseling theories. Although it is recognized that delinquency is the behavior of individuals and that some individual delinquents may indeed have some form of emotional problem, we want to call attention to the influence exerted by the structures which surround the delinquent. In doing so, our approach is not as much concerned with problems "in the head" of the delinquent as it is with the "world out there," which may leave the young person with a well-developed troublesome identity and few options other than trouble.

The premise behind this difference should be obvious. If the problem lies solely in the head of the deviant, then adjustment strategies which counsel or treat the individual to lift him out of his troublesome state are appropriate. The accumulated evidence of such treatment in psychiatry, psychology, social work, and counseling does not lead us to be optimistic about the potential of clinical models to deal with delinquency. Our logic, and its supporting evidence, suggest that clinical programs which do not simultaneously engage in specific structural changes can have only limited effect, if any, because structural features may be operating which exert strong pressures to lock the young person into a deviant role.

The approach used here is more closely allied to the analysis of the delinquent subculture as portrayed by Albert K. Cohen.[1] Cohen argues that delinquency is a working-class phenomenon that represents a collective response of working-class boys to their experience of failure in the middle-

---

[1]Albert K. Cohen, *Delinquent Boys* (New York: The Free Press of Glencoe, Inc., 1955).

4

class school environment. We extend this form of sociological analysis, however, in order to account for rebellious behavior that crosses class lines and also to focus more intensively than does Cohen on the *organizational features* of the school that play a critical role in defining careers of youthful deviance.

One of the functions of an introduction is to indicate not only what a book is about, but why it is worth reading. The great volume of works on youthful rebellion, unrest, and delinquency reflect the concern of many with troublesome adolescent behavior. We hope our analysis aids not only in understanding such behavior, but also in the development of more appropriate responses to adolescent misbehavior.

Certainly the concern itself is easy to understand. Many forms of criminal behavior are fundamentally youthful crimes. The *Uniform Crime Reports* compiled by the FBI show that in 1969 over half of all arrests for property offenses involve persons under the age of 18 (54.0 percent to be exact), and over half (51.4 percent) of *all* arrests are accounted for by persons under the age of 25. Furthermore, the numbers and percentages of youth involved in law violations are staggering. Over one million young people are referred to the juvenile courts each year, the number representing close to 3 percent of all children between the ages of 10 and 17 (the population at risk).

Furthermore, we know that these figures underrepresent the actual volumes. There is the well-established sieving process that removes many known law violations from the official books. In a study made in Los Angeles a few years ago (See figure), it was shown that of 52,398 juvenile acts which had come to the attention of the police, only 8,615 individuals were brought to the court, with a small number—875—sent to an institution for care and correction.[2] Although the 52,398 figure does, to be sure, represent an overestimate of the number of individuals involved (since a person might appear more than once in these police records), the drastic reduction from one level to the next (police to courts) is one indication of how official court referrals underestimate the actual number of offenses and offenders. The effect of the sieving process also can be seen in the self-report studies, which suggest that perhaps as many as 90 percent of all young persons have committed at least one act for which they could have been brought to juvenile court.[3]

---

[2]Joseph W. Eaton and Kenneth Polk, *Measuring Delinquency* (Pittsburgh: University of Pittsburgh Press, 1961).

[3]Austin L. Porterfield, "Delinquency and Its Outcome in Court and College," *American Journal of Sociology* 49 (November 1943): 199–208; idem, "The Complainant in the Juvenile Court," *Sociology and Social Research* 28 (January 1944): 171–81; James F. Short, Jr. and F. Ivan Nye, "Reported Behavior as a Criterion of Deviant Behavior," *Social Problems* 5 (Winter 1957): 205–13; John P. Clark and Eugene P. Wenninger, "Socioeconomic Class and Area as Correlates of Illegal Behavior Among Juveniles," *American Sociological Review* 27 (December 1962): 826–34.

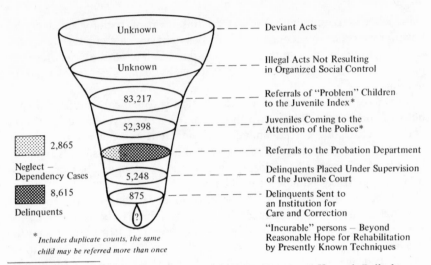

The Delinquency Process Sieve. Screening of "Problem" Children in Los Angeles County to Effect Social Control—1956.

In addition, recent research in the Pacific Northwest reveals that although the yearly rate of official delinquency may vary between 2 or 3 percent, the chance of becoming a delinquent at some time before the eighteenth birthday, for males at least, is much higher and ranges somewhere between 20 and 25 percent.[4] That is, roughly one young male in every four or five will have some encounter with the juvenile court before he reaches the age which puts him under the jurisdiction of adult criminal law and courts. Comparable rates have been reported elsewhere.[5]

As we take this brief glance at juvenile misconduct, we must join the growing group of sociologists who point out that what constitutes delinquency consists of acts which can be roughly subdivided into two parts:

---

[4]Figures obtained from a sample of over 1,200 adolescent males being investigated by the Marion County Youth Study, a study in Marion County, Oregon (1960 population: 120,888) funded by the National Institute of Mental Health (Grant No. MHI4806 "Maturational Reform and Rural Delinquency"). Virtually identical results were obtained in similar research undertaken by the author in Lane County, Oregon (1960 population: 180,000).

[5]The President's Commission on Law Enforcement and the Administration of Justice has estimates that, although still large, are a shade lower: one in six for males. See The President's Commission on Law Enforcement and the Administration of Justice, *The Challenge of Crime in a Free Society* (New York: Avon Books, 1968), p. 170.

(a) *behavior* which comes to be defined as *deviant,* and (b) *a process of reaction* to the act which gives rise to the label of *delinquency.* While we will delve into the specific components of this labeling process, and some of the problems created by the process, in the sections which follow there is a more general problem of the reaction process that gives this book urgency.

Ours is a time of obsession with law and order. One manifestation of this obsession is the development of what amounts to a virtual war on youth. Prompted by civil rights activism, increasingly violent student protests, and the challenge of traditional standards of morality as reflected in sexual behavior and drugs, society is creating and utilizing increasingly punitive legal mechanisms to control youthful misbehavior.

We hope to establish that this legalistic and punitive approach comes at the problem from the wrong direction. More effective laws, police, courts, and prisons, however desirable on other grounds, will not resolve basic structural weaknesses that create youthful discontents. To put it another way, no matter how effective we make our prison or court experiences, these cannot be counted on to deal with the circumstances that bring the young person to the prison or court in the first place.

If there are structurally defined problems in the way institutions relate to young people, and if these problems are a part of the process that creates youthful deviance, then it is these institutions that must be corrected, not the young who are its casualties. In considering changes in social conditions to prevent and reduce delinquency, we are immediately faced with this question: What specific existing conditions around certain youth heighten their attraction to delinquency? Most who have studied the problem agree that commitment to illegitimate rather than legitimate patterns of behavior results from a multitude of conditions and forces: defective families, overcrowded housing, adult criminal influences, access to automobiles, poverty and lack of economic opportunity, decline of influence of the church, and many others. Most also agree that anything approaching complete elimination of delinquency rests on major social changes at each of these and other points.

At the same time, available evidence strongly suggests that delinquent commitments result in part from adverse or negative school experiences, and that there are fundamental defects within the educational system—especially as it touches lower-income youth—that actively contribute to these negative experiences, thereby increasing rather than decreasing the chances that some youth will choose the illegitimate alternative. Despite the fact that the schools are meant to be the major agency for promoting progress along legitimate avenues to adulthood, prevailing conditions in education deter such progress for some youth and make the delinquent alternative more attractive. Evidence also suggests that because of its central and strategic place in the lives of youth, the school has the potential to at least partly offset or neutralize pressures toward delinquency set in motion by non-educational forces in the family and community but that this potential is not now being realized.

If these positions are valid, then major educational changes are crucial for large-scale and effective prevention and reduction of delinquency. Because of the size of the present problem, such changes must be aimed at reducing law violations among currently delinquent and predelinquent youth; but, at the same time, large-scale prevention calls for broad educational changes that will reduce pressures toward delinquency in the first place. We believe that unless these underlying educational conditions that help produce delinquency are altered, efforts to deal with particular delinquent or delinquency-prone youth will have little effect in the long run.

This should not be interpreted as a call not to hold young persons accountable for their acts. It can be anticipated that our society will continue to hold individuals responsible for violations of criminal law. The issue here is how we respond to large-scale *patterns* of violations which demonstrate institutional failure. In this case responding by means of institutional change makes more sense than further elaboration of positive sanctions applied to individual deviants. What such institutional changes require, however, is an analysis of the structural conditions that relate to the problem. That is what this book is about. By accepting the premise calling for institutional changes, perhaps we can create an alternative to the war-on-youth response which, if allowed to continue, can only lead to a widening of the gap between established adult interests and youth and, by a simple logical extension, to an increase in rates of youthful rebellion and deviance.

the
changing
context
of education

Some General Trends

One basic premise of this book is that the educational experience in our society is emerging as one of the fundamental determinants of the individual's economic and social position. Competence in negotiating through achievement-oriented educational institutions, then, has been replacing the older system of social stratification where the position of one's family (the ascription of status) provided the major clue to the individual's social standing. This is not to say that the socioeconomic status of one's parents is irrelevant; clearly it remains as one of the factors affecting social and economic attainment. What appears to be happening today is that the educational experience functions as an achievement-based mechanism that exerts a mediating and at times independent effect between one's social origins and his ultimate position.

Much of the basis for this shift can be found in the changes in the work world that have accompanied the process of technological development aud urbanization. As manpower needs have changed, so schools have been called on to alter their objectives, programs, and techniques to produce new generations adequately prepared to enter available positions in the world of work.

Rapid changes in technology have resulted in the wholesale creation and elimination of jobs. As Corwin has observed, "It is estimated that one-half of jobs now available to high school graduates were not in existence when they were in the sixth grade, and they will not be in existence in ten years."[1] A feature of this trend which Venn has noted has been the shift from manipulative to cognitive work; more and more workers deal with symbols and people, while fewer deal with objects.[2] As a result, the overall level of required skill and education is increasing and ". . . employers in both plant and office look for people with higher levels of education and more marketable skills to perform the more cognitive work functions required."[3]

It is in the specifics of these changes that we see the problems posed for education. For example, there has been a marked decline in the need for farm workers. In 1910 almost one out of every three workers was on the farm; the ratio today is below one in ten and is still going down. There is a closely related constriction of blue-collar and manual occupations and

---

[1] Ronald G. Corwin, *A Sociology of Education* (New York: Appleton-Century-Crofts, 1965), p. 124.

[2] Grant Venn, *Man, Education, and Work* (Washington, D.C.: American Council on Education, 1964), p. 76.

[3] Ibid., p. 7.

an expansion of white-collar and nonmanual positions. In 1910 more than one in three employed persons was a blue-collar worker and only about one in five a white-collar worker; now white-collar workers outnumber blue-collar workers, and this trend is expected to accelerate in the future. Greatest expansion is occurring in the professional, clerical, and sales ranks.

As part of these trends, there is a particularly notable increase in the need for scientific and engineering technicians. This increase is reflected in the fact that "during some of the space flights from Cape Kennedy, the control center was manned by 20 scientists and engineers and 60 technicians." Grant Venn of the United States Office of Education states that although no precise estimate has been made of how many additional technicians will be needed in the years ahead ". . . the creation and expansion of technical occupations suggest that the demand for technically trained personnel will be high and continually growing."[4]

Of major significance for education has been the growing number of professional and subprofessional workers in the public sector of the economy, especially in human services areas such as health, education, welfare, and recreation. Arthur Pearl has called attention to this change:

> Today, there are no more people working for private employers than there were five years ago, but there are far more persons working for public employers now than there were five years ago. Most of these increases in employment have taken place in health, education, and welfare fields. These fields are going to increase more in the next ten years. We can reach this conclusion simply by looking at the population projections. For instance, by 1975 there are going to be about one and a half times the number of people of school age than was the case in 1960. Obviously then, we are going to need many more teachers. By 1970 there are going to be one-third again as many people over the age of 65 than there were in 1960. These people have severe health needs *now*. We are going to have an even greater need for persons to work in health services in the future. Similar conditions will prevail in welfare, recreation, and conservation.[5]

The recent report of the National Commission on Technology, Automation, and Economic Progress[6] gives the following estimates of new jobs needed in the human services to take care of "important social needs" in the near

---

[4]Ibid., p. 132.

[5]Arthur Pearl, "New Careers as a Solution to Poverty," in *Poverty: Four Approaches, Four Solutions* (Eugene, Oregon: Associated Students of the University of Oregon, 1966), p. 14.

[6]National Commission on Technology, Automation, and Economic Progress, *Technology and the American Economy,* vol. I. (Washington, D.C.: U.S. Government Printing Office, 1966), p. 36.

future: medical and health, 1.2 million; education, 1.1 million; national beautification, 1.3 million; welfare and home care, 700,000; public protection, 350,000; urban renewal and sanitation, 650,000.

These trends have altered both the structure and the meaning of the educational experience. Quantitatively, one consequence has been that more young people are involved in education for longer periods of time. The percentage of adolescents completing high school has gone from less than 4 percent of the age eligible in 1900 to over 40 percent in 1960. The emergence of science and human service manpower needs have produced a spectacular growth of graduate enrollments, a trend especially notable at the present time as students born during the post-World War II baby boom move into the postgraduate years.

These quantitative shifts are undergirded by a host of qualitative alterations in the lives of adolescents. It was not so long ago that a man's life work was pretty much determined by the occupation of his father. In what is a relatively short period of time historically, the phenomenon of *occupational inheritance* has, for millions of American adolescents, been supplanted by the phenomenon of *occupational choice*. One of the social functions of schools is to develop and maintain the basic flows, or pathways, whereby students move through childhood, adolescence, and adulthood. These flows in most cases are not neat and tight couplings of the educational experience to specific jobs. Most commonly, each category (the high school dropout, the high school graduate, or the college graduate) has available a set of optional work rates, with levels of salary and status positively (but not perfectly) correlated with level of education.

For most students, in other words, the American educational system does not provide skills and training for specific jobs. Instead, what is provided is a series of status platforms (and a jumble of consequent academic and social skills) from which individuals launch themselves into the adult world of work, with the probability of successful entry closely geared to higher levels of education attainment. The actual choice facing a student is quite complex, then, and can be viewed as a series of decisions regarding, first, his flow through the educational system (where general decisions regarding the character of the curriculum and specific decisions regarding actual courses are made), and second, his flow out of the educational system into work. Our argument is that these complex flow mechanisms are of relatively recent origin and have fundamentally altered the American adolescent life style. Most adolescents must contend with the system, not simply because school itself is legally compulsory well into adolescence in most jurisdictions, but also because their own occupational aspirations require the successful negotiation of one or another of these interlocking flows.

Implications for the Student Role

Other implications of these trends may not be so obvious. The concentration of the training experience in the school setting has altered the older patterns of socialization. To give one illustration, the functions of the family are significantly altered. In part, this is a product of economic factors. When American society was less technological, especially in the early years of this country when most families made their living off the land, the adolescent was ordinarily expected to play the role of economic producer within the family unit. In families in which the adolescent contributed something to the social well being of the familial unit, mechanisms existed to communicate a sense of belonging and a sense of competence. These conditions are noticeably absent in the typical contemporary family. Today, the adolescent is a dependent. Not only does he not contribute to the economic well being of the family—instead he is a cost. There is little in the economic organization of the unit to communicate to the adolescent a significant sense of contribution or competence.

What we have developed to replace these occupational socialization functions is the school. The young person's future economic status, and the learning appropriate to it, are contained in the school experience. The identity a person is to assume, then, flows not out of a set of experiences within the family but out of his negotiation, successful or not, through school.

Over time, the pattern of education adopted by this society has heightened the dependence of the youth on the school. The age-segregation and cloistering that is so characteristic of schools today has made the school the basic conduit through which community and adult influences enter into the lives of adolescents. What and how one learns about much of the community around him is set by the school and its agents.

The high school, then, has come to dominate the life of the adolescent significantly; it has come to serve functions having to do with the social life of the student as well. School is not simply an 8:00 a.m. to 3:00 p.m., Monday through Friday experience. Many of the freetime activities of the student also are school-based (even when they take place elsewhere). Games, parties, dances, or even just fooling around are likely to be engaged in with peers when the peer relationships derive from the school setting.

Further, there are important qualities of the adolescent school experience that have become, we think, problematic. First, the school experience is increasingly segregative rather than integrative. The school grounds or campuses have become virtual prison compounds, where youth are kept safely out of public sight and mind during school hours. There is little or no opportunity even for communication between young people and adults, let alone any chance for collaborative working through of any problem. Such segregation denies the young person the chance to participate in community decisions, regardless of what he might have at stake. The world of politics, then, is an alien one which students read about (in what they come to know is a distorted description) but which they never see, let alone become involved in. The world of work, similarly, is alien. The opportunities to observe adults at work are few, so that the further and much more critical process of engagement in work is precluded.

Second, the role defined for the student in school is passive, rather than active. Education is something we do to young people, not with them. The model student thus becomes a receptacle into which the wisdom of the teacher is poured. Among the many consequences which flow from this noncollaborative, passive definition of the student role we find a cluster of moral norms which support the seen-but-not-heard expectation. One difficulty, then, in arguing for more active involvement of students is that this position generates moral outrage in some quarters.

Third, the student role is defined to assure a meaningless rather than meaningful existence. The student has little or no opportunity to make any difference to, or to have an impact upon, the community in which he lives or even on his school. Perhaps this can be seen most poignantly when we ask what happens when a student dies. Aside from family bereavement, what notice will be taken? What important social task must be taken over by someone else? Which reins must be gripped by other hands? Most often, nothing happens. The student disappears without even a slight social ripple to show that he existed. The reason is simple. As a social being he hardly exists. In all probability he makes no difference at all to the world outside the school (except within the family), and he has little positive weight to throw around inside the school.

So, although the school has come to dominate the life of the adolescent, it has done so in particular and peculiar ways. Important differential roles are played by students, but cutting across these roles are the facts of the adolescent experience generally—its segregated, passive, and meaningless nature. Although these may press down on virtually all adolescents, we argue later that they generate special problems for the troublesome groups.

Putting all this together, we propose that present day adolescents derive much of their identity out of what happens to them in the flows through the school. It is the school that sets them into tracks or streams from which present and future social and economic status is derived. The school provides the framework for the emerging social life of the young person, yielding not only activity settings but pools of peers from which appropriate peer groupings emerge. "Smart" students, "dumb" students, "good" students, "bad" students (of varied types) in the typical high school are able to find things to do, places to do them, and friends to do them with. In the next chapter we discuss specific aspects of the academic and social experiences of the school that are central in the development of deviant careers.

Some
perspectives
on
delinquency

This chapter is a logical extension of earlier attempts of social scientists to account for youthful misconduct. Some existing accounts have focused on delinquency as a product of the articulation between the class system and the school experience. Others have examined delinquency as it flows out of a lack of commitment to school or educationally related processes. Further, some recent theorizing has treated the process of *labeling* as it relates to delinquency, which by direct implication raises question about the role of the school. All of these streams of thought can be found in our arguments.

Delinquency as a Result of Blocked Goal Attainment

Two major theories of delinquency causation argue that delinquent commitments result from blockages in the attainment of highly valued success goals. The works of Albert Cohen and of Richard Cloward and Lloyd Ohlin hold that, although nearly all youth are exposed to and internalize the goals of educational attainment and later of financial and occupational success, not all of them have equal opportunities or are equally equipped to reach those goals.[1] Lower-class youth are at a particular disadvantage. Lack of accessibility to educational opportunities and adverse home experiences make it difficult for lower-class youth to measure up to middle-class standards of conduct and performance. As a result, some youth fail to achieve the goal of educational attainment and perceive little likelihood of achieving later occupational rewards. When internal controls are sufficiently weak or when illegitimate patterns of behavior are readily accessible, some of these youth reject or rebel against legitimate patterns of conduct. At the same time they collectively adopt new illegitimate commitments and standards as an alternative avenue to status and status symbols or as means of striking back at the middle-class world that produced goal-frustration in the first place.

Although we have reviewed only the barest outlines of these theories and have ignored important differences between them, this brief review suggests several possible implications for an analysis of the linkages between school experiences and educational conditions, on one hand, and juvenile delinquency on the other. First, these theories suggest that poor school performance may represent one form of blocked goal attainment. That is,

---

[1]Richard A. Cloward and Lloyd E. Ohlin, *Delinquency and Opportunity* (New York: The Free Press of Glencoe, Inc., 1960); Albert K. Cohen, *Delinquent Boys* (New York: The Free Press of Glencoe, Inc., 1955); for reviews of these and other delinquency theories, see David Bordua, *Sociological Theories and Their Implications for Juvenile Delinquency* (Washington, D.C.: U.S. Government Printing Office, 1960).

failure to receive high grades, to be promoted from one grade to the next, or to receive informal rewards for achievement may be one experience indicating to adolescents that they are not succeeding in reaching a goal which most of them value highly. Second, they suggest that failure to get a good job, or the perception that a good job will not be forthcoming—either as a result of or independent of academic failure—may be another form of blocked goal attainment. Third, they suggest, or at least raise the possibility, that although lower-class youngsters are most likely to be frustrated in the attainment of educational and occupational goals, these same blockages may lead to delinquency among middle-class youth as well. Fourth, the theories raise the possibility that the school itself may contribute to blocked goal attainment among some youth, especially those from lower-class backgrounds. As we will see, each of these implications from the two theories is useful in directing us to linkages between the school and delinquency.

Delinquency as a Result of Lack of Commitment

Although the theories of Walter B. Miller and of Larry Karacki and Jackson Toby contain quite different arguments and refer to different youth populations, they converge on the position that some youth become delinquent because of a basic lack of commitment to conventional, middle-class adult roles and to community standards of behavior.[2] Miller takes the position that many lower-class youth become delinquent because their behavior is a simple reflection of lower-class culture which they have learned rather than because of deprivation or goal frustration. In other words, they have been acculturated into a way of life that calls for behavior consistent with the "focal concerns" of "trouble, toughness, smartness, excitement, fate, and autonomy" but inconsistent with the conventional standards of the larger community. Implicit in this theory is the idea that lower-class youth have become committed, but committed to a set of standards and values that are antithetical to dominant norms and values. Lower-class norms call neither for achievement and conformity in school nor for conformity with community laws.

It should be clear that Miller's theory is inconsistent in some ways with the theories of blocked goal attainment mentioned above. The most

---

[2]Walter B. Miller, "Lower-Class Culture as a Generating Milieu of Gang Delinquency," *Journal of Social Issues* 14 (1958, No. 3): 5–19; Larry Karacki and Jackson Toby, "The Uncommitted Adolescent: Candidate for Gang Socialization," *Sociological Inquiry* 32 (Spring 1962): 203–15.

important difference is that, whereas Miller points to a lack of commitment to achievement goals and community standards, Cohen and Cloward and Ohlin argue that, at least initially, lower-class youth do generally have such a commitment. We suggest that, although the two positions are not consistent, they may both be correct in that they refer to different populations of youth. It is entirely possible, as Bordua has suggested, that Miller's theory fits certain ethnic and bottom status groups in the cities, but that this Cohen and the Cloward and Ohlin theories refer to the more populous working class in the cities and elsewhere as well.

The theory of Karacki and Toby also holds that delinquency sometimes results from a lack of commitment, but their theory pertains especially to middle class delinquency and is based on a different set of premises. They argue that most middle-class youth have ample exposure to dominant norms and values and ample opportunity to become committed to them, but that through "imperfect socialization" or simple choice, not all adolescents do become committed. As a result, they become more oriented to fun and trouble than to conformity and achievement, and the frequent outcome is delinquency.

For our analysis of the schools and delinquency, an important possible implication of these theories is that the school itself may directly contribute to lack of commitment, or at least may not capitalize on the chance to foster a commitment to the legitimate system when that commitment is lacking. At the same time that we recognize the possibility that socialization into "lower-class culture," "imperfect socialization," or plain choice may partly account for low commitment to the school, to community standards, and to adult values, we also raise the question of whether characteristics of the authority and decision-making systems of the school, or its basic teaching-learning structure, might generate lack of commitment and thereby inadvertently contribute to delinquency. This possibility is explored later.

Deviant Behavior, Group Sanctions, and Delinquency

A sociological conception of deviant behavior that recently has received widespread attention sees the phenomenon as a joint product of actions of certain persons and of social definitions of those actions as unacceptable. "Deviance is not a property *inherent in* certain forms of behavior; it is a property *conferred upon* these forms by the audiences which directly or indirectly witness them.[3] Deviance thus becomes an attribute of exchanges

---

[3]Kai T. Erikson, "Notes on the Sociology of Deviance," in *The Other Side: Perspectives on Deviance,* ed. Howard S. Becker (New York: The Free Press of Glencoe, Inc., 1964), p. 11.

or interactions between the individual and the group, rather than of the individual alone.

> Social groups create deviance by making the rules whose infraction constitutes deviance, and by applying those rules to particular people and labeling them as outsiders. From this point of view, deviance is not a quality of the act the person commits, but rather a consequence of the application by others of rules and sanctions to an "offender." The deviant is one to whom that label has successfully been applied; deviant behavior is behavior that people so label.[4]

This view gives rise to a number of important considerations for the understanding and analysis of deviant behavior. One is that there is nothing inherent in an act that makes that act either deviant or conforming.[5] Rather, the perceptions and definitions of those who enforce group standards determine whether an act is or is not acceptable. Consequently, an individual may or may not be defined as deviant for a particular behavior, depending on such things as his own status characteristics—how he looks, who his friends are—and what his reputation is, on the situation, and on who is enforcing group standards.[6]

Second, the process of labeling is itself a critical determinant of the subsequent deviant or conforming career of the individual.[7] Both the way in which the label is applied and the nature of that label are likely to have several future consequences for the individual. An important component of an emerging commitment to a deviant career is a person's definition of himself as a deviant; the extent to which such a self-concept develops is partly determined by how degrading and public the "labeling ceremony" is. If an individual is reacted to in a highly derogatory or demeaning fashion or if he is set apart from those applying the label or observing its application, he is likely to come to see himself as deviant. Partly as a matter of "right" and of rebellion and rejection, then, the individual may be likely to increase rather than decrease his deviant conduct in the future.

Another consequence of the labeling process is that if it is highly exposed to the view of others—directly or through later communication—they are likely to develop and maintain a conception of the individual as

[4]Howard S. Becker, *Outsiders: Studies in the Sociology of Deviance* (New York: The Free Press of Glencoe, Inc. (1963), p. 9.

[5]Ibid., p. 8; Erikson, "Notes on the Sociology of Deviance," p. 11.

[6]Walter E. Schafer, "Deviance in the Public Schools: An Interactional Approach," in *Behavioral Science for Social Workers,* ed. Edwin J. Thomas (New York: The Free Press of Glencoe, Inc., 1967).

[7]John I. Kitsuse, "Societal Reaction to Deviant Behavior: Problems of Method and Theory," in Becker, *The Other Side,* pp. 87–102; Erikson, "Notes on the Sociology of Deviance," p. 11.

"bad" or, in the words of Becker, as an "outsider."[8] As a result, the person is likely to be perceived, treated, and reacted to in the future as a "bad guy," an "exconvict," a "hoodlum," or a "delinquent," as the case may be. Such perceptions, treatment, and reactions may be independent of the individual's own motivation—or of his actual behavior. Still another consequence of the labeling process is that the kind of label applied to the individual determines the kind of reaction that others will have.[9] For example, if an individual who violates a law is labeled "mentally ill," he will be handled quite differently than if he is labeled "criminal." In one case he may go to a mental hospital, in the other to jail.

A third implication of this perspective is that one of the factors determining the chances that deviancy will be reduced, or that it will be repeated or even broadened to include a wider range of acts in the future, is the nature of the reactions of the group to the initial act.[10] Those reactions may have several possible effects. They may cut off or prevent future deviancy through the imposition of firm sanctions combined with deliberate attempts to involve the individual in legitimate activities and to reward him for conformity to legitimate standards, or by changing the conditions in and around him that generated deviant pressures in the first place.

On the other hand, those reactions may inadvertently heighten the chances of future deviancy, perhaps of a more serious nature, by being excessively punitive and thereby alienating the individual further, or by closing off future opportunities to become involved in and committed to legitimate activities, thereby pushing the deviant away—ultimately out of the group entirely—rather than pulling him back into the system. Moreover, the responses of others may inadvertently lock the individual into the role of deviant and hinder rather than facilitate his return to a conventional place in the group, even when he seeks to do so. Once assumed, the public identity of "deviant" may be extremely difficult to shed, despite changes in one's own motivation and behavior.[11]

A Suggested Perspective on Delinquency

Two general propositions can be derived from the foregoing: (1) School experience is emerging as a fundamental determinant of adolescent status,

---

[8]Becker, *Outsiders.*

[9]John I. Kitsuse and Aaron V. Cicourel, *The Educational Decision-Makers* (New York: The Bobbs-Merrill Co., Inc., 1963).

[10]Kitsuse, "Societal Reaction to Deviant Behavior," pp. 87–102; Albert K. Cohen, "The Sociology of the Deviant Act: Anomie Theory and Beyond," *American Sociological Review* 30 (February 1965): 5–14.

[11]Erikson, "Notes on the Sociology of Deviance"; Schafer, "Deviance in the Public Schools."

and (2) the manner in which a youngster is identified within the status system of the school exerts a basic influence on the development of deviant careers. Now we must expand upon these propositions to give them additional meaning, especially with regard to the school's contribution to the problem of delinquency.

THE GOAL OF SUCCESS. It is critical at the onset to underscore the importance of the school as it plays a role in the definition and achievement of "success" in contemporary American society. The theory we are developing here makes several key assumptions. First, we live in a society that places a heavy emphasis on success. As the term is used here, success is not necessarily translatable into specific and concrete objectives or goals that can be applied to all individuals. It is intended to convey an orientation to the world, or a set of operating assumptions, that exert a push so that an individual wants to "be somebody."

In this society, being somebody ordinarily conveys some economic meaning. Its components in actuality are extremely varied, however, and can derive from such things as money, job, inherited position, life style, social status, and the like. Success can be obtained in adult life along a number of different dimensions, and these dimensions may or may not converge. One can obtain a great deal of money, for example, by means of illicit activity (such as gambling) and as a consequence obtain success in a limited economic sense and still be denied success in a social or reputational sense. The very diversity of success goals, however, provides important room to maneuver and makes it possible for the generalized achievement success ethic to apply. Thus, with a wide range of goals and diverse standards for gauging success, people can be encouraged to start from quite different vantage points, with different routes or success mechanisms available to them, and still be encouraged to make their own way.

THE SCHOOL AND SUCCESS. Second, our theory assumes that schools, fundamentally, are about success. Running along underneath a covering rhetoric of learning or liberalizing education that dictates much of the substance of what is supposed to be studied, we encounter the hard reality that what schools do—regardless of the educational rhetoric—is to process individuals differentially and thereby affect very directly their life chances for success. In our present technologically oriented society, the school has become the gatekeeper of success. Possession of one or another set of formal skills becomes a basic mechanism for achievement of success. Thus, how well one does within the institution established to provide such skills comes to the fore as a factor influencing success achievement.

One of the peculiarities of the school experience that makes this a difficult point to make is that, in the current educational logic and thinking, the substance of education is often defined as being nonvocational in character. The content of what studies make one an educated man, according to many who pass for educational philosophers, is not and should not be vocationally based. Literature, music, politics, history, or art, to name but a few, are provided in the curriculum to prepare people for life, not for a job. But if the *content* of education is deemed irrelevant to future work, the *process* is not gauged by simply how much of it one possesses. For example, the more education one has, the more life success is improved. Many jobs are open only to those who possess degrees, even when the field of the degree bears no relationship to the character of the work. More important to our present concern with the adolescent, the school also processes people by virtue of their academic success into various categories which have both immediate and long-range effects on the definition of success status. It is likely that many students doing well in school will go on to college (and then on to better jobs). Yet, in addition to this future implication of school status, doing well serves also to fix the adolescent's present identity within the setting of the school as well as in the eyes of his teachers, his fellow students, and himself.

THE BUREAUCRATIC ORGANIZATION OF SUCCESS AND FAILURE: THE SYSTEMATIC BLOCKAGE OF SUCCESS GOALS. Third, we assume that schools will, as a consequence, develop mechanisms for processing students differentially with regard to their access to the avenues leading to success. It is at this point we encounter the important difficulties, for it is here that we encounter the phenomenon of *locking-out*. Differential access means that while some win, others lose. The locking-out process appears to have three problematic dimensions, or biases: (1) class biases, (2) ethnic biases, and (3) ability-assumption biases.

The class and ethnic biases of school are well known. Thus, the school relates to children within a standard code framework of values, norms, and intellectual orientation, this standard code containing biases regarding class, ethnic, and (increasingly) intellectual orientation. This can be seen both in the content and in the process of education. By now we have all become familiar with the fact that Dick-and-Jane type readers depict suburban, middle-class, and white scenes at the expense of depicting events in other class-culture and ethnic settings. Such illustrations are bountiful—we learn that when whites lose a battle with Indians it is a massacre, not a battle.

What may not be quite so clear is the bias in intellectual style. These same Dick-and-Jane scenes and the language and procedures used to depict and explain them are about a particular style of life. There ain't no hippies in them books. Ain't no four letter words, neither. Why, there ain't no ain'ts.

But it is not just these content biases that pose the problem. Over time and reflected in the differential flows of students through the school, these biases are translated into *bureaucratic or organizational mechanisms.* At one level this can be seen as a consequence of the development of a relatively unidimensional concept of ability that functions both at a professional level (reflected in the concept *intelligence*) and at a common sense, or folk-concept, level (reflected in such terms as *bright* or *dull*). Although adult success may require a range of job-related and social skills, the school has selected a very narrow range of particular intellectual skills (which emphasize such abilities as memorization and arithmetic reasoning, for example) upon which to base judgments of individuals.

From this logic flows a virtual ideology of intelligence which assumes that there is some correspondence between one's ability and the legitimacy of his claims to success. Important implications flow from this assumption. If successfully applied to the range of students, it can serve as an important device for social control. If it is granted that dull persons have no legitimate claim to demanding occupations (because they are not able enough to qualify for the necessary educational experience) and that dullness is correctly assessed by procedures utilized by the school, then the individual dull person will come to see his lack of success as a product of his own intellectual weakness. He will, in short, not see his failure as unjust depreciation. In the words of the professional thief, he will be "cooled out."

If, on the other hand, he becomes aware that there exist important subcultural biases in both the measurement devices and in the concept of ability itself, and if he becomes aware that he fits some category against which there is systematic bias (such as lower-class black), then the situation becomes unstable. No longer will he see the judgment of his ability, and therefore of the consequences for his academic success, as legitimate. At least some of the recent educational protest among blacks is centered precisely on this issue.

A consequence of relevance to the present discussion is that maintaining the notions of ability in the school requires that some students be seen as having limited potential. Simply put, in order to have smart students, there must be dumb students. Given the notion of unidimensional ability that operates in the school: (1) there must be dumb students for the logic to work, and further, (2) there will be developed a supporting belief in the general trait of limited potential possessed by some students. Dumbness comes to be seen not as an attribute operating in only one academic endeavor (in history, or English, or mathematics), but as a general attribute or trait of some students.

Success and ability concepts are important, not only as ideas but also in the way they become translated into bureaucratic structures. Once ability is identified, it becomes relevant for the grouping of students into homogeneous categories, giving rise to ability grouping and tracking. As the student career develops, it is these grouping mechanisms that convey the direct assessment of success. In the elementary years, the grouping conveys differential levels of, say, reading skill. By the time students reach high school, the grouping mechanisms—especially the college-prep and non-college-prep distinction—are more clearly related to later-life success concepts. The cumulative design of many course offerings in the high school assures that, as the junior and senior years approach, transfer from non-college to college preparatory classes becomes difficult or impossible because the student will not have the prerequisite experiences. Thus, one feature of the tracking system is that the student becomes increasingly locked-in to the noncollege role as the years progress by virtue of the design of these organizational processes.

THE EMERGING IMPORTANCE OF SCHOOL STATUS FLOWS. Fourth, the impact of technological changes may be functioning to change the nature of the connective links between class origins, school status, and class destination. As our society becomes more concerned about searching out intellectual talent, it emphasizes academic achievement somewhat at the expense of class origins. Cicourel and Kitsuse have argued that orientation to college has significantly reduced crude class pressures that operated in earlier periods of our history:

> The differentiation of college-going and noncollege-going students defines the standards of performance by which they are evaluated by the school personnel and by which students are urged to evaluate themselves. It is the college-going student more than his noncollege-going peer who is continually reminded by his teachers, counselor, parents, and peers of the decisive importance of academic achievement to the realization of his ambitions and who becomes progressively committed to this singular standard of self-evaluation. He becomes the future-oriented student interested in a delimited occupational specialty, with little time to give thought to the present or to question the implications of his choice and the meaning of his strivings.[12]

It is within this framework that the functional relationship between class background and school behavior may be changing:

> We suggest that the influence of social class upon the way students are processed in the high school today is reflected in new and more subtle family-school relations than the direct and often blatant manipulation of

---

[12]Kitsuse and Cicourel, *The Educational Decision-Makers,* p. 146.

family class pressure documented by Hollingshead. . . .Insofar as the high school is committed to the task of identifying talent and increasing the proportions of college-going students, counselors will tend to devote more of their time and activities to those students who plan and are most likely to go to college and whose parents actively support their plans and make frequent inquiries at the school about their progress—namely, the students from the middle and upper social classes.[13]

Class and ethnic biases will continue to exist and exert their influence on school and student. What we can expect, however, is that there will continue to be a development of an ideology of achievement. As this gains in momentum, an increasingly large component of the student's identity will be established by where he stands within the status flows through school, independent of his class and ethnic origins.

ACADEMIC FLOWS AND COMMITMENT TO CONFORMITY. Fifth, it is assumed that placement into educational categories is an important determinant of the stake an individual student has in conformity. On the positive side, this means that the student who is identified as being academically able and who is firmly fixed into the college preparatory track has much to lose by engaging in troublesome behavior. While it certainly is no absolute guarantee against delinquency, such an identity for a late adolescent means that delinquency becomes irrational. A police record may mean that a career (in such areas as education, medicine, or law) will be closed to him, thus rendering his academic life useless and nonsensical. Turning it around somewhat, the bright, college-prep student has a rational reason for not engaging in troublesome behavior, a reason flowing out of the logic behind his educational career.

The dull noncollege student does not possess the same rational barrier against delinquency. This does not mean that a delinquent career is in any sense inevitable. It does mean that there is a lowered stake in conformity, because deviance does not threaten the noncollege student in the same way it threatens the person in a success track or flow.

ACADEMIC FLOWS AND DEVIANCE. Sixth, it is assumed that the implication of deviance for success is of such importance that the school will develop organizational procedures for misbehavior comparable to those developed around ability, except that these operate in reverse. If a troublesome identity is seen as a threat to success, it is natural that, given its stake in the development and maintenance of successful careers, the school will develop mechanisms for dealing with maladaptive behavior.

The consequence is that a good-bad dimension of organizational

---

[13]Ibid., pp. 144–45.

behavior emerges to supplement and complement the smart-dumb grouping mechanisms. Initial concerns about individual-based emotional disturbance or behavior problems become organizationally transformed into special adjustment classes. Whatever the professional intent, the result is to create within the school the structure to maintain and support "bad" identities whereby the mere presence of the individual student in the special setting makes visible to teachers, other students, and parents the problematic character of the student's behavior. We argue in sections to follow that these mechanisms often function to lock students into the deviant role. For the person already in a nonsuccess, low ability track, placement in the public "bad" role may serve to make even more clear that whatever chances the student has to be somebody must be sought outside the school setting. The school's response to deviance, in other words, may actually serve to reinforce the deviant role, rather than serving any corrective or rehabilitative function. If a basic factor in the drift into deviant roles is the low stake in conformity that results from identity with nonsuccessful academic tracks, heightening the problematic aspect of a student's role can be expected to accelerate that drift.

THE GROUP RESPONSE TO LOCKING-OUT. Seventh, we assume that as the school makes clear through its mechanisms that the youngster is not wanted, a group response of pessimism and hostility results. For the unwelcome student, school is not a pleasant place. Such a view emphasizes the role of the school in the life of the individual and focuses on the question of the consequences that accrue to those who are unable to achieve within the school system. Vinter and Sarri have pointed out that the school has a multitude of punishments which it can mete out to the malperforming youngster.[14] In Valley City, Call reports that not only were delinquent youth likely to do poor academic work, they were also less likely to participate in school activities and more likely to see themselves as outside the school setting.[15]

For such youth the future begins to take on a different meaning. If they lack an orientation to the future and appear unwilling to defer immediate gratifications in order to achieve long-range future goals, it may be that they see fairly clearly that for them there is little future. Pearl suggests that such youth ". . . develop a basic pessimism because they have a fair fix on reality. They rely on fate because no rational transition by system

---

[14]Robert D. Vinter and Rosemary C. Sarri, "Malperformance in the Public School: A Group Work Approach," *Social Work* 10 (January 1965): 3–13 (see especially p. 9).

[15]Donald J. Call, "Delinquency, Frustration, and Noncommitment" (Ph.D. dissertation, University of Oregon, 1965).

is open to them. They react against schools because schools are characteristically hostile to them." [16]

The hostility engendered is not simply individual hostility. Consider
the observations of Empey and Rabow in a small city in Utah:

> Despite the fact that Utah County is not a highly urbanized area when
> compared to large metropolitan centers, the concept of a "parent" delin-
> quent subculture has real meaning for it. While there are no clear-cut
> gangs, per se, it is surprising to observe the extent to which delinquent boys
> from the entire county, who have never met, know each other by reputa-
> tion, go with the same girls, use the same language, or can seek each other
> out when they change high schools. About half of them are permanently
> out of school, do not participate in any regular institutional activities, are
> reliant almost entirely upon the delinquent system for social acceptance and
> participation. [17]

Call presents evidence that delinquent youth are more likely to spend
their spare time with friends and that their friends are much more likely to be
outside the school system. [18] Polk and Halferty's factor analysis study suggests that delinquency fits into a pattern of rejection of commitment to school
success accompanied by a concomitant involvement in a pattern of peer
rebellion against adults. [19] In enabling youngsters to cope with the locking-
out process, "A limited gratification exists in striving for the impossible and
as a consequence poor youth create styles, coping mechanisms, and groups
in relation to the systems which they can and cannot negotiate. Group
values and identification emerge in relation to the forces opposing them." [20]

The point of this discussion is that these youth are not passive
receptors of the stigma that develops within the school setting. When
locked out, they respond by seeking an interactional setting where they
can function comfortably. The fact that the resulting subculture has built-in
oppositional forces becomes an important aspect of the delinquency problem encountered in a community. We deal not with isolated alienated
youth, but with a loosely organized subculture which provides important
group supports for the deviancy observed. Individualized treatment aimed
at such youth, which does not take into account the importance and functioning of the group supports within this culture, can have limited, if any,

---

[16]Arthur Pearl, "Youth in Lower-Class Settings," in *Problems of Youth*, eds. M.
Sherif and C. Sherif (Chicago: Aldine Publishing Co., 1968), pp. 89–109.

[17]Lamar T. Empey and Jerome Rabow, "The Provo Experiment in Delinquency
Rehabilitation," *American Sociological Review* 26 (October 1961): 674–95.

[18]Call, "Delinquency, Frustration, and Noncommitment."

[19]Kenneth Polk and David Halferty, "Adolescence, Commitment, and Delinquency," *Journal of Research in Crime and Delinquency*, 4 (July 1966): 82–96.

[20]Pearl, "Youth in Lower-Class Settings."

impact. An approach is needed that will counteract the system processes which generate this subcultural response.

This, in brief, is our general theoretical overview. In the sections which follow, these propositions are expanded upon, and evidence is introduced to justify our assertions. In Part II which follows immediately we bring together bits of evidence that support our argument that such features of school as tracking, grading, and the like can be linked to delinquency. In Part III we will weave these and other findings together to provide a more complete statement of our theoretical positions. In Part IV we present some of our specific recommendations concerning changes that might be made in educational practice and process.

2

Some supporting studies

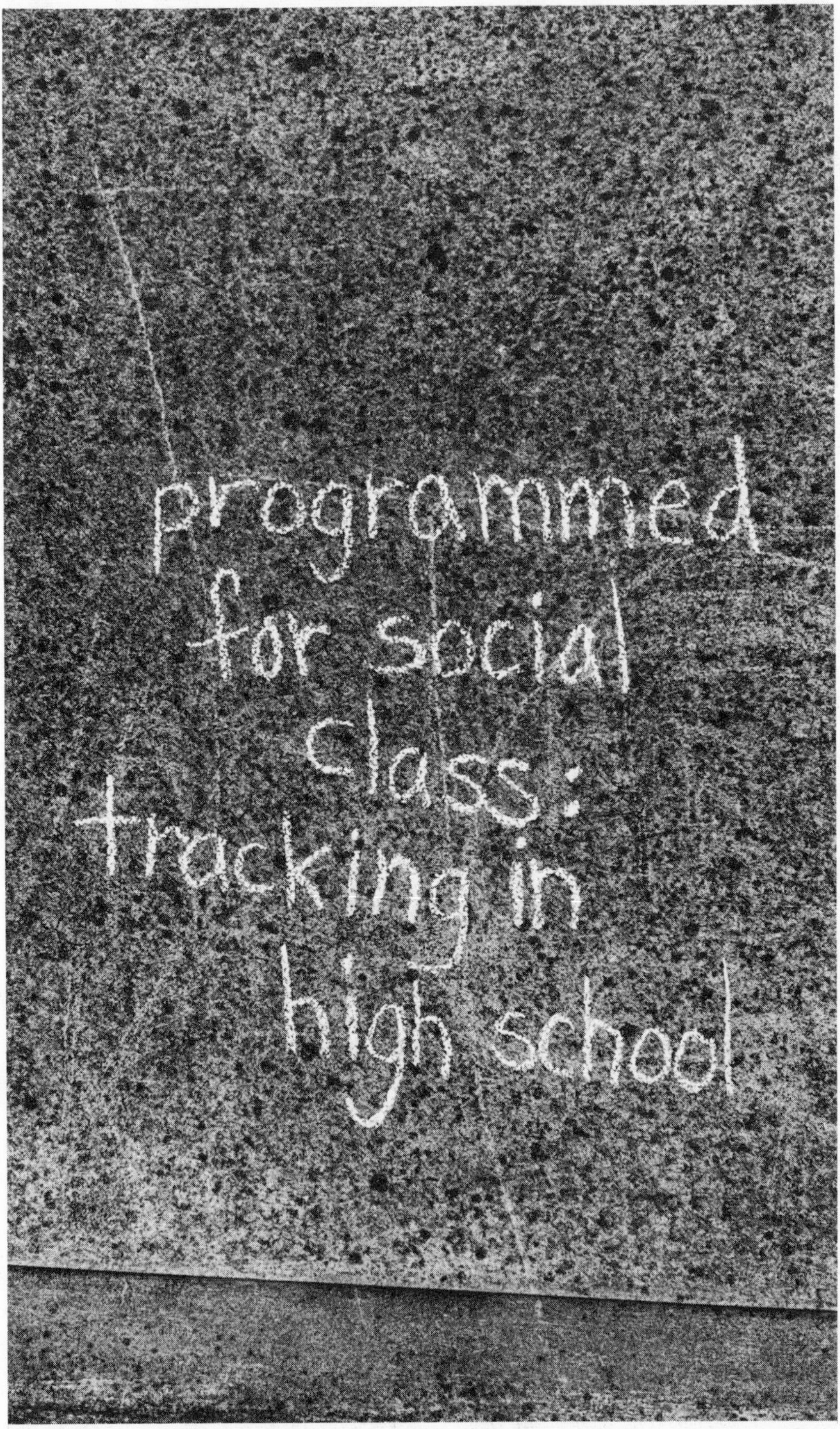
programmed
for social
class:
tracking in
high school

It is conceivable that the detrimental effects of segregation based upon intellect are similar to the known detrimental effects of schools segregated on the basis of class, nationality, or race.

Kenneth B. Clark[1]

Children from higher social strata usually enter the "higher quality" groups and those from lower strata the "lower" ones. School decisions about a child's ability will greatly influence the kind and quality of education he receives, as well as his future life, including whether he goes to college, the job he will get, and his feelings about himself and others.

Patricia Sexton[2]

... "special ability classes," "basic track," or "slow learner classes" are various names for another means of systematically denying the poor adequate access to education.

Arthur Pearl[3]

The evidence is clear: Children from low-income and minority group families more often find themselves in low-ability groups and noncollege-bound tracks than in high-ability groups or college-bound tracks. But does this result in decreased educational and life chances? Does it dampen the self-image and foster alienation and rebellion? By the way it groups and tracks students, is the school itself a barrier to equality of educational opportunity and a cause of failure, the dropout problem, and delinquency? Before presenting new data on these questions—and proposing an alternative to present tracking practices, it is important to discuss the background of the high school tracking system.

Tracking in Perspective

Since the turn of the century, a number of trends have converged to increase the pressure on American adolescents to enter and graduate from high school; the disappearance of work roles for adolescents, the upgrading of

"Programmed for Social Class: Tracking in High School," by Walter E. Schafer, Carol Olexa, and Kenneth Polk. A more complete report of this research may be found in Walter E. Schafer and Carol Olexa, Tracking and Opportunity: The Locking-Out Process and Beyond *(Scranton: Chandler Publishing Co., 1971). A condensed version of this article appeared in* Trans action 7, no. 12 (October 1970): 39–46.

[1]Kenneth B. Clark, "Educational Stimulation of Racially Disadvantaged Children," in A. Harry Passow (ed.), *Education in Depressed Areas* (New York: Teachers College, Columbia, 1963), p. 152.

[2]Patricia C. Sexton, *The American School: A Sociological Analysis* (Englewood Cliffs, New Jersey: Prentice-Hall, Inc., 1967), p. 57.

[3]Arthur Pearl, "Youth in Lower Class Settings," in Muzafer Sherif and Carolyn W. Sherif, eds., *Problems of Youth* (Chicago: Aldine Publishing Company, 1965), p. 92.

educational requirements for job entry, and the declining need for teen-agers to contribute to family income. The effect of these pressures is reflected in the fact that 94 percent of the high-school-age population was in school in 1968, compared to 7 percent in 1890.[4] This vast increase in the size of enrollment has forced the educational system not only to increase its facilities and manpower, but also to broaden its objectives and programs in order to serve student populations with much greater diversity in abilities, interests, and aspirations.

While some school systems, especially in the large cities, have adapted by creating separate high schools for students with different abilities or occupational destinations, most communities have developed comprehensive high schools serving all the youngsters in a neighborhood or community. A common structural arrangement for serving the presumed needs and abilities of different student groups now used by about half the high schools in the United States, is some form of tracking system, usually consisting of two or more relatively distinct career lines with such titles as college preparatory, vocational, technical, industrial, business, general, basic and remedial. While students on different tracks may take some courses together in the same classroom, they are usually separated into entirely different courses or different sections of the same course.

Several different rationale are given for tracking systems. Common to most rationale, however, is that college-bound students are academically more able, learn more rapidly, should not be deterred in their progress by slower, noncollege-bound students, and need courses for college prepara-tion which noncollege-bound students do not need. It is thought that non-college-bound students, on the other hand, are less bright, learn more slowly, should not be expected to progress as fast or learn as much as college-bound students, and need only a general education or work-oriented training to prepare them for immediate entry into the world of work or a business or vocational school.

Numerous critics contend that schools inadvertently close off oppor-tunities for achievement and success for those who do not make it into the upper track and thereby help cause the very problems of low motivation, alienation, and rebellion which they are trying to prevent.

If these critics are correct, the American comprehensive high school, which is assumed to be more open and democratic than, say, English schools where students of different presumed ability and potential are early assigned to different schools, may not really be open and democratic at all. Rather than facilitating equality of educational opportunity, the school may be a barrier for those assigned to the lower tracks.

---

[4]United States Office of Education, *Digest of Educational Statistics* (Washington, D.C.: U.S. Government Printing Office, 1969), p. 25.

Until now, evidence in support of this position of the critics has been skimpy and mixed. Studies on the effects of ability grouping have shown mixed results, but they have not examined the cumulative effects of career-long tracking in high school. While the Coleman report found no difference in student achievement in schools where tracking was present or absent, any conclusions must be very cautiously drawn, because of the unknown variations in curriculum organization in schools in both categories.[5]

We contend that a more fruitful approach than the Coleman report's between-school analysis is to examine within-school differences in educational outcomes for students located on different tracks. Following this approach, we have collected data from two three-year, midwestern high schools, which strongly indicate the criticisms we have cited may be valid. If our data and conclusions are in fact valid, then not only must the present tracking system be abolished, but an entirely new way of structuring the learning-teaching process and of linking the educational and occupational careers must be developed.

Data and Methods

During the summer of 1964, a variety of data was collected from official school transcripts on the classes which had entered two midwestern, three-year high schools in September of 1961. At the time the data were collected, nearly all members of the sample had graduated. The larger school, located in a predominantly middle-class, academic community of about 70,000, had a total enrollment of 2,641 in the fall of 1963. The smaller school, with an enrollment of 1,272 students in the fall of 1963, was located in a nearby predominantly working-class, industrial community of about 20,000. The respective classes of 753 and 404 for each school were combined into a single sample for this study, except where indicated, since the findings were virtually identical for each school.

The independent variable, track position, was indicated by whether the student took tenth grade English in the "college prep" or the "general" section. If they were enrolled in the college prep section, they almost always took other college prep sections or courses such as advanced math or foreign language in which almost all enrollees were college prep. In this study, the two college prep tracks of the larger school were combined, as were the five noncollege prep subdivisions. The smaller school had only two tracks.

The first dependent variable, academic achievement, was indicated by grade point average for all major courses for the tenth through the twelfth grades. Trends in grades were indicated by comparing grade point averages

---

[5]James S. Coleman, et al., *Equality of Educational Opportunity* (Washington, D.C.: U.S. Government Printing Office, 1966).

(GPA's) for each of the six semesters. The second dependent variable, participation in extracurricular activities, was measured by the number of yearbook entries (in addition to the class picture) for each student for each of the three years. This variable was measured only in the larger school. The third dependent variable, dropout, was measured by whether those who did not graduate with their class were still enrolled because they had fallen behind, had had a transcript sent to another school or had not had a transcript sent. Those who were no longer enrolled and had not had a transcript sent were classified as dropouts. The fourth dependent variable, misbehavior in school, which was collected only for the larger school, was indicated by entries by the vice principal on cards kept in his office for serious enough violations of school or classroom rules to result in the student being sent to him. The fifth dependent variable, delinquency, was measured by whether a student had an official juvenile court record. Court records, of course, are known to be incomplete and must be viewed as only a gross underestimation of actual offenses. Court data were collected in 1967, but only offenses before high school graduation were recorded for this study.

Three control variables were employed: father's occupation, indicated by school records and divided into blue collar and white collar; measured intelligence, indicated by scores on the transcripts and dichotomized for this study; and GPA for the second semester of the ninth grade, also obtained from the transcripts. The method for controlling these factors is a mean weighted percentage approach called test factor standardization.

Assignment to Tracks

In both schools we studied, a majority of incoming students were assigned to the college prep track: 58 percent in the smaller school, 71 percent in the larger school. Socioeconomic and racial background had a substantial effect on assignment to different tracks. Whereas 83 percent of those from white-collar homes were assigned to the college prep track, this was true of only 48 percent of those from blue collar homes. The effect of race was even stronger; 71 percent of whites and 30 percent of blacks were assigned to the college prep track.

Just how students were assigned to—or chose—tracks is somewhat of a mystery. Interviews in both high schools and their feeder junior highs indicated that selection into the different tracks resulted from a combination of student desires and aspirations, teacher advice, achievement test scores, grades, pressure from parents, and counselor assessment of academic promise. Cicourel and Kitsuse have shown in their study, *The Educational Decision-Makers,* that assumptions made by counselors about the character, adjustment, and potential of incoming students are vitally important in track assignment.[6] Whatever the precise dynamics of this decision, the outcome was clear in the schools we studied: socioeconomic and racial background had an effect on track selection independent of either measured ability or achievement in junior high. As a result, lower-income and black students were disproportionately subject to whatever negative effects there were from the noncollege-bound track—which, as we will see, were substantial.

This decision point in the students' school careers was of great significance for their future—probably greater than most realized, since it was virtually irreversible. Only 7 percent of those who began on the college prep track moved down to the noncollege prep track, while 7 percent of those who began there moved up. Clearly, these small figures indicate a high degree of intraschool segregation and closedness. In fact, greater mobility between levels has been reported in English secondary modern schools, where streaming is usually thought to be more rigid and fixed than tracking in this country. (It must be remembered, of course, that in England the more rigid break is between modern secondary and grammar schools.) And, as we will see, separation of students into fixed tracks results in the creation of relatively distinct student subcultures.

Effects of Track Position

Track Position and Academic Achievement

Does track position independently affect grades? Although we cannot be entirely certain because of simultaneous influence of other factors, the data strongly suggest that it does. Table 1 shows that a far greater percentage of college prep than noncollege prep students achieved in the top quarter

Table 1: Grade Point Average by Track Position

	GPA				
	Top Quarter of class	Second Quarter of class	Third Quarter of class	Bottom Quarter of class	Total (No.)
College prep	37%	29%	23%	11%	100% (752)
Noncollege prep	2%	16%	30%	52%	100% (405)

[6]John I. Kitsuse and Aaron V. Cicourel, *The Educational Decision-Makers* (Indianapolis: The Bobbs-Merrill Co., Inc., 1963).

of their class (37 percent vs. 2 percent), while over four times a greater percentage of noncollege prep students fell in the lower quarter (52 percent vs. 11 percent).

Clearly, this is a great difference in achievement. But to what extent is it caused by track position itself, as against other factors? It is often argued, for example, that noncollege-bound students do less well in schoolwork because of family background; they more often come from blue-collar homes where less value is placed on grades and college, achievement is encouraged less, books and help in schoolwork are less available and the quality of language is poor. Others would argue that the difference in grades in Table 1 can be explained by the fact that college prep students are simply brighter; after all, this is one of the reasons they were selected into college prep courses. Still others would contend that lower-track students get lower grades because they performed less well in elementary and junior high, have fallen behind in the accumulation of learning, and probably try less hard in high school.

**Table 2: Grade Point Average by Track Position,
Controlling for Father's Occupation, IQ, and Ninth-Grade
GPA**[a]

		GPA			
	Top Quarter of class	Second Quarter of class	Third Quarter of class	Bottom Quarter of class	Total (No.)
College prep	30%	31%	27%	12%	100% (681)
Noncollege prep	4%	23%	38%	35%	100% (326)

[a]In this and later tables, the procedure for controlling is a weighted mean percentage technique known as test factor standardization.

Each of these alternative explanations is quite plausible and must be taken seriously. That is, lower-track students indeed might get lower grades partly because they more often come from lower-class families, have lower IQ's, and have developed an accumulated deficit in learning through lower performance in the past. Fortunately, it is possible with our data to separate out the influence of track position from these other factors by "controlling" or "holding constant" the effects of father's occupation, IQ, and grade point average (GPA) for the last semester of junior high school.

Table 2 shows that even when the effects of these confounding factors are eliminated (through a weighted percentage technique known as *test factor standardization*), a very sizeable difference in GPA between tracks remains. For instance, an average of 35 percent of noncollege-bound students fell in the bottom quarter, compared with 12 percent of college prep students. These figures, which are similar for both boys and girls, clearly suggest that assignment to the noncollege prep track has a rather strong negative influence on grades. While family background, ability, and past performance clearly affect achievement, these data indicate it is too simplistic to attribute track differences in GPA entirely to these factors. In fact, we found the independent effect of track position on GPA to be greater than the independent effect of father's occupation, IQ, or previous GPA. And, while there was a moderate difference in ninth-grade GPA between those assigned to the college prep and noncollege prep tracks, this difference had greatly increased by the senior year. This widening gap resulted from the fact that a higher percentage of college prep students improved in GPA between the sophomore and senior years, while a higher percentage of the noncollege-bound declined. A number of possible reasons for this widening difference in achievement will be discussed later.

Track Position and Participation in Extracurricular Activities

Selection into the lower track has negative effects which are not singular and isolated. Rather, the effects are woven together into a complex pattern of attitudes toward self, others, school, and the future behavior and performance in school; relations with other students and teachers; and even out-of-school behavior. Within the school itself, the noncollege bound are usually outside the mainstream of student life, partly because of self-exclusion and partly because of intentional or unintentional exclusion by other students and teachers.

Table 3: Amount of Participation in Extracurricular Activities During High School[a]

	No Activities	One or Two Activities	Three or More Activities	Total (No.)
College prep	21%	35%	44%	100% (537)
Noncollege prep	58%	31%	11%	100% (216)

[a]Data for larger school only.

This is illustrated by the figures in Table 3 on participation in extra-curricular activities in one of the schools for which data were available. Whereas 44 percent of college prep students participated in three or more activities during high school, only 11 percent of noncollege bound students participated that much. The social marginality reflected here, among the noncollege-bound, probably resulted in further alienation because of isolation from the positive educational influences from participating students and the teachers who sponsored their activities.

Track Position and Dropout Rate

Does track position also influence the chance that students will stay in high school through graduation or drop out? Table 4 indicates that the chances of dropping out were nine times greater if the student was on a noncollege-bound track (36 percent vs. 4 percent). Of course, it is again possible that it is not track position itself that exerts this adverse effect, but initial differences in educational ability, aspiration, or commitment which students brought with them at the beginning of high school. Since this is a

Table 4: Dropout Rate by Track Position Career by End of Senior Year

CAREER BY END OF SENIOR YEAR

	Graduated[a]	Transferred to Another school	Dropped out	Total (No.)
College prep	86%	10%	4%	100% (752)
Noncollege prep	57%	7%	36%	100% (405)

[a]A small number in this category were delayed in graduating until one year after their class.

Table 5: Dropout Rate by Track Position, Controlling for Father's Occupation, IQ, and Ninth-Grade GPA

CAREER BY END OF SENIOR YEAR

	Graduated	Transferred to Another school	Dropped out	Total (No.)
College prep	88%	8%	4%	100% (681)
Noncollege prep	74%	7%	19%	100% (326)

real possibility, we have separated out some of these "selection" influences, just as we did with academic achievement, by controlling for father's occupation, IQ, and previous GPA. Table 5 shows that noncollege-bound students still dropped out in considerably greater proportion than college-bound students (19 percent vs. 4 percent). As before, the relationship holds among boys and girls alike.

Further analyses not shown here revealed that track position made very little difference in dropout rate among students who were average or high achievers. However, among low achievers it made a great deal of difference. For instance, 43 percent of noncollege prep students who achieved in the bottom half of their class dropped out, compared with 9 percent of low achieving college prep students. The overall independent influence of track position on the dropout rate was greater than the influence of father's occupation, previous achievement, or IQ, just as it was on academic achievement.

The findings reported so far strongly suggest that the noncollege prep experience has a negative, dampening effect on commitment to school and that it independently contributes to resentment, frustration, and hostility finally ending in active withdrawal from the alienating situation of school.

Track Position and Misbehavior in School

Every principal is confronted with continuous pressures to maintain order in his school. These pressures come from outside the school (the community expects teen-agers to be kept off the streets during the day and to obey school authorities while in attendance), as well as inside (teachers expect the bureaucracy to run reasonably quietly and on schedule so they can get on with the job of teaching—and instilling respect for authority—and so they will not be unduly threatened by their students). The sheer size of most schools makes the management of masses of students difficult enough, but the fact that many are there only because they have to be exacerbates the task still further.

When students misbehave and violate school rules, most teachers and principals point their fingers at the parents, at bad influences from the student's friends, or at the students' own personality defects. But the data in Table 6 suggests that rebellion and misbehavior may be partly caused by the school itself, through its tracking system. Utilizing discipline records kept in his office by the vice principal of the larger of the two schools, we recorded a variety of information on types of offenses, disciplinary action taken, and attributes of offenders during the senior year of the students in our sample. (The resulting data, then, are on a sample of all students in the school, not just those from one graduating class.) As shown in the table, while noncollege prep students comprised 29 percent of the total class we studied, they comprised 53 percent of all students who were disciplined at least once during the year by the vice principal, 70 percent of those who were disciplined three or more times, and 51 percent of those who were suspended. While our data do not establish a definite causal linkage between track position and misbehavior, they lend strong additional support to the conclusion that assignment to the noncollege-prep track often leads to resentment, declining commitment to school, and rebellion. If large size and compulsory attendance make the job of behavior management difficult, the tracking system may make it more formidable yet.

Track Position and Delinquency

As a principal agency of adolescent socialization, the school must seek to foster a commitment to law-abiding behavior among teen-agers. Among the vast majority of youth, the school is fairly successful. But if noncollege-prep track position generates a sense of frustration and alienation, a tendency to drop out, and greater misconduct in school, might it not also result in rebelliousness and delinquency outside the school? The top part of Table 7 indicates that when juvenile court records are used as the indicator of delinquency 16 percent of the noncollege prep students were delinquent while in high school, compared to less than half as high a percentage (6 percent) of the college prep students. Of course this may be the result of greater delinquency proneness in the first place among students who entered the

Table 6: Misconduct in School by Track Position[a]

| | TRACK POSITION | | | |
	College Prep	Noncollege Prep	Unknown	Total (No.)
A. One or more recorded violations	36%	53%	11%	100% (220)
B. Three or more recorded violations	19%	70%	11%	100% (37)
C. Suspended from school	37%	51%	12%	100% (65)
D. Percentage of all students in each track[b]	71%	29%	0%	100% (753)

[a]The data on misconduct are based on violations recorded in the vice principal's office for students from all three classes during the 1963–1964 school year in the larger school.

[b]These data are only for the class which entered as sophomores in the fall, 1961, in the larger school (most of whom were seniors during the year when the misconduct data were collected). There is no reason to believe this class differed from others in distribution between tracks.

lower track. However, when we limit the analysis to those students who did not have a court record before high school the difference still remains, as shown in the lower part of Table 7.

Table 7: Recorded Delinquency by Track Position

A. TOTAL DELINQUENCY RATES

	Nondelinquent	*Delinquent*	*Total (No.)*
College prep	94%	6%	100% (752)
Noncollege prep	84%	16%	100% (405)

B. DELINQUENCY RATES ACCORDING TO DATE OF FIRST ENTRY

	Non-delinquent	*Delinquent Before and During High School*	*Became Delinquent During High School*	*Total (No.)*
College prep	94%	1%	5%	100% (752)
Noncollege prep	84%	5%	11%	100% (405)

As Albert Cohen argued over a decade ago in *Delinquent Boys,* delinquency may well be largely a rebellion against the school and its standards.[7] At least being outside the mainstream of success and involvement in school may leave many of the noncollege-bound more open and susceptible to deviant influences from other youth. Our analysis suggests that the key factor in rebellion or "drift" into delinquency may not be working-class background as in Cohen's analysis, but rather noncollege prep status in the school's tracking system, with the low achievement and marginal standing that go along. This conclusion is consistent with Hargreaves' findings on the effect of streaming at Lumley:

> . . . There is a real sense in which the school can be regarded as a generating factor of delinquency. Although the aims and efforts of the teachers are directed towards deleting such tendencies, the organization of the school and its influence on subcultural development unintentionally foster delinquent values. . . . For low-stream boys . . . , school simultaneously exposes them to these values and deprives them of status in these terms. It is at this point they may begin to reject the values because they cannot succeed in them. More than this the school provides a mechanism through the streaming system whereby their failure is effected and institutionalized, and also provides a situation in which they can congregate together in low streams.[8]

---

[7] Albert K. Cohen, *Delinquent Boys* (Glencoe, Ill.: Free Press, 1955).
[8] David H. Hargreaves, *Social Relations in a Secondary School* (New York: Humanities Press, 1968), p. 173.

Interpretation

We have seen, then, that when compared with college prep students, non-college prep students experience lower achievement, greater deterioration of achievement, less participation in extra-curricular activities, a greater tendency to drop out, more misbehavior in school, and more delinquency. Further, we have argued that these differences are partly *caused by* the student's position in the tracking system.

What are the influences accounting for these differences? What is there about taking college prep or noncollege prep courses which leads to these differences in success, involvement and continuation in school, and conformity or deviancy? Our data themselves do not provide the explanations, but several other studies, as well as social psychological theory do provide a number of probable answers.

The Self-fulfilling Prophecy

The best lead for explaining our findings comes from David Hargreaves' *Social Relations in a Secondary School,* a study of the psychological, behavioral, and educational consequences of the student's position in the streaming system of an English secondary modern school.[9] In "Lumley School," the students (all boys) were assigned to one of five streams on the basis of ability and achievement, with the score on the "11 plus" examination playing the major role. Like the schools we studied, students in the different streams were publicly recognized as high or low in status and were fairly segregated, both formally in different classes and informally in friendship groups. It is quite probable, then, that his explanations for the greater antischool attitudes, animosity toward teachers, academic failure, disruptive behavior, and delinquency among the low-stream boys apply to the noncollege prep students we studied as well. In fact, the negative effects of the tracking system on noncollege-bound students may be even stronger in our two high schools, since the Lumley streaming system was much more open and flexible, with students moving between streams several times during their four-year careers.

As we noted, a popular explanation for the greater failure and misbehavior among low-stream or noncollege-bound students is that they come from homes that fail to provide the same skills, ambition, or conforming attitude as higher-stream or college-bound students. Hargreaves demonstrates that there is some validity to this position: in his study low-stream boys more often came from homes that provided less encouragement for

[9] Ibid.

academic achievement and higher level occupations, and that were less oriented to the other values of the school and teachers. Similar differences may have existed among the students we studied, although their effects have been markedly reduced by our control for father's occupation, intelligence, and previous achievement.

But Hargreaves provides a convincing case for the position that whatever differences in skills, ambition, self-esteem, or educational commitment high- or low-stream students brought to school were magnified by what happened to them in school, largely because low-stream boys were the victims of a self-fulfilling prophecy in their relations with teachers, with respect to both academic performance and classroom behavior. Teachers of higher-stream boys expected higher performance and got it. Similarly, boys who wore the label of streams "C" or "D" were more likely to be expected by teachers to be limited in ability and to be trouble-makers and were treated accordingly.

> In a streamed school the teacher categorizes the pupils not only in terms of the inferences he makes of the child's classroom behaviour but also from the child's stream level. It is for this reason that the teacher can rebuke an A stream boy for being like a D stream boy. The teacher has learned to *expect* certain kinds of behaviour from members of different streams. . . . It would be hardly surprising if 'good' pupils thus became 'better' and the 'bad' pupils become 'worse.' It is, in short, an example of a self-fulfilling prophecy. The negative expectations of the teacher reinforce the negative behavioral tendencies.[10]

A recent study by Rosenthal and Jacobson in an American elementary school lends further evidence to the position that teacher expectations influence students' performance.[11] In this study, the influence is a positive one. Teachers of children randomly assigned to experimental groups were told at the beginning of the year to expect "unusual intellectual" gains while teachers of the control group children were told nothing. After eight months, and again after two years, the experimental group children showed significantly greater gains in IQ and grades. Further, they were rated by the teachers as being significantly more curious, interesting, happy, and more likely to succeed in the future. Such findings are consistent with theories of interpersonal influence and with the interactional or labelling view of deviant behavior.

If, as often claimed, American teachers underestimate the learning potential of low-track students and expect more negative attitudes and greater trouble from them, it may well be that they partially cause the very failure, alienation, lack of involvement, dropping out, and rebellion they are

---

[10]Ibid., pp. 105–6.

[11]Robert Rosenthal and Lenore Jacobson, *Pygmalion in the Classroom* (New York: Holt, Rinehart and Winston, 1968).

seeking to prevent. As Hargreaves points out at Lumley, "It is important to stress that if this effect of categorization is real, it is entirely unintended by the teachers. They do not wish to make low streams more difficult than they are!" [12] Yet the negative self-fulfilling prophecy was probably real, if unintended and unrecognized, in our two schools as in Lumley.

Stigma

Assignment to the lower track in the schools we studied carried with it a strong stigma, just as it did at Lumley. As David Mallory was told by an American boy, "Around here you are *nothing* if you're not college prep." [13] A noncollege prep girl in one of the schools we studied told one of the authors she always carried her "general" track books upside down, because of the humiliation she felt from having them seen by other students as she walked through the halls.

The corroding effect of such stigmatizing on self-esteem is well known. As Patricia Sexton has put it, "He (the low track student) is bright enough to catch on very quickly to the fact that he is not considered very bright. He comes to accept this unflattering appraisal because, after all, the school should know." [14]

One ex-delinquent in Washington, D.C. told one of the authors in the following words how the stigma from his low track affected him:

> It really don't have to be the tests, but after the tests, there shouldn't be no separation in the classes. Because, as I say again, I felt good when I was with my class, but when they went and separated us—that changed us. That changed our ideas, our thinking, the way we thought about each other and turned us to enemies toward each other—because they said I was dumb and they were smart.
>
> When you first go to junior high school you do feel something inside—its like ego. You have been from elementary to junior high, you feel great inside. You say, well, daggone, I'm going to deal with the *people* here now, I am in junior high school. You get this shirt that says Brown Junior High or whatever the name is and you are proud of that shirt. But then you go up there and the teacher says—"Well, so and so, you're in the basic section, you can't go with the other kids." The devil with the whole thing—you lose—something in you—like it just goes out of you.
>
> *(Did you think the other guys were smarter than you?)* Not at first—I used to think I was just as smart as anybody in the school—I knew I was smart.

---

[12] Hargreaves, *Social Relations in a Secondary School*, p. 106.

[13] David Mallery, *High School Students Speak Out* (New York: Harper & Brothers, 1962), p. 113.

[14] Patricia C. Sexton, *Education and Income: Inequality of Opportunity in the Public Schools* (New York: The Viking Press, Inc., © 1961), p. 52.

I *wanted* to go to school, I wanted to get a diploma and go to college and help people and everything. I stepped into there in junior high—I felt like a fool going to school—I really felt like a fool. *(Why?)* Because I felt like I wasn't a part of the school. I couldn't get on special patrols, because I wasn't qualified. *(What happened between the seventh and ninth grades?)* I started losing faith in myself—after the teachers kept downing me, you know. You hear "a guy's in basic section, he's dumb" and all this. Each year—"you're ignorant—you're stupid."[15]

Considerable research shows that such erosion of self-esteem greatly increases the chances of academic failure, dropping out, and causing "trouble" both inside and outside of school.

The Student Subculture

Assignment to a lower stream at Lumley also meant a boy was immediately immersed in a student subculture which stressed and rewarded antagonistic attitudes and behavior toward teachers and all they stood for.[16] If a boy was assigned to the "A" stream, he was drawn toward the values of teachers, not only by the higher expectations and more positive rewards by teachers themselves, but by other students as well. The converse was true of lower-stream boys, who accorded each other high status for doing the *opposite* of what teachers wanted. Because of class scheduling, little opportunity developed for interaction and friendship across streams, with negative stereotyping developing instead. The result was a progressive polarization and hardening of the high- and low-stream subcultures between first and fourth years and a progressively greater negative attitude across stream lines, with quite predictable consequences.

The informal pressures within the low streams tend to work directly against the assumption of the teachers that boys will regard promotion into a higher stream as a desirable goal. The boys from the low streams were very reluctant to ascend to higher streams because their stereotypes of "A" and "B" stream boys were defined in terms of values alien to their own and because promotion would involve rejection by their low-stream friends. The teachers were not fully aware that this unwillingness to be promoted to a higher stream led high informal status boys to depress their performance in examinations. This fear of promotion adds to our list of factors leading to the formation of anti-academic attitudes among low stream boys.[17]

---

[15]Walter E. Schafer and Kenneth Polk, "Delinquency and the Schools," in *Task Force Report: Juvenile Delinquency and Youth Crime,* The Presidents' Commission on Law Enforcement and Administration of Justice (Washington, D.C.: U.S. Government Printing Office, 1967), p. 241.

[16]Ibid.

[17]Ibid., p. 77.

Observations and interviews in the two American schools we studied confirmed a similar polarization and reluctance by noncollege prep students to pursue the academic goals rewarded by teachers and college prep students. However, teachers seldom saw the antischool attitudes of noncollege prep students as arising out of the tracking system—or anything else about the school itself—but out of adverse home influence, limited intelligence, or psychological problems.

Future Payoff

Noncollege-bound students also develop progressively more negative attitudes toward school, especially formal academic work, because they see grades—and indeed school itself—as having little future relevance or payoff. Grades are seen as more important for the future among college prep students. For them, grades are a means toward the identifiable and meaningful end of qualifying for college. Among the noncollege bound, grades are seen as far less important for entry into an occupation or a vocational school. This difference in the instrumental importance of grades is magnified by the perception among noncollege-bound students that it is pointless to put much effort into school work, since it will be unrelated to the later world of work anyway. In *Rebellion in a High School,* Arthur Stinchcombe came to a similar conclusion about the alienating effects of lack of effective articulation of the noncollege-bound high school career with the future occupational career:

> The major practical conclusion of the analysis above is that rebellious behavior is largely a reaction to the school itself and to its promises, not a failure of the family or community. High school students can be motivated to conform by paying them in the realistic coin of future advantage. Except perhaps for pathological cases, any student can be motivated to conform if the school can realistically promise something valuable to him as a reward for working hard. But for a large part of the population, especially the adolescent who will enter the male working class or the female candidates for early marriage, the school has nothing to offer. . . . In order to secure conformity from students, a high school must articulate academic work with careers of students.[18]

Grading Policies

Interviews in the schools we studied suggested the operation of grade ceilings for noncollege prep students and grade floors for college-bound stu-

---

[18]Arthur Stinchcombe, *Rebellion in a High School* (Chicago: Quadrangle Books, 1964), p. 179. © 1964 by Arthur L. Stinchcombe.

dents. That is, by virtue of being located in a college preparatory section or course, college prep students could seldom receive any grade lower than "B" or "C," while students in noncollege-bound sections or courses found it difficult to gain any grade higher than "C," even though their objective performance may have been equivalent to a college prep "B." Several teachers explicitly called our attention to this practice, the rationale being that noncollege prep students do not deserve the same objective grade rewards as college prep students, since they "clearly" are less bright and perform less well. To the extent that grade ceilings do operate for noncollege-bound students, lower grades will only be further insured by the absence of available potential rewards for achievement, with resulting deterioration of motivation and commitment.

Teaching Effectiveness

Finally, numerous investigations of ability grouping, as well as the English study by Hargreaves, have reported that teachers of higher-ability groups are likely to teach in a more interesting and effective manner than teachers of lower-ability groups. Such a difference is predictable from what we know about the effects of reciprocal interaction between teacher and class. Even when the same individual teaches both types of classes in the course of the day, as was the case for most teachers in the two schools in this study, he is likely to be "up" for college prep classes and "down" for noncollege prep classes—and to bring out the same reaction from his students.

Implications.

These, then, are some of the ways the schools we studied contributed to the greater rates of failure, academic decline, uninvolvement in school activities, misbehavior, and delinquency among noncollege-bound students. We can only speculate, of course, about the generalizability of these findings to other schools. However, there is little reason to think the two schools we studied were unusual or unrepresentative and, despite differences in size and social class composition, the findings are virtually identical in both—and are consistent with the speculations, criticisms, and unsystematic observations of numerous writers. To the extent the findings are valid and general, they strongly suggest that, through their tracking system, the schools are partly causing many of the very problems they are trying to solve and are posing an important barrier to equal educational opportunity to lower-income and black students, who are disproportionately assigned to the noncollege prep track. The notion that schools help cause low achievement, deterioration of educational commitment and involvement, the dropout problem, misbehavior, and delinquency is foreign and repulsive to many teachers, administrators, and parents. Yet our evidence is entirely consistent with Kai Erikson's observation that ". . . deviant forms of conduct often seem to derive nourishment from the very agencies devised to inhibit them." [19]

What, then, are the implications from this study? Some might argue that, despite the negative side effects we have shown, tracking systems are essential for effective teaching, especially for students with high ability, as well as for adjusting students early in their careers to the status levels they will occupy in the adult occupational system. We contend that however reasonable this may sound, the negative effects demonstrated here offset and call into serious question any presumed gains from tracking.

Others might contend that the negative outcomes we have documented can be eliminated by raising teachers' expectations of noncollege track students, making concerted efforts to reduce the stigma attached to noncollege classes, assigning good teachers to noncollege track classes, rewarding them for doing an effective job at turning on their students, and developing fair and equitable grading practices in both college prep and noncollege prep classes.

Attractive as they may appear, efforts like these will be fruitless, so long as tracking systems, and indeed schools as we know them, remain unchanged. What is needed are wholly new, experimental environments of teaching-learning-living—even outside today's public schools, if necessary. Such schools of the future must address themselves to two sets of problems highlighted by our findings: ensuring equality of opportunity for students now "locked out" by tracking, and offering—to all students—a far more fulfilling and satisfying learning process.

One approach to building greater equality of opportunity, as well as fulfillment, into existing or new secondary schools is the New Careers model. This model, which provides for fundamentally different linkages between educational and occupational careers, is based on the recognition that present options for entering the world of work are narrowly limited: one acquires a high school diploma and goes to work, or he first goes to college and perhaps then to a graduate or professional school. (Along the way, of course, young men must cope with the draft.)

The New Careers model provides for new options. Here the youth who does not want to attend college or would not qualify according to usual criteria, is given the opportunity to attend high school part time while work-

---

[19]Kai Erikson, *Wayward Puritans: A Study in the Sociology of Deviance.* (New York: John Wiley & Sons, Inc., 1966), p. 14.

ing in a lower-level position in an expanded professional career hierarchy (including such new positions as teacher aide and teacher associate in education). Such a person would then have the options of moving up through progressively more demanding educational and work stages; and moving back and forth between the work place, the high school, and then the college. As ideally conceived, this model would allow able and aspiring persons ultimately to progress to the level of the fully certified teacher, nurse, librarian, social worker, or public administrator. While the New Careers model has been developed and tried primarily in the human service sector of the economy, we have pointed out elsewhere that it is also applicable to the industrial and business sector as well. (See Walter E. Shafer and Kenneth Polk, "Delinquency and the Schools," *Task Force Report: Juvenile Delinquency and Youth Crime.* The President's Commission on Law Enforcement and Administration of Justice, U. S. Government Printing Office, 1967.)

This alternative means of linking education with work has a number of advantages. Students can try different occupations while still in school; students can earn while studying; they can spend more time outside the four walls of the school, learning what can best be learned in the work place; less stigma will accrue to those not immediately college-bound, since they too will have a future; studying and learning will be inherently more relevant because it will relate to a career in which they are actively involved; teachers of such students will be less likely to develop lower expectations because these youth too will have an unlimited, open-ended future; and antischool subcultures will be less likely to develop, since education will not be so negative, frustrating, or stigmatizing.

To ensure equality of opportunity is not enough. Merely to open the channels for lower-income youth to flow into educational careers that are now turning off millions of middle-class, college-bound youth is hardly doing anyone a favor by itself. Though not reflected in our data, many middle-class students now find school even less tolerable than do low-income youth. The empty grade-scrambling, teacher-pleasing, and stultifying passivity such youth must endure stands in greater and greater contrast to their home and other nonschool environments which usually yield much greater excitement, challenge, and reward. More and more are dropping out psychologically, turning instead to drugs, apathy, or political activism, often of an unthinking and self-defeating kind.

What is needed, then, are entirely new and different models that will assure equality of opportunity but also much more in the way of an enriching and rewarding process of growth. Educational environments of the future, incorporating New Careers as well as other new forms, must follow several simple guidelines.

First, successful new learning environments must be based on the recognition and acceptance of each individual's uniqueness. Each person must be allowed and stimulated to develop, learn, and grow as individuals, not as standardized occupants of gross human categories. As Kenneth Keniston stated in *The Uncommitted,* "Human diversity and variety must not only be tolerated, but rejoiced in, applauded, and encouraged." [20]

At the beginning, we pointed out that tracking was an educational response to the increased pupil diversity created by pressure on adolecents to stay in school longer from employers, parents, and educators themselves. While it may be an efficient way to screen large numbers of youth out of the educational and economic systems, and while it may be bureaucratically convenient, tracking is crude at best and destructive at worst in psychological and educational terms. Predictably, the occupants of the categories created by tracking come to be perceived, treated, and taught according to what they are thought to have in common: college material or not college material, bright or not bright, motivated or not motivated, fast or not fast. Yet psychologists of individual differences and learning have told us for years what every parent already knows from common sense and experience: each child is unique in aptitudes, style of interaction, learning style and rate, energy level, interests, self-attitudes, reactions to challenge and stress, and in countless other ways. New educational environments must be adaptable to these differences.

The second guideline must be that the potential for individual growth and development is virtually unlimited and must be freed and stimulated to develop as fully as possible during each student's lifetime. We must stop assuming human potential is somehow fixed or circumscribed. Tragically, tracking—and indeed the whole structure of schooling—is founded on this premise. George Leonard puts it well in his *Education and Ecstacy:* ". . . the task of *preventing* the new generation from changing in any deep or significant way is precisely what most societies require of their educators." [21] Not surprisingly, then, "The most obvious barrier between our children and the kind of education that can free their enormous potential seems to be the educational system itself: a vast, suffocating web of people, practices, and presumptions, kindly in intent, ponderous in response." In building new environments-for-becoming—with rich and limitless opportunities for exploration into self and others, other places, times, and ideas, and the unknown—educators can play a part in seeing to it that more than today's mere fraction of potential learning and growing is unleashed.

The third guideline must be that "learning is sheer delight," to quote Leonard. For the noncollege bound—indeed for the vast majority, including neat and tidy "high achievers"—"schooling" (we can hardly call it learning)

---

[20] Kenneth Keniston, *The Uncommitted: Alienated Youth in American Society* (New York: Dell Publishing Co., 1967).

[21] George Leonard, *Education and Ecstasy* (New York: Dell Publishing Co., 1968).

is the very opposite. Tragically, Leonard may be all too right: "A visitor from another planet might conclude that our schools are hell-bent on creating—in a society that offers leisure and demands creativity—a generation of joyless drudges . . . when joy is absent, the effectiveness of the learning process falls and falls until the human being is operating hesitantly, grudgingly, fearfully at only a tiny fraction of his potential." [22] For joy to enter learning, "cognitive learning" must be reunited with affective, physical, and behavioral growth. The payoff must be now. Will learning then stop with the diploma?

If new learning-teaching-living environments follow these simple guidelines, not only will the negative effects of tracking be eliminated, but several features of the student role that alienate all types of students can also be avoided: passivity, subordination, forced separation from self, fragmented sequencing of learning, age segregation, isolation from community life with the unrealities of school that follow, an almost exclusive instrumental emphasis on future gains from schooling.

In summary, then, the education must afford a chance for every student to experience an individualized, mind-expanding, joy-producing educational process, based on equity of opportunity. But it must do even more. Education must, in the final analysis, address itself to vital issues of man and his survival. Educators then can take a long step toward preserving life itself.

> "Right answers," specialization, standardization, narrow competition, eager acquisition, aggression, detachment from the self. Without them, it has seemed, the social machinery would break down. Do not call the schools cruel or unnatural for furthering what society has demanded. The reason we now need radical reform in education is that society's demands are changing radically. It is quite safe to say that the human characteristics now being inculcated will not work much longer. Already they are not only inappropriate, but destructive. If education continues along the old tack, humanity sooner or later will simply destroy itself. [23]

We must start now.

---

[22]Ibid.
[23]Ibid.

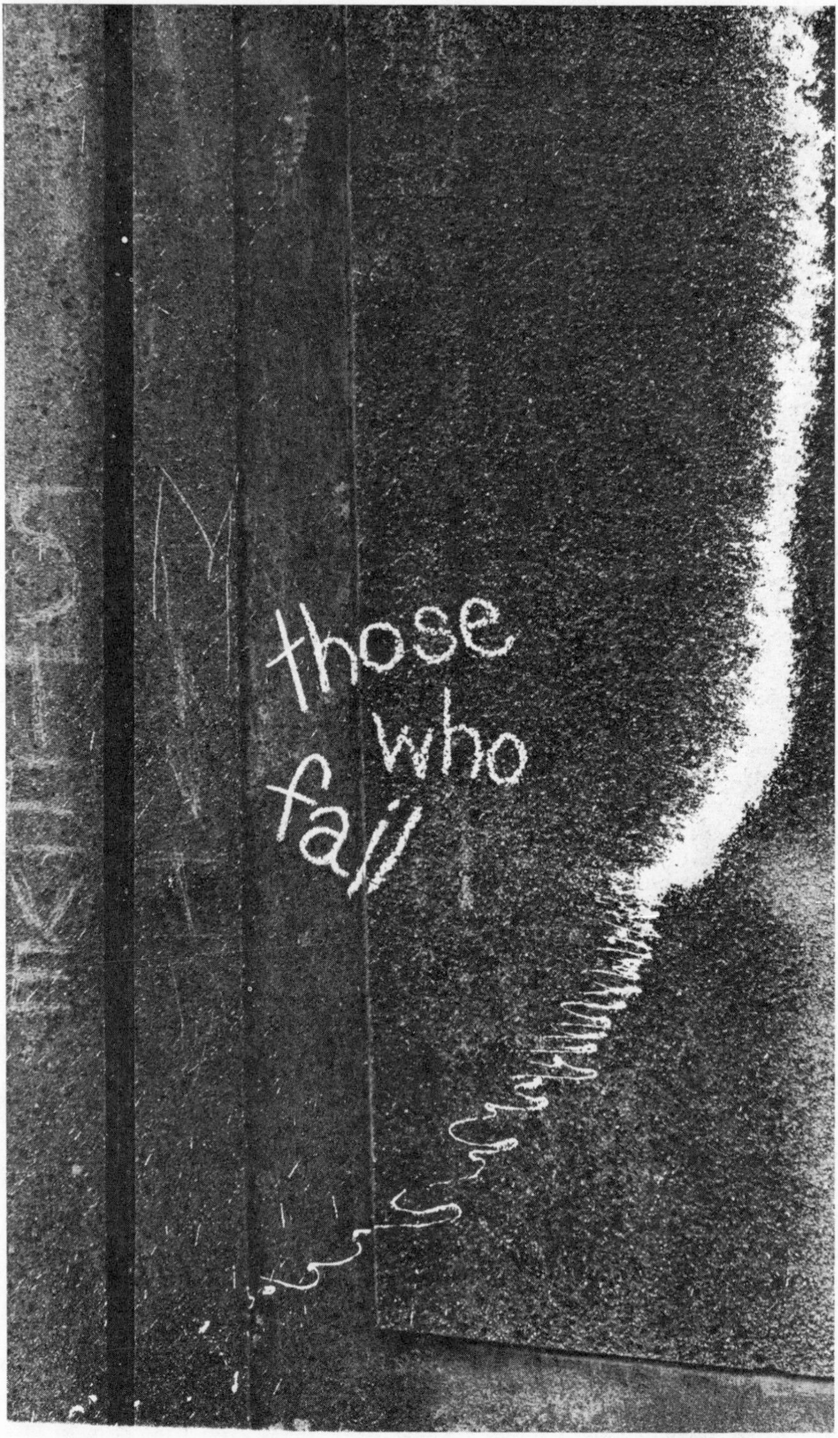
those
who
fail

As our society becomes more specialized economically, a corresponding dependence has developed on formal education for occupational preparation and training. The school's role in society changes, and the relationship of individuals to the school takes on greater significance. Success or failure in this institutional setting becomes an important object of study because academic failure begins to take on implications not present in earlier periods of our history. The educational preparation an individual possesses comes to be one of the fundamental factors in rooting that individual in the occupational world; educational failure can be assumed to be an important precondition to later failure in the adult world.

Various components of the academic adjustment of high school students have come under careful scrutiny in recent literature. In the study of achievement, dropouts, and college orientation, social class has been a dominant factor which recurs as an important explanatory variable. Toby has underscored the role that social class position plays in establishing an orientation to education which has implications for the school maladjustment of lower-class children:

> To sum up, the middle-class child has the following advantages in school compared with the lower-class child: (1) his parents are probably better educated and are therefore more capable of helping him with his school work if this should be necessary; (2) his parents are more eager to make his school work seem meaningful to him by indicating, implicitly or explicitly, the occupational applications of long division or history; (3) the verbal skills which he acquires as part of child training on the middle-class status level prepare him for the type of training that goes on in school and give him an initial (and cumulating) advantage over the lower-class child in the class-room learning situation; and (4) the coordinated pressure of parents, friends, and neighbors reinforce his motivation for scholastic success and increase the probability of good school adjustment.[1]

Hollingshead's classic study of Elmtown provides empirical evidence of the strong relationship between social class position and academic failure.[2] In Elmtown, not a single member of the two upper-class groupings earned a mean grade in the failing range, while one in four of the lower-class students received mean grades in this same failing range. Further, only a slight percentage (8.3 percent) of youth in Class V (the lowest class) earned grades in the highest range, compared with over half (51.4 percent) of the upper class students (see Table 1).

"Those Who Fail" by Kenneth Polk and F. Lynn Richmond. Reprinted with permission of the co-author.

[1]Jackson Toby, "Orientation to Education as a Factor in the School Maladjustment of Lower-Class Children," *Social Forces* 35 (March 1957): 259–66.

[2]A. B. Hollingshead, *Elmtown's Youth* (New York: John Wiley & Sons, Inc., 1949), pp. 172–73. Reprinted by permission of the publisher.

Table 1: Grades Earned by Social Class Level in Elmtown High School

PERCENT WITH MEAN GRADE

Class	85–100	70–84	50–69
I and II	51.4	48.6	00.0
III	35.5	63.2	1.3
IV	18.4	69.2	12.4
V	8.3	66.7	25.0
Total	23.8	66.3	9.9

Source: A. B. Hollingshead, *Elmtown's Youth* (New York: John Wiley & Sons, Inc., 1949), p. 172.

Drawing upon a study of youth in a small city (1960 population, approximately 50,000) in the Pacific Northwest, the phenomenon of academic failure can be examined in further detail. The data for this investigation are provided by a questionnaire submitted to youth in a comprehensive high school (Valley City High School) of about 1,800 students. The instrument was administered to the total high school population present during one day of the spring term of 1963. In addition to the questionnaire, information on academic achievement was obtained from a survey of school records, while the delinquency status of the students was elicited from a survey of county juvenile court records. Because of the interests of this research, the study was restricted to males, yielding a study population of 803.

In this population of adolescents, school failure does not appear to be as closely determined by social class as was true in Elmtown. There is some relationship between the class and achievement variables. More blue-collar boys than white-collar boys (25 versus 15 percent) are earning grades of "D" or "F" (see Table 2). At the same time, the relatively weak correla-

Table 2: Modal Grade Earned by Social Class of Father, Valley City High School Males[a]

	SOCIAL CLASS[b]	
Modal Grade	White Collar (N = 431)	Blue Collar (N = 292)
A and B	44	29
C	41	46
DF	15	25
Total	100%	100%

[a]These data were obtained from questionnaire responses and inspection of school records for 803 male youth enrolled in a relatively large high school in a Pacific Northwest city of roughly 50,000 population. Data are available for slightly more than 90 percent of all males attending the high school.

[b]Social class was defined in terms of father's occupation. Students whose fathers were employed as executives, proprietors, professionals, administrators, owners of small businesses, and as clerical or sales workers were classified as white-collar. Blue-collar fathers were those employed as skilled manual workers, machine operators, and semi-skilled or unskilled workers. Roughly 8 percent could not be classified into one of these two categories.

tion between those two variables suggests that it might be well to look else-where for factors that explain the phenomenon of academic achievement.

In a recent study of youth in River City, it was suggested that factors in addition to social class—factors such as ability, personal and social adjust-ment, and personal motivation—should be considered in order to understand academic achievement.[3] Cicourel and Kitsuse have described the importance of one such additional component, whether or not the individual is in the college-bound track established by the school system.[4] If this identity is as significant as Cicourel and Kitsuse indicate, a strong relationship between college orientation and academic performance would be expected among students in Valley City. This is, in fact, what is found. In Valley City High School, failure (32 percent) is more common among students enrolled in noncollege preparatory courses than it is (7 percent) among those in the college-bound curriculum (see Table 3).

Table 3: Modal Grade Earned by Enrollment in College Preparatory Courses

	ORIENTATION OF COURSES	
Modal Grade	*College Preparatory* (N = 378)	*Not College Preparatory* (N = 382)
A and B	57	20
C	36	48
DF	7	32
Total	100%	100%

But the real significance of these data does not hinge upon this observa-tion. After all, some relationship is to be expected, because college attend-ance ordinarily requires relatively high academic performance in high school. The key findings can emerge only when the interplay between social class, college plans, and academic performance is observed.

Such an analysis substantiates even more forcefully the observations of Cicourel and Kitsuse. When college plans and social class are run simul-taneously against academic achievement, college plans materialize as the more powerful explanatory factor relating to academic success. Using first a relatively imprecise technique, it can be seen that a comparison of the percentage of students with low ("C," "D," or "F") modal grades yields

[3] Robert J. Havighurst et al., *Growing Up In River City* (New York: John Wiley & Sons, Inc., 1962), p. 57.

[4] Aaron V. Cicourel and John I. Kitsuse, *The Educational Decision-Makers* (Indianapolis, Ind.: The Bobbs-Merrill Company, Inc., 1963), p. 146.

greater differences when comparisons are made between levels of college orientation (74–38 = 36, 85–51 = 34) than is the case for social class background (51–38 = 13, 84–74 = 11). (See Table 4.) These differences can be

Table 4: Modal Grades Earned by Social Class and enrollment in College Preparatory Courses

	COLLEGE ORIENTATION				
	COLLEGE PREPARATORY			NOT COLLEGE PREPARATORY	
	Social Class			Social Class	
Grades	White Collar (N = 205)	Blue Collar (N = 136)	Grades	White Collar (N = 119)	Blue Collar (N = 197)
A and B	62	49	A and B	26	15
C, D, and F	38	51	C, D, and F	74	85
Total	100%	100%	Total	100%	100%

expressed more rigorously by comparing the *phi* coefficiencies between college orientation and modal grades when class is held constant, that is .35 and .36 (the corresponding *phi/phi-max* coefficients being .47 and .47), with those obtained between social class and modal grades with college orientation held constant, that is, .14 and .13 (the *phi/phi-max* terms here being .15 and .21). In other words, the effect of college orientation on academic success when social class is held constant is higher than is the effect of social class on grades when college orientation is held constant.

It may be concluded from these findings that this high school is very different from the high school in Elmtown. In Elmtown, one's social class position was an effective shield against academic failure, almost without regard to any other condition. In the present setting, one's economic status will protect the individual from low grades only as long as the student is part of the approved curriculum. Let him fall from that track, and low grades are a likely concomitant. Nearly three-quarters (74 percent) of noncollege preparatory white-collar students earn modal grades of "C" or less, and only slightly less than half (42 percent) have modal grades of "D" or "F." In fact, seven of every ten (71 percent) white-collar students with modal grades of "D" or "F" are found in the noncollege preparatory curriculum.

For the blue-collar youth, on the other hand, there is an avenue of escape from the negative effects of social class as noted in Elmtown. Roughly half (49 percent) of those who identify with the dominant goal of this institution, that is, preparation of students for college, are able to achieve high grades (modal grades of "A" or "B"). Failure to identify with this success goal, however, makes the youth from a working-class background more vulnerable to the grades sanctions administered by this system, since a very high proportion (84 percent) of these noncollege oriented, blue-collar youth earn modal grades of "C" or less.

In suggesting that class is not as directly relevant a factor as is college orientation for the prediction of academic failure, support is given here to the conclusion of Cicourel and Kitsuse that the effects of class origins increasingly are being mediated by academic achievement. The high school sees itself as a training ground for the university, and it is the college bound who receive its academic and status rewards.[5]

On the positive side of the ledger, it can be pointed out that the search for talent in Valley City appears to make school personnel somewhat less sensitive to the effects of class background, as long as the blue-collar youth identifies with the goal of going on to college. On the negative side, it should be remembered that a majority of blue-collar youth are not oriented to college. For many of these students, the high school represents the terminal point in their formal education. These are the students who will pay the high price of economic vulnerability when they become adults. And their vulnerability will be due to the lack of concern, so typical of the middle-class, college-oriented comprehensive high school, for the adequate education of noncollege, work-bound students.

To this deferred penalty can be added the myriad of punishments applied to these youngsters while they are still in high school. Concomitant with other changes that have altered the structure of American education, schools are expected to serve an ever-widening set of socializing functions. The high school is required to enter more directly into the social as well as the academic life of students. In such a system, academic failure could become a double-edged sword, resulting in failure in the social or activity dimension of student life as well. Evidence for this double failure in terms of lowered participation in activities is reported in an earlier study by Vinter and Sarri. Here in Valley City High School as well, academically unsuccessful youth are less likely to spend time in extracurricular activities at school than are more successful students (42 *versus* 58 and 70 percent spending at least one or more hours a week participating in extracurricular activities). (See Table 5.) Vinter and Sarri see this as fitting into a pattern of punishments, including denial of a wide variety of privileges and opportunities within the school, the loss of esteem among classmates, being chosen but seldom for minor but prestigeful classroom or school assignments, and exclusion from participation in certain extracurricular activities. This

---

[5]Ibid., pp. 144–45.

Table 5: Involvement in School Activities by Modal Grade Earned

	MODAL GRADE		
Hours spent during week in extra-curricular activities at school	*A and B (N = 301)*	*C (N = 343)*	*D and F (N = 159)*
None	27	41	54
One or more	70	58	42
Unknown	3	2	5
Total	100%	101%	101%

process, in turn, often resulted in negative parental responses, representing a third penalty.[6]

The systematic patterning of punishments resembles closely a process of *identity spoilage* that accompanies stigmatization. Goffman describes the meaning of stigma in a way that is all too easy to relate to the situation of the unsuccessful student in the school setting:

> By definition, of course, we believe the person with a stigma is not quite human. On this assumption we exercise varieties of discrimination, through which we effectively, if often unthinkingly, reduce his life chances. We construct a stigma-theory, an ideology to explain his inferiority and account for the danger he represents, sometimes rationalizing an animosity based on other differences, such as social class.[7]

There can be little doubt that the life chances of the unsuccessful student are dramatically affected by the range of sanctions imposed on him by the school. These data illustrate further some of the specific components of the process of identity spoilage. The faculty of this high school, as is quite common, are called upon at regular intervals not only to make judgments regarding the academic performance of students, but to make judgments about personality attributes as well. On such dimensions as *responsibility* and *industry* teachers might be expected to rate unsuccessful students disproportionately low, as they do (35 *versus* 11 and 2 percent being rated low on responsibility, 53 *versus* 21 and 5 percent low on industry). What is significant is that these teachers also rate the failing students low on *emotional stability* (31 *versus* 8 and 2 percent). (See Table 6.) In this questioning of psychological competence, one can observe a

---

[6]Robert D. Vinter and Rosemary C. Sarri, "Malperformance in the Public School: A Group Work Approach," *Social Work* 10 (January 1965): 3–13 (p. 9).

[7]Erving Goffman, *Stigma: Notes on the Management of Spoiled Identity,* (Englewood Cliffs, New Jersey: Prentice-Hall, Inc., 1963), p. 5.

Table 6: Teacher Evaluation of Selected Student Attributes by Modal Grade Earned

		MODAL GRADE		
		A and B (N = 301)	C (N = 343)	D and F (N = 159)
Item A:	Low	2	11	35
Teacher evaluation	Medium and high	93	80	58
of "responsibility"	Unknown	6	9	6
	Total	101%	100%	99%
Item B:	Low	5	21	53
Teacher evaluation	Medium and high	87	72	42
of "industry"	Unknown	8	8	5
	Total	100%	101%	100%
Item C:	Low	2	8	31
Teacher evaluation of	Medium and high	91	84	65
"emotional stability"	Unknown	8	9	5
	Total	101%	101%	101%

"stigma theory" at work. The ideology of instability permits the teacher to place malperforming students in a defective human category, so that they may be dealt with accordingly.

But what of the students? How do they respond? Data from Valley City High School adolescents provide some clues, although it must be cautioned that these are viewed as hypothesized responses. Because the data all were gathered at one point in time, it is impossible to isolate which condition actually is antecedent.

One place the effects of identity spoilage could be expected to appear would be in the conception these youth have of themselves. As an illustration, it was found that they do not only accurately perceive themselves more often as "not doing well in school" (71 versus 49 and 20 percent), but also they are not as likely to view themselves as "being close to the center of things" (26 versus 34 and 42 percent). (See Table 7.)

One could not expect these youngsters to be passive receptors of stigma. Such an environment creates a considerable amount of psychological pain for many of these unsuccessful youths. Given present compulsory attendance laws, these students find themselves in the position of being forced to attend an institution to which they are, by and large, uncommitted. One way of contending with this situation consists of the development of a set of techniques which allows these students to neutralize the values permeating the school environment. The mechanisms involved

Table 7: Self-Concept Attitudes by Modal Grade Earned

| | | MODAL GRADE | | |
		A and B (N = 301)	C (N = 343)	D and F (N = 159)
Item A:	Agree	20	49	71
Agreement with the	Disagree	78	50	29
statement: "I am	Unknown	2	2	2
not doing well in school"	Total	100%	101%	102%
Item B:	Near the center	42	34	26
Extent to which student	Not near the center	50	54	61
perceives that he is	Unknown	9	12	14
"near the center of things"	Total	101%	100%	101%

are analogous to the technique noted among delinquent youth by Sykes and Matza, whereby these youth "condemn the condemners."[8] or, as phrased by McCorkle and Korn in their study of prison inmates, there occurs a "rejection of the rejectors."[9] This reaction, as Sykes and Matza note, can be very important to the self-protection of the individual by "deflecting" the sanctions which result from failure to conform to expectations:

> This orientation toward the conforming world may be of particular importance when it hardens into a bitter cynicism directed against those assigned the task of enforcing or expressing the norms of the dominant society. . . . By a slight extension, the rewards of conformity—such as material success— become a matter of pull or luck, thus decreasing still further the stature of those who stand on the side of the law-abiding. The validity of this jaundiced viewpoint is not so important as its function in turning back or deflecting the negative sanctions attached to violations of the norms. The delinquent, in effect, has changed the subject of the conversation in the dialogue between his own deviant impulses and the reactions of others; and by attacking others, the wrongfulness of his own behavior is more easily repressed or lost to view.[10]

What are the specific components of the neutralization process? A number of different things appear to be involved. First, the student's failure, coupled with the other punishments that accompany failure, give the school

---

[8]Gresham M. Sykes and David Matza, "Techniques of Neutralization: A Theory of Delinquency," *American Sociological Review* 22 (December 1957): 664–70.

[9]Lloyd W. McCorkle and Richard Korn, "Resocialization Within Walls," *The Annals of the American Academy of Political and Social Science* 293 (May 1954): 88–89.

[10]Sykes and Matza, *"Techniques of Neutralization,"* p. 668.

a different affective coloration for the unsuccessful youngster. Such a student is more likely to see the school in negative terms. Evidence for this can be seen in the lowered tendency on the part of malperforming youth to rate the school system as "very good" (33 versus 50 and 60 percent) and an increased likelihood of agreeing that school is "dull and boring" (46 versus 31 and 23 percent). (See Items *A* and *B,* Table 8.)

Once the school takes on a negative coloration, a second aspect of the neutralization process consists of the rejection of the goals of the institution. It has been posited that one major goal is the preparation of students for college, and that a strong relationship exists between grades and college orientation. This goal, of course, is a stepping stone to a later accomplishment assumed to follow, namely, entry into some type of white-collar employment. When the occupational plans of these students are examined, it is evident that their spurning of the goals of the high school is reflected in the decreased likelihood that they intend to enter white-collar employment (38 versus 54 and 66 percent). (See Item *C,* Table 8.) In addition, the suggestion of possible ambiguity and uncertainty regarding occupational

Table 8: Neutralizing Attitudes by Modal Grade Earned

		MODAL GRADE		
		A and B (N = 301)	*C* (N = 343)	*D and F* (N = 159)
Item A:	Very good	60	50	33
"How would you	Good; not very good	37	45	58
rate the public	Unknown	2	6	9
school system?"	Total	99%	101%	100%
Item B:	Agree	23	31	46
"School is dull	Disagree	74	66	54
and boring"	Unknown	4	4	1
	Total	101%	101%	101%
Item C:	White Collar	66	54	38
Occupational	Blue Collar	3	12	18
Expectation	Not classifiable or unknown	30	35	44
	Total	99%	101%	100%
Item D:	Agree	40	51	64
"If a person wants to	Disagree	59	47	33
be successful, he some-	Unknown	2	3	3
times has to go against his principles."	Total	101%	101%	100%

alternatives is shown in the higher proportion of "don't know" or nonclassi-
fiable responses among failing youth (44 versus 35 and 30 percent).

Successful neutralization, it might be said, requires not only the rejection of the goals seen as legitimate by the high school but a rejection of
the means for the achievement of that success as well. For an example
of this, among the unsuccessful students in Valley City High School
we find a tendency to agree more often with the statement that success
requires an individual to "go against his principles" (64 versus 51 and 40
percent). (See Item *D*, Table 8.) It is only a small jump to the denial of
the success goal itself once legitimacy is withdrawn from the means necessary to achieve success.

But what of group supports for this neutralization? Neutralization
of values and goals as pervasive as those that permeate the contemporary
middle-class high school would be difficult, at best, to carry out individually.
Others have suggested the important role that peers play in influencing
adolescents generally and the specific role that deviant subcultures play in
response to school failure. Coleman has noted the societal changes which
segregate and insulate youth from adults, leading to the development of
adolescent societies:

> This setting-apart of our children in schools—which take on ever more
> functions, ever more "extracurricular activities"—for an ever longer period
> of training has a singular impact on the child of high school age. He is
> "cut off" from the rest of society, forced inward toward his own age group.
> made to carry out his whole social life with others his own age. With his
> fellows, he comes to constitute a small society, one that has most of its
> important interactions *within* itself, and maintains only a few threads of
> connection with the outside adult society. . . . Society is confronted no
> longer with a set of *individuals* to be trained toward adulthood, but with
> distinct *social systems*, which offer a united front to the overtures made by
> adult society.[11]

For even the "normal" youngster, assuming Coleman has been read
correctly, there is a conflict between the expectations of adults and those
of his peers. What about those who fail? For them, the rejection by the
school leaves little room for any alternative other than that of seeking out
a society of their peers. An additional step in the neutralization process, in
other words, consists of the development of group supports for attitudes and
behavior that violate the standards established by the school. Present data
suggests that this peer involvement has both quantitative and qualitative
dimensions.

Quantitatively, unsuccessful youth are much more likely to spend their
evenings with friends than are successful youth (64 versus 48 and 38 percent

---

[11]James S. Coleman, *The Adolescent Society* (New York: The Free Press of
Glencoe, Inc., 1961), pp. 3–4.

spending two or more nights a week with friends). (See Item A, Table 9.) There are, additionally, important qualitative differences in the friendship patterns of unsuccessful youth. First, they are more likely to seek friends outside the school setting, as can be seen in the increased likelihood that they will have friends who have dropped out of school (43 versus 22 and 16 percent). (See Item *B*, Table 9.) Second, there appears to be a different saliency attached to peer involvements of the academically unsuccessful student. Using Coleman's question forcing a choice between going to a rally as requested by the school principal or going riding with friends,[12] the academic failures are more likely to give a peer-oriented response than are successful students (70 versus 63 and 46 percent). (See Item *C*, Table 9.) Looking at the perception that youth has of peer expectations, unsuccessful students are less likely to think grades (35 versus 53 and 50 percent) or being a leader in activities (65 versus 76 and 84 percent) are important for "making a boy really rate with the other fellows." (See Items *D* and *F*, Table 9.)

Table 9: Peer Culture Involvement by Modal Grade

		MODAL GRADE		
		A and B (N = 301)	C (N = 343)	D and F (N = 159)
Item A:	One or none	59	48	33
Evenings a week spent	Two or more	38	48	64
with friends	Unknown	2	3	3
	Total	99%	99%	100%
Item B:	None	67	55	40
"How many of your	Some	16	22	43
friends have dropped out	Unknown	17	22	18
of high school?"	Total	100%	99%	101%
Item C:	Go to rally	49	32	25
"Suppose school was	Go with friends	46	63	70
dismissed an hour early	Unknown	5	5	5
one day for a pep rally	Total	100%	100%	100%
down at the athletic field,				
and the principal urged				
everyone to go to the				
rally, although it wasn't				
compulsory. On the way,				
some of your friends				
asked you to go riding				
instead of to the pep rally.				
What do you think you				
would do?"				

[12]Ibid., Appendix II, p. 6.

Table 9: Peer Culture Involvement by Modal Grade (Cont.)

		MODAL GRADE		
		A and B (N = 301)	C (N = 343)	D and F (N = 159)
Items D and F: "What things are important for making a boy really rate with the other fellows?"	High Grades			
	Rates high	50	53	35
	Rates low; doesn't matter	45	41	54
	Unknown	5	6	10
	Total	100%	100%	99%
	Being a leader in activities or athletics			
	Rates high	84	76	65
	Rates low; doesn't matter	13	19	30
	Unknown	2	5	4
	Total	99%	100%	99%

The web of evidence here supports the notion of neutralization generally, and implies the existence of a subculture which buttresses this neutralization. Ultimately, concern with the subcultural response leads to the subject of delinquency. Cohen has suggested that working-class delinquency may be a function of the working-class boy's reaction against the status frustration which results, fundamentally, from his measurement in school by the middle-class measuring rod. He then argues that the specific components of delinquency—such as maliciousness, nonutilitarianism, and negativism—allow the youth to strike back at the basic values of the middle class, especially as these are reflected by the school.[13]

These data suggest that delinquency in this setting may be interpreted as a reaction against the school regardless of class position. In fact, a comparison of the incidence of delinquency by academic grade and social class level shows virtually no effect being produced by economic status at the same time that rather striking relationships obtain between differing grade levels. For both white-collar and blue-collar students, delinquency is low where students have earned modal grades of "A" or "B" (white-collar 4 percent, blue-collar 4 percent); it is higher at the "C" level (white-collar 11 percent, blue-collar 12 percent), and reaches its highest level among students who have modal grades of "D" or "F" (white-collar 20 percent, blue-collar 27 percent).

---

[13]Albert K. Cohen, *Delinquent Boys* (New York: The Free Press of Glencoe, Inc., 1955), p. 84.

This finding, that school adjustment shows a much higher relationship to delinquency than does social class, serves to emphasize again the extent to which trouble appears as a direct consequence of academic failure. This may be a direct reflection of the impact that varied changes in economic and social structure have on the school setting. Margaret Mead has emphasized the changing role of the American parent, whereby parents are not able to give children a final status by rooting them for a life in a highly structured and dependable social structure. Instead, their children must be trained for a race that youth will run alone.[14] This is another way of saying that, as the division of labor becomes more elaborate, there is ever expanding dependence on achievement as opposed to ascription as a basis for adult success. Achievement, furthermore, is generally dependent upon possession of formalized skills, skills provided primarily by schools. This school becomes, then, the initial battleground where success struggles take place. Although success in school is no guarantee of later adult success, failure in school has the general effect of excluding an individual from performing those successful occupational roles requiring formal and technical skills.

There are three major implications of these conditions. First, when and if society does become genuinely involved in a search for talent, wherever that talent might lie, the effects of social class on occupational and academic achievement are bound to be diminished. Although the intellectual and cultural orientations of middle-class parents may help place their child "one leg up," the concern of the educational system with such programs and terms as *early enrichment, college work-study programs for the impoverished,* or *compensatory education* demonstrates the direction being taken to reduce, especially for the talented, the initial advantage that the middle-class child might possess.

Second, for both middle-class and working-class youth the school becomes an environment that must be contended with if any adult success is to obtain. For middle-class youth this will mean that, unlike Elmtown of a generation ago, the class position is no longer sufficient to protect the individual from academic failure *and all that goes with it.* For the working-class youth, the pattern of ignoring school is becoming less and less possible. Successful participation in the adult world is changing from success resulting from the possession of more rather than less skills to success in which the possession of some formalized or technical skill is an absolute necessity.

Third, failure in school, regardless of other factors, generates wider patterns of failure and problems. The inability to contend successfully with school will mark the individual and set up wider patterns of troublesome behavior for him and the community. It is suggested here that the resultant

---

[14]Margaret Mead, *And Keep Your Powder Dry* (New York: William Morrow & Co., Inc., 1942), cited in Cohen, *Delinquent Boys,* p. 89.

trouble may follow a sequence close to that suggested by Cohen in his description of reaction formation as a factor generating the delinquent subculture.[15] In the case of academic failure, it is found that the unsuccessful student also fails in the activity, or social, dimension of the school. This double failure, the data suggest, sets into motion techniques of neutralization that deflect the sanctions applied by the school. This neutralization functions by permitting the individual to withdraw from the wider definition of success, which includes withdrawal of the legitimacy attaching to the means for achieving success.

One fundamentally important aspect of this neutralization process is that it results in group supports of hostility and aggression against the system. One does not find isolated, alienated individuals attempting to contend with failure on their own. Instead, evidence suggests the existence of a subculture of alienated youth who work in concert both to provide effective neutralization and to generate trouble for the system. The high incidence of delinquency among this group represents one of the symptoms of this reaction against the school and community. What these data intimate is that class-linked theories of delinquency may become outdated as the class variable per se becomes less relevant for school adjustment and, therefore, less relevant in the generation of delinquency.

---

[15]Cohen, *Delinquent Boys,* p. 132.

school cultures
adolescent commitment
and delinquency

7·75

Recent sociological literature on youth has made extensive use of such terms as "adolescent subculture,""adolescent society," and "youth culture" to argue for the centrality of peer relations in teen-age life. Coleman, in particular, has argued that a formalized educational institution set apart from the rest of society has emerged to replace family-centered, "natural processes" of education:

> As an unintended consequence, society is confronted no longer with a set of individuals to be trained toward adulthood, but with distinct social systems which offer a united front to the overtures made by adult society.[1]

Ernest Smith sees direct conflict arising from extensive involvement in adolescent peer relationships:

> Youth culture enforces a conformity upon its members, which is intensified by the withdrawal of youth from adult socializing institutions and by the resulting secrecy, which acts as an obstacle to the supervision and control of adults over youth activities. From this secrecy, there arises the series of conflicts between youth culture and adult culture that is characteristic of American society.[2]

Not all commentators share this view. Some have contended that the existence of a distinct adolescent peer culture is a myth,[3] with perhaps detrimental effects on our understanding of the behavior of youth.[4] Some recent writers have skirted the question of whether the thing called youth culture exists, and instead have focused on questions related to when and under what conditions the influence of peers can be observed in behavior, or on analyses of the relationship of youth culture to drinking, delinquency, or sexual behavior.[5]

"School Cultures, Adolescent Commitments, and Delinquency" by Kenneth Polk and David Halferty. This chapter was previously published in the Journal of Research in Crime and Delinquency *4 (July 1966): 82–96. Reprinted by permission of the co-author and the Council on Crime and Delinquency.*

---

[1]James S. Coleman, *The Adolescent Society* (New York: The Free Press of Glencoe, Inc., 1961), p. 4.

[2]Ernest A. Smith, *American Youth Culture* (New York: The Free Press of Glencoe, Inc., 1962), p. 7.

[3]Frederick Elkin and William A. Westley, "The Myth of Adolescent Culture," *American Sociological Review* 20 (December 1955): 680–84.

[4]Robert C. Bealer, Fern K. Willits, and Peter R. Maida, "The Myth of a Rebellious Adolescent Subculture," in *Rural Youth in Crisis*, ed. Lee G. Burchinal (Washington, D.C.: U.S. Department of Health, Education, and Welfare, 1965).

[5]For examples, see George L. Maddox and Bevode C. McCall, *Drinking Among Teen-Agers* (New Haven: College and University Press, 1964); Herbert Bloch and Arthur Niederhoffer, *The Gang: A Study in Adolescent Behavior* (New York: Philosophical Library, 1958); and Ira L. Reiss, "Sexual Codes in Teen-Age Culture," *Annals of the American Academy of Political and Social Science* 338 (November 1961): 53–62.

The purpose of this paper is to examine a set of empirical data to throw light on the nature of the things which are supposed to make up the adolescent subculture and to analyze the extent to which this concept can add to the understanding of juvenile delinquency.

The data are provided by a questionnaire submitted to all the youth present during one day of the spring term of 1963 in a high school of about 1,800 students in a small city (1960 population, approximately 51,000) in the Pacific Northwest. In addition to the questionnaire, information on academic achievement was obtained from a survey of school records, while the delinquency status of the students was elicited by a survey of county juvenile court records. Because of the research interest in delinquency, and because of the assumption that it is a predominantly male phenomenon, this study is restricted to boys of high school age. For this investigation, a sample of half the males was drawn—a population of 410—for the correlational analysis.

Adolescent Behavior

What are the dimensions of adolescent behavior? Factor analysis might supply some interesting answers to this question. To explore the underlying order in the general domain of adolescent attitudes and behavior, we selected the following variables for analysis. (The italicized terms refer to the code name of the item as it appears in the intercorrelation matrix and subsequent tables.)

1. "Modal" grade—the grade that appears most frequently on a boy's high school record. (*Grades.*)
2. Agreement or disagreement with the statement: "I am not doing so well in school." (*Doing well.*)
3. Agreement or disagreement with the statement: "School is dull and boring." (*School attitude.*)
4. Do you plan to go to college? (*College plans.*)
5. What three subjects that you are taking (or have taken) do you like best? (*Academic subjects.*)
6. In general, how do you feel about your high school? (*Alienation.*)
7. In the average week, how many hours do you spend at schoolwork at home? (*Homework.*)
8. In the average week, how many hours do you spend at extracurricular activities at school? (*Extracurricular activities.*)
9. In the average week, how many evenings do you spend at school-related activities? (*School-related activities.*)
10. In the average week, how many evenings do you spend at club or other organized group activities? (*Organized group activities.*)
11. What kind of work do you intend to go into when you finish schooling? (*Occupational aspirations.*)

12. What is your father's (or stepfather's) occupation? (*Father's occupation.*)
13. How much education does your father have? (*Father's education.*)
14. Suppose school were dismissed an hour early one day for a rally, and the principal urged everyone to go to the rally, although no one had to go. On the way, some of your best friends asked you to go somewhere instead of to the rally. What do you think you would do? (*Friends/rally.*)
15. Let's say you had always wanted to belong to a particular club at school, and then finally you were asked to join. But then you found out that your parents didn't approve of the group. Do you think you would join? (*Club/parents.*)
16. Generally speaking, which one of these things would be hardest for you to take—your parents' disapproval, your teachers' disapproval, or your best friends' disapproval? (*Friend/parent.*)
17. What things are important for making a boy really rate with the other fellows? Stirring up a little excitement? (*Rate "excitement."*)
18. Agreement with the following statement: "My parents always know where I am and what I'm doing." (*Whereabouts known.*)
19. In the average week, how many evenings do you spend at home with your family? (*Time with family.*)
20. In the average week, how many hours do you spend visiting friends in their home? (*Visiting, their home.*)
21. In the average week, how many hours do you spend with friends at your house? (*Visiting, your home.*)
22. In the average week, how many hours do you spend going out with friends? (*Going out.*)
23. In the average week, how many hours do you spend going out on dates? (*Dating.*)
24. Do you have a car of your own? (*Own a car.*)

As a first step, an intercorrelational matrix of the twenty-four variables was computed (Table 1). This matrix was factored by use of Hotelling's principal components method. Four of the nine factors extracted were subsequently omitted from further analysis because of minimal loadings on the factors and the resultant small contribution to the variance of the items (in no case over 4 percent of the common variance). The five factors remaining accounted for 39 percent of the common variance.

Rotations of the factors were accomplished graphically. This technique permitted continuous inspection of the factor patterns that emerged from the data. Thus the rotations were reviewed in light of the interpretations that derived from the structures as they were isolated.

Following the procedure suggested by Cattell, a loading of .30 or higher is arbitrarily defined as significant, while loadings under .30 are treated as zero loadings.[6] By use of this criterion, and as a result of rotation, Factors

---

[6]Raymond B. Cattell, *Factor Analysis* (New York: Harper & Row, Publishers, 1952), p. 284.

Table 1: Intercorrelation Matrix

Items	1	2	3	4	5	6	7	8	9	10	11	12	13	14	15	16	17	18	19	20	21	22	23	24	25	26	27	28
1. Grades	1.0	45	24	41	30	-19	38	18	12	02	20	13	22	-25	-04	-11	00	05	09	-20	-14	-16	-12	-18	-23	-26	-29	21
2. Doing well		1.0	33	38	16	-17	32	19	10	05	26	11	13	-19	02	-10	02	06	03	-04	-08	-08	-04	-10	-12	-12	-16	20
3. School attitude			1.0	43	22	-31	29	22	16	14	28	09	16	-37	-08	-11	-08	20	20	-08	-07	-13	-08	-15	-18	-23	-27	21
4. College plans				1.0	37	-29	47	30	24	20	45	29	31	-28	-01	-10	-01	05	05	-08	-03	-09	-06	-10	-21	-24	-33	28
5. Academic subjects					1.0	-10	29	12	11	13	14	24	20	-12	-03	-06	08	-06	-03	-13	-12	-04	-09	-10	-17	-24	-17	18
6. Alienation						1.0	-17	18	-12	-01	-20	-05	-12	-08	-11	02	08	-17	-13	12	-01	-05	-04	-14	-23	-15	-24	-18
7. Homework							1.0	24	25	13	14	15	20	-23	-26	-04	-11	08	-05	12	08	-10	-01	05	-04	00	07	19
8. Extracurricular activities								1.0	37	23	16	13	21	-13	-04	-11	05	12	08	-12	-01	05	01	21	13	17	15	11
9. School-related activities									1.0	28	20	-01	23	-17	-02	-04	-10	05	-03	-05	-01	05	13	10	15	14	13	11
10. Organized group activities										1.0	11	-01	05	-12	06	02	00	-03	-08	04	-05	01	10	06	-02	-08	-07	15
11. Occupational aspirations											1.0	13	11	-19	-01	-12	-09	13	09	03	-02	11	10	06	-05	-10	-19	16
12. Father's occupation												1.0	48	-08	-01	-01	02	13	-07	-04	05	-10	-12	-06	-03	-05	-08	08
13. Father's education													1.0	-12	06	02	-06	13	14	05	-14	-17	-06	-11	06	11	-11	06
14. Friend's/rally														1.0	20	15	18	-27	-22	15	08	24	11	17	22	36	38	-28
15. Club/parents															1.0	25	13	-32	-14	09	11	17	16	08	14	20	17	-08
16. Friend/parents																1.0	08	-14	-19	-05	01	06	05	00	07	11	13	10
17. Rate "excitement"																	1.0	-08	-12	03	03	04	08	12	07	11	10	-07
18. Whereabouts known																		1.0	23	-16	-24	-17	-07	-23	-19	-18	-22	17
19. Time with family																			1.0	23	30	-16	-24	-17	10	-20	-22	12
20. Visiting, their home																				1.0	62	51	30	10	17	15	21	-12
21. Visiting, your home																					1.0	48	23	11	15	14	17	-05
22. Going out																						1.0	42	19	18	27	30	-11
23. Dating																							1.0	25	21	14	26	-10
24. Own a car																								1.0	22	34	28	-04
25. Delinquency																									1.0	34	34	-13
26. Drinking																										1.0	59	-24
27. Smoking																											1.0	-25
28. Truant delinquent																												1.0

III and V can be eliminated from further analysis since they show no loadings in the rotated matrix above .30. Accordingly, three major orthogonal dimensions emerge from these data (see Table 2).

Factor A contains the following items:

19. Time with family.
20. Visiting, their home.
21. Visiting, your home.
22. Going out.
23. Dating.
24. Own a car.

These items represent a sociability dimension of adolescent life that has to do with extensiveness of the involvement of youth with their peers. The Visiting, Going Out (with friends), and Dating variables lend themselves directly to this interpretation. Possession of a car may be viewed as necessary for peer involvement to take place, while the negative loading of Time with Family may be evidence of the erosion of family involvement demanded if the youth is to spend time with his peers. This dimension has been named the *Peer Involvement Factor.*

Factor B contains the following items:

1. Grades.
2. Doing well.
3. School attitudes.
4. College plans.
5. Academic subjects.
6. Alienation.
7. Homework.
8. Extracurricular activities.
9. School-related activities.
10. Organized group activities.
11. Occupational aspirations.
12. Father's occupation.
13. Father's education.
14. Friends/rally.

These items comprise a wide range of variables relating to the successful engagement of youth in school affairs. In part, Factor B consists of such behaviorally relevant activities as studying and getting good grades. The plans that a youngster has, for both college and career, appear here, as do his attitudes toward scholastic subject matter, his progress, and the school itself. The rounded character of this school involvement is shown by the appearance here of the variables having to do with participation in activi-

Table 2: Factor Matrix of Adolescent Culture Items

Items	ORIGINAL MATRIX						ROTATED MATRIX						FACTOR PATTERN		
	I	II	III^a	VI	V^a	h²	I"	II"	IV"	III^a	V^a	h²	I"	II"	IV"
1. Grades	-10	47	-24	-36	08	.42	-24	53	01	27	13	.43	0	+	0
2. Doing well	03	39	-27	-32	14	.35	-09	53	-07	21	14	.36	0	+	0
3. School attitude	-04	41	-37	-10	33	.43	-17	48	-36	17	11	.43	0	+	-
4. College plans	-02	30	-65	-33	02	.62	-14	77	-07	-05	-06	.62	0	+	0
5. Academic subject	-00	38	-16	-46	-00	.38	-13	50	16	25	17	.38	0	+	0
6. Alienation	-12	-10	48	-11	-18	.30	16	-33	36	17	11	.30	0	-	+
7. Homework	09	49	-31	-27	10	.43	-07	58	-09	29	05	.44	0	+	0
8. Extracurricular activities	27	26	-40	-12	18	.35	17	50	-24	10	01	.35	0	+	0
9. School-related activities	32	33	-21	-06	09	.27	21	36	-17	26	-04	.27	0	+	0
10. Organized group activities	36	19	-20	-03	05	.21	28	30	-14	16	-06	.22	0	+	0
11. Occupational aspirations	-07	04	-58	-04	12	.36	-10	46	-25	-26	-09	.36	0	+	0
12. Father's occupation	-29	-07	-36	-49	-14	.48	-28	47	29	-28	10	.47	0	+	0
13. Father's education	-25	06	-36	-50	-09	.45	-27	52	25	-18	12	.45	0	+	0
14. Friends/rally	17	-31	42	-20	-21	.39	25	-30	45	-03	17	.38	0	-	+
15. Club/parents	21	-28	-08	-19	-35	.29	27	10	37	-23	-13	.29	0	0	+
16. Friend/parent	15	-11	21	-24	-14	.16	17	-05	31	04	13	.15	0	0	+
17. Rate "excitement"	-20	-22	01	-17	-28	.20	-13	-03	35	-23	-05	.20	0	0	+
18. Whereabouts known	-26	16	-19	42	28	.38	-29	-06	-52	-01	-13	.38	0	0	-
19. Time with family	-32	36	09	17	34	.38	-41	-07	-36	27	13	.39	-	0	-
20. Visiting friends, their home	69	-22	-01	07	03	.53	72	-02	-06	-03	-01	.52	+	0	0
21. Visiting friends, your home	68	-15	-04	13	05	.51	69	01	-14	01	-06	.50	+	0	0
22. Going out	73	-20	-01	-01	-05	.58	76	05	03	00	-04	.58	+	0	0
23. Dating	62	-15	-07	01	01	.41	64	08	-04	-02	-03	.42	+	0	0
24. Own a car	26	-19	17	-04	02	.13	31	-13	08	-02	12	.13	+	0	0

^a Not included in final analysis.

ties. Finally, the socioeconomic variables which serve to set the back-drop for engagement are also present. This dimension is called the *Commitment Factor*.

Factor C contains the following items:

3. School attitude.
6. Alienation.
14. Friends/rally.
15. Club/parents.
17. Rate "excitement."
18. Whereabouts known.
19. Time with family.

This dimension comprises a measure of the salience of peer pressure, an approximation of the attitudes and behavior expected of "rebellious" adolescents. This is shown most clearly in the items taken from Coleman which pose a direct choice between peers and adults. The Excitement aspect may be some indication of the hedonism often attached descriptively to the oppositional youth culture. The negative loading of the Family items reinforces the interpretation of the rejection of adult demands in the face of peer involvement, while the School Attitude items suggest some attitudinal estrangement from school, an estrangement which, interestingly enough, does not appear to be accompanied to any great degree by a behavioral withdrawal from the school. This dimension is labeled the *Rebellion Factor*.

Interpretation of Findings

What do these findings suggest about the nature of adolescent attitudes and behavior? For one thing, the results are not necessarily what we might expect after reading some of the current literature on adolescence. Many sociologists have argued that emphasis on peers and peer culture acts as a deterrent to academic endeavor. Smith, for example, states:

> Cliques set up norms contrary to those of the school. There are generally deterrents to academic achievement, diverting interest into athletics and social activities.[7]

Coleman expresses the same thought, and then goes on to indicate what he perceives to be the social consequences of this effect:

---

[7]Smith, *American Youth Culture*, p. 79.

The relative unimportance of academic achievement, together with the effects shown above, suggest that the adolescent subcultures in these schools exert a rather strong deterrent to academic achievement. . . .

The implications for American society as a whole are clear. Because high schools allow adolescent societies to divert energies into athletics, social activities, and the like, they recruit into adult intellectual activities many people with a rather mediocre level of ability, and fail to attract many with high levels of ability.[8]

Our data, however, do not provide strong supports for such assertions. Sheer involvement with peers does not seem to have any particularly strong relationship to grades, specifically, or to the more general dimension of Commitment. Individually, none of the six variables included within the Peer Involvement dimension has correlations with grades that are above .20 (Visiting, their home, $r = -.20$; Own a car, $r = -.18$; Going out, $r = -.16$; Visiting, your home, $r = -.14$; Dating, $r = -.12$; Time with family, $r = .09$). More important is the general independence of Peer Involvement and Commitment. None of the variables included within the Peer Involvement dimension is loaded on the Commitment dimension, and none of the Commitment variables appears in the Peer Involvement dimension. Whatever problems there may be in the nature of adolescent commitments, the commitment itself appears to be affected by factors other than simple involvement with peers.

Even more startling is the general independence of Commitment and Rebellion. Of the fourteen variables included in Commitment, only three show significant loadings on the Rebellion dimension. Two of these have to do with psychological rejection of school (School attitude and Alienation). The third is the peer-adult authority choice item that specifically relates to the pull between peers and school officials within a school situation which might reasonably be expected to appear in both dimensions (Friend/rally). Significantly, such important school behaviors as grades received, time spent on homework, and participation in activities are not loaded on the Rebellion factor. These findings lend support to Berger's contention that the sources of the adolescent's commitment to school success lie in the nature of the wider society, rather than in the fact of adolescent rebellion alone.[9]

In addition, these data suggest a close relationship between activities and academic achievement. A crucial assumption, for both Coleman and Smith, is that social activities divert energies from academic achievement. Were this actually the case, a negative relationship could be expected between grades and participation in activities. Instead, in this study, these two

[8]Coleman, *The Adolescent Society,* pp. 265–66.
[9]Bennett M. Berger, "Adolescence and Beyond," *Social Problems* 10, no. 4 (Spring 1963): 394–408.

variables are found side by side as part of a total pattern of commitment that a "successful" youngster makes to the school system. The definition of adolescent success implied in the Commitment dimension derives from behavior of various kinds and is not specifically confined to grades or social activities. Others have observed this broad character in the nature of adolescent commitments—commitments which include involvement in social activities along with at least adequate academic performance. Parsons, for example, observes:

> Given the importance of the whole complex which leads toward occupational status, particularly for boys, the peer group has a special set of significances beyond that of easing a difficult transition. For the more successful groups it becomes the principal field for learning skills which in an organizationally complex society must be of the greatest significance, namely skills in "getting along with others." Though the picture is highly variegated, it seems to be broadly true that the leadership of the more prestigeful youth groups, in and out of the school context, coincides broadly with a level of academic achievement which is comparable with high occupational status.[10]

Similarly, Havighurst and Taba note:

> To achieve success in the adolescent peer culture, a boy or girl must stay in school, be a reasonably good student, take part in school activities, and go to the school dances and parties. In the process of adjusting successfully in these ways, he would be learning middle-class morality. The majority of young people attempted to fit themselves into this situation.[11]

The term "commitment' as used here would appear consistent with the usage suggested by Becker.[12] Involvement in the generalized success system of the school may be thought of as consisting of a series of "side bets," which serve to "lock in" the involvement of the student. While at least adequate academic performance may constitute a minimum basic ingredient of his commitment, the "side bets" that a student makes serve an important role in reinforcing his commitment to success within the system. Participation in student activities provides one of the clearest examples of this kind of bet. Once he becomes involved in activities, the adolescent adds a link to the chain locking him to the system. This involvement in activities gives him an increased stake in academic performance, since in all probability con-

---

[10]Talcott Parsons, "A Sociologist's View," in *Values and Ideals of American Youth,* ed. Eli Ginzburg (New York: Columbia University Press, 1961), p. 281.

[11]Robert J. Havighurst and Hilda Taba, *Adolescent Character and Personality* (New York: John Wiley & Sons, Inc., 1949), p. 36.

[12]Howard S. Becker, "Notes on the Concept of Commitment," *American Journal of Sociology* 66, no. 1 (July 1960): 35–36.

tinued engagement in activities will depend to some degree on continued academic success.

The perception of future success, in terms of both occupational and educational aspirations, illustrates another kind of protective bet. The expectation developed by a student that he is going on to college, and his plans to take a white-collar job, serve to commit him to a certain course of academic study and endeavor. As long as he is doing well in school, he can maintain the gamble that he is going to college. If he begins to slip academically, the hedging bet becomes relevant, since its maintenance depends on the main chance of academic success. His involvement in the "side bet," in other words, works back on his concern with academic success, so that a web of engagement is created which might appropriately be termed "commitment."

Such a view reinforces the need for logical clarity in the study of adolescence. The comments of Parsons, and of Havighurst and Taba, make reference to peer influences on behavior through the use of either "peer group" or "adolescent peer culture." It seems that the source of school-based success commitment does not lie solely within the influence of adolescents but is affected by agents from the wider society as well. For example, Havighurst and Taba make reference specifically to the role teachers play with regard to adolescent activities:

> The high school was the principal locus of the adolescent peer culture. School dances, athletic contests, hay rides, and club activities, as well as study halls and classrooms, are the places where boys and girls learn how to behave socially and morally. . . . Thus, the two most powerful groups in the school, the teachers and the leading clique among adolescents, worked pretty much together in setting standards. Most of the students followed their lead.[13]

Berger, in particular, argues that much of what Coleman sees as specifically adolescent behavior is, in fact, behavior directly affected by adults and adult culture:

> In attempting to account for the "frivolous," leisure-oriented values of adolescents, Coleman tells us that good grades and concentration on academic work are seen by adolescents as acquiescence and conformity to adult pressures, whereas social affairs, extracurricular activities, and athletics are seen as "their own." But these activities do not "belong" to adolescents nearly so much as Coleman imagines. How could they when they are initiated and supported by the schools, sponsored and run by the faculty advisors, coaches, and local advisory groups, and considered by grownups to be organized training grounds for the assumptions of adult responsibilities? Such activities are apparently considered by educators to

---

[13]Havighurst and Taba, *Adolescent Character and Personality*, p. 35.

be so important to the overall purposes of the schools that many high schools force student participation in them by building an "activities" period into the regular curriculum.[14]

There are two distinct points to be made here: (1) the major success commitment made by adolescents is quite broad and includes such divergent aspects as academic achievements and social activities of various sorts; (2) the source of these commitments may lie in the adult culture rather than within an adolescent subculture.

It is only too easy to assume that, because adolescents engage in a particular pattern of behavior, the behavior is distinctively adolescent. Adults enter into the lives of adolescents by guiding and directing activities engaged in by youth, and the pattern of values reflected in the success commitment of youth has as its source the values of the wider, adult society.

The use of the "commitment" concept raises questions about the uncommitted. It has been argued that problems of adolescent commitments are central to such adolescent problems as delinquency. Karacki and Toby, for example, report that commitment was crucial in the emergence of a pattern of gang delinquency which they observed.

> It is our impression that the Dukes failed to develop early in adolescence commitments to adult roles and values which would have mobilized their interests and energies and which would have served to relate them to school and work. In lieu of this, they drew instead upon the youth culture for meaning and purpose, and out of this emerged a delinquent gang. . . .
>
> This involvement in the youth culture was incompatible with diligent performance in school. School was not viewed by the Dukes as an opportunity to prepare for adult occupations or for college. Nor did they select their courses or pursue grades with the future in mind. Instead, they regarded school within the framework of adolescent interests.[15]

It is obvious that the referent for the term "youth culture" as used by Karacki and Toby is different from the analogous terms used by either Parsons or Havighurst and Taba. The different varieties of "youth culture" become clear when in one instance "diligent performance" in school is a *requirement for,* and, in another instance, *incompatible with,* participation in the culture. Karacki and Toby clarify their meaning somewhat in the following:

> Much of their delinquent behavior was an expression of three "youth culture" values: (1) desire for immediate gratification, (2) loyalty to peers, and (3) assertion of masculinity through physical aggression.[16]

---

[14]Berger, "Adolescence and Beyond," pp. 396–97.

[15]Larry Karacki and Jackson Toby, "The Uncommitted Adolescent: Candidate for Gang Socialization," *Sociological Inquiry* 32 (Spring 1962): 208.

[16]Ibid., p. 211.

The "youth culture" referred to in this citation, with its linkage of peer influence and hedonism, resembles what in this study is called the Rebellion factor. In fact, the findings of these authors suggest that the variable Delinquency, if included in the present study, should emerge negatively in the Commitment dimension and positively in the Rebellion dimension. If it is true that delinquent youth fail to develop early commitments to adult roles and values, one would expect them to do poorly in school, not to be oriented to college, to be less likely to plan for a white-collar occupation, and to feel less positive about their school—in short, to show a pattern of uncommitment. At the same time, one would expect them to turn more to their peers and more often to reject adults as guides to their behavior, evidencing what this paper has called Rebellion.

Four additional variables are added to the original matrix to test this hypothesis. The first of these is Delinquency itself, defined officially in terms of the youngster's appearance in juvenile court record for any offense other than a minor traffic violation. Self-report data on drinking and smoking were included as the second and third of these variables, partly because either may constitute actual delinquent behavior, but more because of the possible role of these acts in a pattern of hedonism and rejection of adult authority. Finally, a fourth measure included as an indication of attitudinal predisposition to delinquency was determined from response to the question, "Is a youth delinquent when he habitually skips school?" This item was selected because of the linkage between school behavior and delinquency; i.e., its centrality to the commitment hypothesis. These "trouble" items (with italicized terms referring to their code names as shown in Table 1 and Table 3), as they appeared in the questionnaire, were:

25. Delinquency data gathered from county juvenile court records. (*Delinquency.*)
26. Do you drink? (*Drinking.*)
27. Do you smoke? (*Smoking.*)
28. Is a youth delinquent when he habitually skips school? (*Truant delinquency.*)

The four variables were added to the original intercorrelation matrix and the matrix was factored again by the principal components solution. Rotations were accomplished graphically as before, but this time an attempt was made to isolate the structure specified by the hypothesis. The hypothesis called for a location of the three original factors, with the four measures of "trouble" showing zero loadings on the Peer Involvement factor, negative loadings on the Commitment factor, and positive loadings on the Rebellion factor.

A close approximation of the hypothesized structure did, in fact, emerge (see Table 3). The original three factors were located, with some slight modifications, and the "trouble" variables largely occupied the positions hypothesized.

The first factor contains the following:

12. Father's occupation.
13. Father's education.
20. Visiting, their home.
21. Visiting, your home.
22. Going Out.
23. Dating.

The second factor contains the following:

1. Grades.
2. Doing well.
3. School attitude.
4. College plans.
5. Academic subjects.
6. Alienation.
7. Homework.
8. Extracurricular activities.
9. School-related activities.
10. Organized group activities.
11. Occupational aspirations.
12. Father's occupation.
13. Father's education.
14. Friends/rally.
25. Delinquency.
26. Drinking.
27. Smoking.
28. Truant delinquent.

The third factor:

6. Alienation.
14. Friends/rally.
15. Club/parents.
16. Friend/parent.
18. Whereabouts known.
19. Time with family.
25. Delinquency.
26. Drinking.
27. Smoking.

The Peer Involvement factor in the expanded matrix contains four of the original six variables (Visiting Friends, Their Home; Visiting Friends, Your Home; Going Out; and Dating) with the two socioeconomic background variables making unexpected (and negative) entrance into this dimension. Of the two variables formerly part of this factor, Time with Family shifts over to the Rebellion factor, and Own a Car drops out of the three-

Table 3. Factor Matrix of Adolescent Culture Items with "Trouble" Items Included

Items	ORIGINAL MATRIX						ROTATED MATRIX						FACTOR PATTERN		
	I	II	III[a]	IV	V[a]	h^2	I"	II"	IV"	III"[a]	V'[a]	h^2	I"	II"	IV"
1. Grades	−29	48	−04	−24	−08	.38	−23	49	07	26	−01	.37	0	+	0
2. Doing well	−12	47	−09	02	−12	.26	−01	43	01	19	−19	.26	0	+	0
3. School attitude	−24	50	−15	−08	23	.39	−03	56	−17	17	13	.39	0	+	0
4. College plans	−25	52	−47	−26	02	.62	−15	76	04	−08	05	.61	0	+	0
5. Academic subject	−16	40	−01	−38	−14	.35	−23	42	26	23	06	.35	0	+	+
6. Alienation	23	−24	36	−11	−21	.29	00	−41	31	15	−03	.29	0	−	0
7. Homework	−14	57	−09	−17	−02	.38	−03	56	09	25	−01	.38	0	+	0
8. Extracurricular activities	04	46	−28	−14	24	.37	20	55	−01	01	18	.38	0	+	0
9. School-related activities	12	46	−06	−00	07	.23	24	37	04	19	−01	.23	0	+	0
10. Organized group activities	17	36	−11	−01	13	.19	28	33	03	09	04	.20	0	+	0
11. Occupational aspirations	−18	25	−49	−06	20	.38	−01	53	−17	−25	09	.38	0	+	0
12. Father's occupation	−28	01	−38	−53	−14	.52	−45	37	27	−28	17	.52	−	+	+
13. Father's education	−28	12	−32	−54	−15	.51	−44	42	29	−17	16	.51	−	+	+
14. Friends/rally	36	−39	21	−27	−18	.43	04	−46	45	−08	11	.43	0	−	+
15. Club/parents	27	−15	−21	−22	−21	.23	04	−04	38	−28	−01	.23	0	0	+
16. Friend/parent	18	−15	08	−32	−08	.17	−04	−13	35	−03	17	.17	0	0	+
17. Rate "excitement"	−05	−25	−08	−16	−29	.18	−26	−14	22	−20	−09	.18	0	0	0
18. Whereabouts known	−32	14	−05	46	22	.38	01	13	−58	07	−15	.38	0	0	−
19. Time with family	−38	19	26	21	13	.31	−17	04	−39	35	−04	.31	0	0	−
20. Visiting friends, their home	59	01	−15	−05	34	.49	59	02	15	−17	29	.48	+	0	0
21. Visiting friends, your home	56	09	−13	03	33	.45	62	04	09	−11	22	.45	+	0	0
22. Going out	65	05	−14	−10	21	.50	59	01	28	−15	22	.50	+	0	0
23. Dating	57	08	−16	−05	21	.40	55	05	21	−15	18	.40	+	0	0
24. Own a car	37	−12	06	−05	06	.16	29	−19	18	−05	10	.17	0	0	0
25. Delinquency	43	−19	18	−11	−04	.27	25	−31	31	00	09	.26	0	−	+
26. Drinking	55	−21	15	−21	−10	.42	29	−33	47	−05	11	.43	0	−	+
27. Smoking	53	−30	19	−18	−11	.45	27	−41	44	−06	10	.45	0	−	+
28. Truant delinquent	−20	40	−01	05	17	.23	01	37	−21	23	03	.23	0	+	0

[a] Not included in final analysis.

factor matrix. As predicted, none of the four "trouble" variables shows loadings above the arbitrarily selected level in the Peer Involvement dimension.

The Commitment factor is found in the same form as in the previous matrix except that, as predicted, the four additional variables are negatively loaded on the dimension. Delinquency, Drinking, Smoking, and a disinclination to view truancy as delinquent behavior, then, all emerge as part of a pattern of noncommitment.

The Rebellion factor is altered slightly in the second matrix. Six of the eight original variables are present (Alienation, Friends/rally, Club/parents, Friend/parent, Whereabouts known, Time with family), with two dropping out (School attitude and rate "excitement"). Three of the trouble measures—Delinquency, Smoking, and Drinking—do occur in this factor.

Commitment Hypothesis

There seems to be general support here, then, for the suggestion of Karacki and Toby that delinquency among at least some youth may be a function of the lack of commitment to school and adult success, on the one hand, and identification with a pattern of peer rebellion on the other. The presence of delinquency in a pattern of noncommitment helps give increased specificity to the commitment hypothesis. The uncommitted delinquent youth, it would appear, is characterized by behavioral withdrawal from school. He does not study, he receives poor grades, and he does not participate in activities. This withdrawal tends to be accompanied by a concomitant withdrawal from identification with pathways to adult status as well, since the educational and occupational aspirations of the uncommitted delinquent youth are lower than those of the successful and committed nondelinquent youth. Just as important is how the youth "feels" about school, these data suggesting that there is a pattern of psychological discomfort and alienation in the attitudes the delinquent and uncommitted youth exhibits toward the school.

The nature of the commitments of delinquent youth suggests a close relationship between the problem of noncommitment and what Short and Strodtbeck have called "social disability":

> Gang life is not conducive to punctuality, dependability on the job every day, discipline, and consistency in job performance . . . all basic requirements of modern industry. . . . The failure of individuals to make satisfactory adjustments in any institutional sphere inevitably handicaps their ability to achieve future goals. Our gang boys fail often in school, on the job, in conventional youth-serving agencies, and in the eyes of law enforcement (and therefore in the public eye). . . . These failures, combined with

limited social and technical skills, and blocked legitimate opportunities, constitute an overwhelming handicap for the achievement of the goals they endorse.[17]

In an earlier paper by Toby, there is a suggestion (perhaps implicit) of a temporal sequence operating between such commitment or social disability, and involvement with delinquent peers. He asks what it is that restrains the youngster with advantages from committing deviant acts, responding that such an individual has much to lose by engaging in delinquency:

> What they have to lose should not be measured exclusively in material terms. True, the middle-class youngster has a spacious home to live in, nutritious food to eat, and fashionable clothes to wear; but he usually has social approval in addition. He comes from a "good" family. He lives in a "respectable" neighborhood. He is "neat and clean." His teachers like him; he gets good marks; and he moves easily from grade to grade. He has a basis for anticipating that this will continue until he completes college and takes up a business or professional career. If he applied his energies to burglary instead of to homework, he would risk not only the ego-flattering rewards currently available but his future prospects as well.
>
> In short, youngsters vary in the extent to which they feel a stake in American society. For those with social honor, disgrace is a powerful sanction. For a boy disapproved of already, there is less incentive to resist the temptation to do what he wants when he wants to do it.[18]

To whom is such a youngster to turn for social approval?

> Psychologically uncommitted to school or job, such a boy "hangs out" on the street corner with other unsuccessful youngsters. He needs their approval as a compensation for the rejection of school authorities and employers. The price for their approval runs high. He must show that he is not "chicken," i.e., cowardly, by manifesting a reckless willingness to fight, to try anything once. He must repudiate the bourgeois virtues associated with school and job: diligence, neatness, truthfulness, thrift. He becomes known as a "loafer" and a "troublemaker" in the community. When family and neighbors add their condemnations to those of teachers and employer, all bridges to respectability are burned, and he becomes progressively more concerned with winning "rep" inside the gang. For him, stealing is not primarily a way to make money. It is primarily a means of gaining approval within a clique of outcasts. The gang offers a heroic rather than an economic basis for self-respect.[19]

---

[17]James F. Short, Jr. and Fred L. Strodtbeck, *Group Process and Gang Delinquency* (Chicago: University of Chicago Press, 1965), p. 230.

[18]Jackson Toby, "Social Disorganization and Stake in Conformity," *Journal of Criminal Law, Criminology, and Police Science* 48, no. 1 (May-June 1957): 17. © 1957 by Northwestern University School of Law. Reprinted by special permission.

[19]Ibid., p. 15.

Such an orientation is consistent with the argument developed from the present data and serves to explicate the hypothesized temporal sequence. Within this view, the lowering of a boy's commitments increases the probability of his being involved in rebellious peer associations which, in turn, affect the probability that he will become delinquent.

Such a view of delinquency has three advantages over the more established status-frustration theories. First, as Matza[20] and others[21] have urged, it is essentially a probabilistic hypothesis and as such is consistent with the intermittent delinquent character of the activities of those youths labeled delinquent. Delinquency is a status, and it must be differentiated from the incumbents who occupy that status. As Matza points out so persuasively, delinquent youth are perfectly capable of conventional activity in a wide range of situations, so that they play both conventional and delinquent roles. The "stake in conformity" hypothesis states that some individuals have a higher probability of playing both delinquent and conventional roles, while others are highly constrained from the commission of delinquent acts by virtue of their commitment to conformity. The casual, intermittent, and transient "drift into delinquency" noted by Matza is consistent, then, with the linkage of delinquency to a pattern of noncommitment. The hypothesis does not state that uncommitted youth will become delinquent; it states, instead, that it is more probable that such youngsters will drift into delinquency.

A second virtue of the commitment hypothesis is that it is consistent with one of the fundamental features of delinquency—namely, its disappearance with the onset of adulthood. Most current delinquency theories, especially those of the status-frustration theorists, have no way of accounting for the phenomenon of "maturational reform." Matza has been one of the keenest observers of the obvious conclusion that such theories posit (by implication) that delinquency will continue into adulthood:

> Most theories of delinquency take no account of maturational reform; those that do often do so at the expense of violating their own assumptions regarding the constrained delinquent. Why and by what process do youngsters once compelled or committed to delinquency cease being constrained? Why and by what process is the easy continuity from juvenile delinquency to adult crime implicit in almost all theories of delinquency not apparent in the world of real events?[22]

The commitment hypothesis as stated in the present study makes no assumption about continuity or deviance into adulthood. It assumes that if

---

[20]David Matza, *Delinquency and Drift* (New York: John Wiley & Sons, Inc., 1964).

[21]Scott Briar and Irving Piliavin, "Delinquency, Situational Inducements, and Commitment to Conformity," *Social Problems* 13, no. 1 (Summer 1965): 35–45.

[22]Matza, *Delinquency and Drift*, p. 23.

alternative commitments are developed as the youth moves into adulthood, he will drift out of delinquency. Such commitments can be expected to develop as the individual becomes rooted firmly in the occupational structure and begins to take on responsibilities as head of a family. Support for

Table 4. Percentage of Male Students Who Are Delinquent, by Modal Grade Earned and by Social Class of Father, "Pacific City" High School, 1963

| | SOCIAL CLASS | | | |
Modal Grade	Blue Collar	(N)	White Collar	(N)
A or B	4%	(189)	4%	(89)
C	11%	(177)	12%	(138)
D or F	20%	(65)	27%	(74)

Note: N = 732. Eighty-seven responses from original sample could not be classified according to socio-economic status.

such an expectation can be found in the investigation of Karacki and Toby,[23] who report a relatively high incidence of successful early adult adjustments, both educationally and occupationally, among their group of previously delinquent youth.

A third advantage of the commitment hypothesis is that it accounts for the present delinquency data better than does status-frustration theory. The correlations between delinquency and the social class background of these youth are not strong (Father's occupation, $r = -.10$; Father's education, $r = -.16$), and they tend to be overshadowed by other correlations within the Commitment dimension. Such overshadowing can be demonstrated most dramatically by executing a different type of analysis, one where the incidence of delinquency is compared by social class and academic achievement level (see Table 4). When this is done, delinquency appears to be much more a function of academic achievement level than of social class. Among those students who perform well (receive *A* or *B* grades) or adequately (receive grades of *C*), the delinquency rates are virtually identical for white- and blue-collar youngsters (4 percent versus 4 percent, 11 percent versus 12 percent). The slight difference in delinquency at the poor performance level—i.e., among those who receive modal grades of *D* or *F*— between white-collar and blue-collar youth (20 percent versus 27 percent) is relatively insignificant, lending, if anything, support to the commitment hypothesis. That is, overall there is corroboration of the hypothesis that the youth who are "making it" are less likely to be delinquent, be they white-

---

[23]Karacki and Toby, "The Uncommitted Adolescent."

or blue-collar. Among youth who are doing poorly in school, there is a higher probability of delinquency involvement for both white- and blue-collar youth, with blue-collar youth showing the highest probability of becoming delinquent. The slightly lower incidence of delinquency among white-collar, academically unsuccessful youth suggest that within this group social class position may exert some minimal, residual effect in holding the youngster's commitment.

The conclusion is inescapable that, regardless of the nature of any alternative explanation, a social class-based theory of delinquency cannot explain the delinquency observed among these boys of a small city. When academic achievement is held constant, the effects of social class on the distribution of delinquency virtually disappear. Conversely, the finding that the relationship between one measure of commitment (grades) and delinquency holds up, regardless of class level, suggests that further exploration of the commitment hypothesis is justified.

Some of these conclusions obviously need to be qualified. The sample consists of boys from one high school in one small city. Whether the findings have application for youth in larger cities (or in other small cities) is something to be established by additional investigation. In fairness, it should be pointed out that Cohen,[24] in particular, has indicated that his theory was developed to account for delinquency in metropolitan areas. Likewise the tentative nature of the hypothesis as it is supported by the factor analysis must be underscored. Additional analyses need to be made to ascertain whether the structure specified here can be isolated in other populations. Given the occasionally perverse nature of factor analysis, identical structures may not emerge in other studies. If the hypothesis advanced is at all tenable, however, it should be possible to locate similar factor patterns.

The important qualification, however, is that the data of this study cannot provide an adequate test of the commitment hypothesis. The essential notion of this view is that, as a result of the lowering of an individual's commitment to success and conformity, there is an increased probability of his turning to a characteristically rebellious peer culture for significant social attachments, which in turn, increases the chance of involvement in delinquency. All that can be said on the basis of the data is that our observations are consistent with this hypothesis of drift, in that delinquency appears as part of a pattern of uncommitment on the one hand and peer rebellion on the other. Its very consistency suggest that establishment of the nature of the temporal sequence over time should have relatively high priority in future research. From the present data, the variables *commitment, delinquency,* and *rebellion* might stand in any of six possible temporal sequences

---

[24]Albert K. Cohen, *Delinquent Boys* (New York: The Free Press of Glencoe, Inc., 1955), p. 13.

(where C refers to Commitment, R to Rebellion, and D to Delinquency, and where for simplicity it is assumed that variables will not occur simultaneously):

1. $C \rightarrow R \rightarrow D$
2. $C \rightarrow D \rightarrow R$
3. $R \rightarrow C \rightarrow D$
4. $R \rightarrow D \rightarrow C$
5. $D \rightarrow C \rightarrow R$
6. $D \rightarrow R \rightarrow C$

Needless to say, there are important reasons for knowing which of these sequences best describes the data of delinquency. Theories of delinquency, in addition to programs to prevent or control delinquency, will vary considerably, say, according to whether delinquency precedes or follows commitment in a temporal sequence. While the present interpretations within the commitment hypothesis have leaned toward the view that commitment is temporally prior to delinquency, it must be said that the present data do not support this sequence over any alternative sequence. As a consequence, the critical aspects of the hypothesis are yet to be tested.

participation
in interscholastic
athletics and
delinquency

Interscholastic athletics share with other competitive sports the distinction of being among the least studied of all social phenomena. Like collegiate, professional, and sand-lot athletics, high school sports are marked by rich and abundant folk wisdom about the reasons for their existence and strength, their internal dynamics, and their consequences for the society, the community, the school, and the participant. Systematic sociological investigations of these issues, however, are only now beginning.[1]

Athletic Participation as a Deterrent to Delinquency: Theoretical Framework

Interscholastic athletics are supported by school administrators partly out of the belief that participation in sports is an effective deterrent to delinquency. Yet the validity of this belief remains untested.[2] Fortunately,

"Participation in Interscholastic Athletics and Delinquency: A Preliminary Study" by Walter E. Schafer. This article appeared in Social Problems *17, no. 1 (Summer 1969): 40–47 and is reprinted by permission of The Society for the Study of Social Problems.*

[1]For general works on the sociology of sport, see *The International Review of Sociology of Sport*; John W. Loy, Jr. and Gerald S. Kenyon (eds.), *Sport, Culture, and Society* (New York: The Macmillan Company, Publishers, 1969); the entire issue of *Current Sociology* 15, no. 3 (1967); Eric Dunning and Norbert Elias (eds.), *Sport and Social Structure;* Gerald S. Kenyon (ed.), *Sociology of Sport* (Chicago: The Athletic Institute, 1969).

For several recent studies on some of the consequences of participation in interscholastic athletics, see Walter E. Schafer and J. Michael Armer, "Athletes are Not Inferior Students," *Trans-action* 6 (November 1968): 21–26, 61–62; Richard A. Rehberg and Walter E. Schafer, "Participation in Interscholastic Athletics and College Expectation," *The American Journal of Sociology* 63 (May 1968): 732–40; Walter E. Schafer, "Athletic Success and Social Mobility," paper presented at annual meetings of the American Association of Health, Physical Education, and Recreation, April 1968, St. Louis, Missouri; Walter E. Schafer and Nico Stehr, "Participation in Competitive Athletics and Social Mobility: Some Intervening Social Processes," paper presented at the bi-annual meetings of the International Committee on Sociology of Sport, October 1968, Vienna, Austria.

[2]For unsupported discussions suggesting that athletic participation is likely to prevent delinquency, see, for example, James B. Nolan, "Athletics and Juvenile Delinquency," *Journal of Educational Sociology* 28 (1954–55): 263–65; Joseph H. Fichter, *Parochial School: A Sociological Study* (Garden City, N.Y.: Anchor Books, 1961), p. 214. For discussions of the position that athletic participation is not likely to prevent delinquency, see Paul W. Tappan, *Juvenile Delinquency* (New York: McGraw-Hill Book Company, 1949), p. 150; and Edwin H. Sutherland and Donald R. Cressey, *Principles of Criminology,* 7th ed. (Chicago: J. B. Lippincott Co., 1966), p. 169. For a sensitive treatment of the relationship between delinquent behavior and participation in athletics outside the institutional framework of the school among urban gangs, see James F. Short, Jr. and Fred L. Strodtbeck, *Group Process and Gang Delinquency* (Chicago: University of Chicago Press, 1965), especially pp. 82–92, 161–72, 244–46. For a related discussion, see Solomon Kobrin, "Sociological Aspects of the Development of a Street Corner Group: An Exploratory Study," *American Journal of Orthopsychiatry* 31 (October 1961): 688.

six general theories of delinquency provide a basis for formulating a hypothesis on this relationship.

Albert Cohen has remarked that adequate theories of deviancy must account for conforming behavior as well.[3] Therefore, we will draw on these theories to predict that other things being equal, participation in interscholastic athletics will have a deterring influence on delinquency. Stated in testable terms, athletes will have a lower delinquency rate than nonathletes, other things being equal.

DELINQUENCY AS A RESULT OF DIFFERENTIAL ASSOCIATION. Sutherland, and many other sociologists since him, posited that delinquency was the result of exposure to deviant influences.[4] From this theory it follows that a lower-class youth in a neighborhood with a high crime rate will be more likely to become delinquent than a lower-class youth in a neighborhood with a low crime rate. Further, a boy who attends a school with a high proportion of delinquents carries a greater risk of delinquency than one who attends a school with few delinquents. It also follows that, within a particular school, the chances of becoming delinquent vary directly with the amount of exposure to deviant subgroups and inversely with exposure to conforming influences.

Coaches usually set strict standards of behavior, not only on the field but off as well. Thus, there are rules prohibiting smoking, drinking, maintaining late hours, wearing beards or long hair—and delinquent behavior in the community. Violation of such rules often results in expulsion from the team. Most athletes internalize these standards, as well as other less formal but just as conventional standards, and, moreover, exert pressures on other athletes to conform to them as well. Since the influence from coaches is likely to be high, as is the amount of intra-athletic friendships and influence, any particular athlete is thus not only less likely than a comparable nonathlete to be exposed to deviant influences, but he is more likely to be exposed to strong conforming influences. Such influences are further reinforced in the wider school and community, where basic training rules are fairly well known and the athlete's behavior is under constant public scrutiny, especially in smaller communities.

In short, athletes should be delinquent less often than nonathletes on the basis of the theoretical reasoning of differential association.

---

[3] Albert K. Cohen, "The Study of Social Disorganization and Deviant Behavior," in *Sociology Today,* Robert Merton, Leonard Broom, and Leonard S. Cottrell (eds.), (New York: Basic Books, Inc., Publishers, 1959), p. 463.

[4] See, for example, Albert K. Cohen, Alfred R. Lindesmith, and Karl Schuessler, (eds.), *The Sutherland Papers* (Bloomington, Ind.: University of Indiana Press, 1956), Part I; Sutherland and Cressey, *Principles of Criminology,* Chap. 4; Donald R. Cressey, *Delinquency, Crime, and Differential Association* (The Hague: Martinus Nijhoff, 1964).

DELINQUENCY AS A RESULT OF WEAK SOCIAL CONTROLS. Reiss, Gold, Cohen, and others have concluded that delinquency is sometimes the result of weak external social controls; other things being equal, boys who are exposed to strong social controls from parents or other authorities are less likely to deviate.[5] It may be that the training rules regulating off-the-field behavior of athletes deter some youth from engaging in delinquent behavior. If so, we would expect athletes to be less delinquent than nonathletes.

DELINQUENCY AS A RESULT OF REBELLION. Albert Cohen, Arthur Stinchcombe, Kenneth Polk, myself and others have contended that delinquency is often a result of rebellion against the school.[6] For Cohen, many youth become delinquent because of a motivation to strike back at the school, where they are measured against universalistic achievement criteria which they cannot reach. For Stinchcombe and Polk, rebellion flows from the perception that the school will be unable to pay off on their occupational aspirations. For Polk and myself, rebellion sometimes arises out of failure, perceived lack of payoff, or resentment against punitive sanctions. Running through each position is that, for some youths, school is frustrating, an outcome of which is overt rebellion in the form of illegal behavior.

For the athlete, especially the successful one, school is less likely to be a source of frustration than for the comparable nonathlete. Rather, school is a source of success-experience and a positive public and private evaluation of self. If school in fact has this meaning, then it follows that athletes will rebel and become delinquent less often than comparable nonathletes.

DELINQUENCY AS A RESULT OF BOREDOM. Several theorists contend that delinquency often arises out of sheer boredom.[7] Slashing tires, stealing, beating on drunks, and smoking pot are simply ways of getting one's kicks.

---

[5]Martin Gold, *Status Forces in Delinquent Boys* (New York: The Free Press of Glencoe, Inc., 1955); Albert J. Reiss, Jr., "Delinquency as a Result of Personal and Social Controls," *American Sociological Review* 16 (1951): 196–207.

[6]Albert K. Cohen, *Delinquent Boys;* Arthur S. Stinchcombe, *Rebellion in High School* (Chicago: Quadrangle Books, 1964); Kenneth Polk, "Delinquency and Community Action in Nonmetropolitan Areas," in *Task Force Report: Juvenile Delinquency and Youth Crime*, President's Commission on Law Enforcement and Administration of Justice (Washington, D.C.: U.S. Government Printing Office, 1967), pp. 343–52; Walter E. Schafer and Kenneth Polk, "Delinquency and the Schools," in *Task Force Report*, pp. 222–27; Walter E. Schafer, "Rural and Small Town Delinquency: New Understanding and Approaches," address to the National Outlook Conference on Rural Youth, October 1967, Washington, D.C. (mimeographed).

[7]See, for example, David Bordua, *Sociological Theories and Their Implications for Juvenile Delinquency* (Washington, D.C.: U.S. Government Printing Office, 1960).

Clearly, athletes are less likely to be bored and thereby be susceptible to delinquency than comparable nonathletes, since sports take up so much after-school and weekend time. Even when not directly occupied in practice or competition, the athlete's psychic energies and loyalties are still directed in a conforming direction.

DELINQUENCY AS A RESULT OF NEED TO ASSERT MASCULINITY. Cohen, Ferdinand, Parsons, and others contend that delinquency sometimes results from the motivation to assert masculinity to themselves and their peers through daring, adventuresome, or illegal acts.[8] It is argued that this is especially true of boys from middle-class homes, for whom conformity is linked to mother. As Ferdinand points out, however, interscholastic athletics, as an institutionalized display of force, skill, strength, and competitiveness, represents a visible nondelinquent means for public and private demonstration of masculine prowess and competence. Insofar as delinquency arises from the need to establish one's manhood, then, athletes can be expected to be lawabiding more often than comparable nonathletes.

DELINQUENCY AS A RESULT OF LABELING. The labeling or interactional view of deviant behavior, as discussed by Lemert, Becker, Erickson, and others, holds that deviancy is not something inherent in an act but is created by the definitions of those who enforce social standards of behavior.[9] Thus, Becker states:

> Social groups create deviance by making the rules whose infraction constitutes deviance, and by applying those rules to particular people and labeling them as outsiders. From this point of view, deviance is not a quality of the act the person commits but rather a consequence of the application by others of rules and sanctions to an "offender." The deviant is one to whom that label has successfully been applied; deviant behavior is behavior that people so label.[10]

Whether or not an act is defined as deviant depends not only on the nature of the act itself but on a number of factors extrinsic to the act: who is

---

[8]Albert K. Cohen, *Delinquent Boys*, pp. 157–69; Talcott Parsons, "Certain Primary Sources and Patterns of Aggression in the Social Structure of the Western World," *Psychiatry* 10 (May 1947): 167–81; Theodore N. Ferdinand, *Typologies of Delinquency* (New York: Random House, Inc., 1966), Chap. 4.

[9]For illustrative statements of the perspective, see Howard S. Becker, *Outsiders: Studies in the Sociology of Deviance* (New York: Free Press, 1963); Kai Erikson, "Notes on the Sociology of Deviance," in Howard S. Becker, ed., *The Other Side: Perspectives on Deviance* (New York: Free Press, 1964); Edwin Lemert, *Human Deviance, Social Problems and Social Control* (Englewood Cliffs, New Jersey: Prentice-Hall, Inc., 1967). Discussions with Gregory Stone were helpful in developing this point.

[10]Howard S. Becker, *Outsiders* (New York: The Free Press of Glencoe, 1964).

enforcing the norm; the situation and its social context; and the status, reputation, and friendship patterns of the actor himself. Thus, for example, a white middle-class youngster may well not be referred to the juvenile authorities for a minor theft. For him, the act is defined as a mere adolescent prank. On the other hand, a lower-class Negro youth is much more likely to be apprehended and referred to the court for the same act.[11]

Similarly, athletes, especially those who are successful and live in small communities, are more likely to be "protected" from apprehension and referral to the court by the public image they enjoy as being clean-cut, all-American boys, even when they commit delinquent acts. They may well be just as delinquent in fact, but turn up less often in delinquency statistics.

The interactional view of deviancy also leads one to predict that athletes are less likely to develop the image of bad boys, cut-ups, or hoods early in their school careers. As a result, they are less likely to get caught in the negative, self-fulfilling cycle of action, labeling, repressive or alienating sanctions by teachers, increasing negative self-images, identification with other troublemakers, rejection of school standards, further deviancy, further labeling, etc., ultimately resulting in overt rebellion in the community. Rather, because of their conforming public and private identities, athletes are more likely to become involved in a positive self-fulfilling prophecy with respect to their conduct.

In short, each theoretical position leads to the same hypothesis: participation in interscholastic athletics can be expected to exert a deterring or negative influence on delinquent behavior. In testable terms, athletes should be delinquent less often than comparable nonathletes.

Data and Methods

During the summer of 1964, complete high school records were examined for all 585 boys who began as tenth graders three years earlier in two midwestern senior high schools. At the time the records were examined, most of the class had already graduated from high school. One of the three-year high schools had a total enrollment of 2,641 in the fall of 1963 and was located in a predominantly middle-class, university community of about 70,000. The other school had a total enrollment of 1,272 and was located in a nearby, predominantly working-class, industrial com-

---

[11]For an application of the labeling perspective to deviance in the school, see Walter E. Schafer, "Deviance in the Public Schools: An Interactional View," in *Behavioral Science for Social Workers,* Edwin J. Thomas (ed.), (New York: The Free Press of Glencoe, 1968). Also reprinted in this volume.

munity of about 20,000. For purposes of this study, boys from the two schools are treated as a single sample.

Of the 585 in the total sample, 164 (28 percent) were classified as athletes. These boys completed at least one full season in any interscholastic sport (varsity or junior varsity) during the three years of high school. Any given boy could participate in three seasons each year; e.g., football in the fall, basketball in the winter, and track in the spring. Thirty percent of the athletes completed one season during the three years, 34 percent completed two or three seasons, 21 percent four or five seasons, and 15 percent six to nine seasons.

Delinquency, the dependent variable, was measured by examination of the juvenile court records of the county in which the two schools are located. Since all those included in the sample were over the legal age of juveniles when the delinquency data were collected (1967), the records used were all in the court's inactive file. Since we are interested in the possible effect of participation in high school sports on delinquency, only those boys who had a court record after the beginning of high school were classified as delinquent.

It must be recognized, of course, that court records underestimate actual delinquent behavior, especially for middle-class boys and perhaps for athletes, as we suggested earlier. Therefore, this measurement must be viewed as only a gross indicator.

Even if we find a relationship in the predicted direction, we will not have proven the hypothesis, of course, since boys who go into sports might not be very apt to become delinquent anyway. In short, the findings might simply be due to selection. As a means for eliminating some selection influences, we will control for academic achievement during the final semester of junior high school and father's occupation. Academic achievement was measured by obtaining the grade point average of all major courses during the second semester of the ninth grade, ranging from 4.00 (all As) to 0.00 (all Fs). For this analysis GPAs were dichotomized into equal categories. Father's occupation was measured using census categories and dichotomized into white collar and blue collar. By controlling on previous GPA and father's occupation, we can also determine whether the original relationship varies among different types of boys.

In addition, athletes were divided into major-minor sports and high-low participation, in order to determine whether the deterrent effect of participation on delinquency varies according to the type of sport and the amount of participation. Football and basketball were labeled major sports, based on their popularity, and all other sports were labeled minor. Boys who completed three or more seasons, either in different years or the same year, were placed in the high participation category, while low participants were those who completed one or two seasons.

Results

The results in Table 1 indicate a negative association between athletic participation and delinquency, as predicted.[12] Seven percent of the athletes had a court record, compared to 17 percent of the nonathletes. This finding suggests that participation in interscholastic sports might well have a deterring influence on delinquency. However, it is entirely possible that athletics simply do not attract the type of boys who have been or are likely to become delinquent. This is, of course, a distinct possibility, which we cannot entirely rule out with available data. However, we can partially assess this alternative explanation by noting (1) whether two factors,

Table 1

	Delinquent	Nondelinquent	Total	N
Athletes	7%	93%	100%	(164)
Nonathletes	17%	83%	100%	(421)

academic achievement and father's occupation, which have shown relationships to delinquency in past research, are related to the independent and dependent variables in this study; and (2) if so, whether controlling for them will lessen or eliminate the relationship reported in Table 1.

In Table 2, we see that previous academic achievement is rather strongly related to athletic participation. That is, 40 percent of the boys who had achieved in the top half of their class in the second semester of the ninth grade completed at least one season of high school sports, compared to 18 percent of the boys who had achieved in the lower half of their

Table 2

	Athlete	Nonathlete	Total	N
Hi 9B GPA	40%	60%	100%	(284)
Lo 9B GPA	18%	82%	100%	(284)

Table 3

	Delinquent	Nondelinquent	Total	N
Hi 9B GPA	7%	93%	100%	(284)
Lo 9B GPA	14%	86%	100%	(284)

[12]Variations among the following tables in total N are due to missing data for some individuals on particular variables.

Table 4

	Athlete	Nonathlete	Total	N
White-Collar	33%	67%	100%	(298)
Blue-Collar	22%	78%	100%	(239)

class. Table 3 indicates that previous academic achievement also relates to delinquency, although somewhat less strongly. Whereas 14 percent of the low achievers developed a court record, this was true of 7 percent of the high achievers. Since previous GPA relates to both the independent and dependent variables, we will control for it and then reexamine the original relationship.

Table 4 reveals that white-collar boys participate more often than blue-collar boys (33 percent versus 22 percent) while Table 5 shows that white-collar boys are less often delinquent (7 percent versus 17 percent). The chance of a confounding influence of father's occupation also arises, then, and suggests that this factor, too, should be controlled.

Table 5

	Delinquent	Nondelinquent	Total	N
White-Collar	7%	93%	100%	(298)
Blue-Collar	17%	83%	100%	(239)

Table 6 contains the delinquency rates for athletes and nonathletes within each of the categories of father's occupation and 9B GPA. Examination of the findings reveals that for white-collar, high GPA boys the relationship declines to a four percentage point difference, while for white-collar, low GPA boys it is slightly reversed. In both cases, then, the relationship virtually disappears.

Among blue-collar, high GPA boys, the relationship is in the predicted direction, although a three percentage point difference can hardly be regarded as a relationship at all. Interestingly enough, however, the relationship among blue-collar, low GPA boys is rather marked: whereas 10 percent of the athletes had a court record, this was true of 23 percent of the nonathletes.

In short, controlling for father's occupation and previous GPA virtually eliminates the relationship, except among low achieving boys from blue-collar homes, for whom athletic participation appears to make a substantial difference in the chances of becoming delinquent. If one is such an athlete, the chances of becoming a delinquent are reduced by more than half. Interestingly enough, this interaction effect directly

Table 6

	Delinquent	*Nondelinquent*	*Total*	*N*
White-Collar				
High 9B GPA				
Athlete	4%	96%	100%	(74)
Nonathlete	8%	92%	100%	(113)
Low 9B GPA				
Athlete	11%	89%	100%	(27)
Nonathlete	5%	95%	100%	(94)
Blue-Collar				
High 9B GPA				
Athlete	8%	92%	100%	(36)
Nonathlete	11%	89%	100%	(57)
Low 9B GPA				
Athlete	10%	90%	100%	(20)
Nonathlete	23%	77%	100%	(126)

parallels earlier findings on academic achievement and college expectations of athletes.[13] It must be pointed out, however, that the difference in size of the Ns for athletes and nonathletes in this category is rather large, making it necessary to draw conclusions with caution.

Is there a difference in delinquency rates among participants in major and minor sports? The data show that the delinquency rates for the two types of athletes are identical at 7 percent. They also reveal that there is a virtually identical rate for boys who completed three or more and one or two seasons (6 percent versus 8 percent).

Conclusions

We have seen that, as predicted, athletes are less often delinquent than nonathletes and that the overall relationship is almost entirely the product of a rather marked association among blue-collar, low achievers. Of course, it is still possible that athletics attract conforming types of boys in the first place. Stated differently, the negative relationship between athletic participation and delinquency may not be the result of the deterrent influence of athletics at all, but rather to selection of conformers into the athletic program. This alternative interpretation must be taken seriously, since we have not controlled out all the selection factors, and since deviant

---

[13]Richard A. Rehberg and Walter E. Schafer, "Participation in Interscholastic Athletics and College Expectation."

boys are likely to have been formally or informally screened out of sports by coaches during junior high school or even before.

Nevertheless, the deterrence hypothesis warrants further investigation, since the data we have presented are consistent with it. If there in fact is a preventive effect of participation in interscholastic sports on delinquency, under what conditions does it occur, in terms of type of school, community, sport, and athlete? Further, what are the processes by which it occurs? Is it because of greater exposure to nondelinquent influences? Stronger social controls? Less internal and external pressure toward rebellion? Less boredom? Less need to assert masculinity through deviant behavior? Or less chance of being labeled and detected? Unfortunately, the data available for this study do not allow us to put these interpretations to a test, although each is plausible.

Hopefully, this preliminary study will stimulate further thinking and research on the consequences of participation in athletics and especially on the role of athletic participation in deterring delinquency.

class, strain,
and rebellion
among adolescents

One of the most serious challenges to the social class theories of youthful deviance as expressed by Albert K. Cohen or Robert D. Cloward and Lloyd E. Ohlin has been advanced by Arthur L. Stinchcombe[1] in his "articulation" hypothesis. Reduced to simple terms, the argument holds that an adolescent's "status prospects" (where he seems to be headed economically) are much more important in the genesis of youthful rebellion than are his "status origins" (his roots in the social class hierarchy). Stinchcombe proposes that alienation and rebellion can be expected with greatest frequency among those young people who face a working-class future in today's universalistic labor market.

Unlike many other deviance theorists, Stinchcombe is not content with a persuasive argument, but introduces data which, by and large, support his basic propositions. He reports that rebellion at all class levels is generally lower among college-oriented or high academic achievement youth. He argues that these measures of current school status assess the future status of adolescents, and concludes that such measures are more important in explaining the nature and content of youthful rebellion than is social class background.

Stinchcombe is not alone in this last conclusion. Call,[2] in a study set like that of Stinchcombe, in a small city, found little difference in the class backgrounds of delinquents, and noted that both white-collar and blue-collar delinquents were similarly alienated from school. Additional confirmation appears in a study by Polk and Halferty,[3] in which delinquency was reported to be uniformly low among white- *and* blue-collar youth who are doing well in school, but high among *both* groups where academic performance is low. The general weight of this evidence suggests that, if we are going to account for patterns of rebellion among adolescents, at least in smaller cities, we will have to rely on some alternative to the classic "status frustration" theories.

Stinchcombe, however, draws upon a theoretical tradition very similar to Cohen's in elaborating ideas which weave together status origins and status prospects. His failure to find any direct link between social class background and rebellion did not lead Stinchcombe to reject the idea that status origins play an important role in the generation of rebellion. In

"Class, Strain, and Rebellion Among Adolescents" by Kenneth Polk. *This article was previously published in* Social Problems *17, no. 2 (Fall 1969): 214–24 and is reprinted with permission of The Society for the Study of Social Problems.*

[1] Arthur L. Stinchcombe, *Rebellion in a High School* (Chicago: Quadrangle Books, 1964).

[2] Donald J. Call, "Frustration and Noncommitment" (Ph.D. dissertation, Dept. of Sociology, University of Oregon, Eugene, Oregon, 1965).

[3] Kenneth Polk and David S. Halferty, "Adolescence, Commitment, and Delinquency," *Journal of Research on Crime and Delinquency* 4 (July 1966): 95. Also reprinted in this volume.

fact, as he develops his argument, Stinchcombe[4] draws upon classic anomie theory to make sense of the school experience:

> The school system, particularly the secondary school, is one of the main institutions in the society where universal standards of success are applied over the whole range of the class system. Students are placed under great pressure to force a decision on the degree of success they expect, and the (symbolic) means of success, especially grades, are deliberately and systematically allocated differentially. Further, the ritual idiom of the school, by defining only middle-class choices positively, allows but a very limited redefinition of the meaning of "occupational success."

Stinchcombe[5], then, sees a direct link between the pressures to succeed in school (which, in turn, assure successful status prospects), and the individual's origin in the class system:

> Normally we would expect that the school's ritual idiom, defining occupational success in middle-class terms, would have greatest resonance among middle-class children. Of course, middle-class children are also more likely to have access to the means of success, by being more intelligent and better trained for the competitive struggle. But there is an essential distinction between *personal* means of success (intelligence, physical beauty, and the like) and *social* means (parental culture, money, grooming, social contacts). Social means of success tend to be highly correlated with social class, and hence with pressure to succeed, but the correlations between parental social status and personal means of success, though positive, are not as high.

It is at this juncture in his argument that Stinchcombe is led to the notion of differential strain. If it is assumed that there is a universality in the definition of economic success, which uses the same standard to judge persons with different opportunities to succeed, Stinchcombe then hypothesizes that those most subject to success pressures are most likely to be rebellious. Accordingly it is his expectation that unsuccessful middle-class students will be under exceptional strain, which will be reflected in a relatively high incidence of rebellion. Furthermore, he predicts that, due to their lack of the "social" means of success, upwardly mobile working-class boys, while less rebellious than their nonmobile working-class peers, will be more rebellious than nonmobile middle-class boys.

When he turns to a test of this stress hypothesis, Stinchcombe finds his data uncomfortably perverse. A pattern of differences emerges whereby unsuccessful lower-middle-class boys are indeed more alienated than their working-class counterparts, but among upper-middle-class boys the predicted responses do not emerge with enough consistency to prevent Stinch-

---

[4]Arthur L. Stinchcombe, *Rebellion in a High School*, p. 135.
[5]Ibid., pp. 135–36.

combe from being "discouraged." He does conclude, however, that among the academically unsuccessful, middle-class boys are the most rebellious.[6]

The purpose of the present work is to examine more closely Stinchcombe's concept of strain as a key element in his theory directing attention to the influence of the external economic system within the school framework. Success in school, within his framework, is related in two fundamental ways to the external economic order. First, success itself is seen as a direct product of the individual's social class position in the community. Second, success in school derives its meaning from its implication for the economic future, i.e., the status prospects, of the adolescent.

This model, which gives such strong weight to the economic implications of adolescent behavior, deserves close examination. As a set of propositions firmly grounded in the anomie tradition, the arguments have a most acceptable sociological pedigree. It may be, however, that such a view undervalues the characteristics of the more immediate status system of the school. While failure may be assumed to have important and recognized implications for the economic future of the individual adolescent, it is possible that the strains of failure may derive from the more immediate degradation and stigma in the at-present social world of the adolescent. If the important meaning of failure for the adolescent is to be found in the countless humiliations the high school can heap upon its "undesirables," then the Stinchcombe argument deflects our attention from the meaningful present to the misleading future.

Given Stinchcombe's brand of economic determinism, the interlocking of status futures as a psychological reality becomes crucial. For his theory to be valid, it is essential that those with the most to lose, i.e., downwardly mobile middle-class boys, be the most rebellious. If we observe such a relationship, then we can substantiate Stinchcombe's view of adolescence. If, on the other hand, we do not find differential responses to failure among white- and blue-collar boys, we shall be faced with the task of constructing an alternative view of the relationship between school experience and rebellion.

Stinchcombe's total theoretical scheme is complex and beyond testing in any short paper. In his first chapter,[7] in which the basic theory is elaborated, four major hypotheses are derived. We shall be concerned here with the fourth of these, stated in the following form: *Whenever the goals of success are strongly internalized but inaccessible, expressive alienation results.* We are interested, actually, in the sentence which precedes this hypothesis, in which Stinchcombe[8] makes explicit his contention that alien-

---

[6]Ibid., p. 168. Again, some confirmation can be found in the work of Call, who also reported that middle-class delinquents typically display a greater pattern of alienation than do working-class delinquents.

[7]Ibid., Chap. 1.

[8]Ibid., p. 8.

ation is a reaction formation which supports the rejection of partially internalized goals of success (italics his):

> We will expect that *among those who are failing in school those under the most pressure to succeed will be most rebellious,* because rebellion is a way of rejecting pressure for success.

In examining this hypothesis, we shall utilize two kinds of measures of academic success. One type of measure is obvious from Stinchcombe's language—academic performance as measured by grade point average (GPA). We shall use a second measure as well, that of orientation toward college. Two reasons can be presented for this procedure. First, it can be argued that what is important is not simply to do well in school, but to be identified with what might be termed the "success stream" through the high school, a major aspect of such a flow concept being the orientation toward college. Second, the use of a second measure permits a type of cross-validation, so that an approximation of a replication check is possible.

It is recognized, however, that utilization of the college orientation variable as a measure of direct success does some violence to Stinchcombe's formulation. In the elaboration and testing of much of the rest of his theory, college orientation represents for him the essential ingredient of the future orientation to the labor market, i.e., the measure of "articulation." If we were testing the other hypotheses of Stinchcombe, such as the hypothesis which examines the connection between articulation and rebellion, then the difference between the present formulation and his might be more problematic. As it is, we will use both measures as direct indicators of one variable, involvement with the successful flow through the high school. Once defined in this way, we also can make tentative inferences about status futures as well, since the present-oriented definition of success stream carries with it obvious implications and meanings regarding status futures. In any case, what will be done here is to reformulate Stinchcombe's hypothesis so that it states: *Among those who have fallen out of the success stream of the high school, those whose social class background place them under the most pressure to succeed, i.e., those from white-collar homes, will be the most rebellious.*

Another important difference between Stinchcombe and the present work is in the conception of rebellion and alienation. Stinchcombe restricted his analyses explicitly to the phenomenon of rebellion within the context of the high school. His first paragraph, for example, reads:

> The student-teacher relation in high school is one of the few authority relations in modern society whose maintenance is consistently problematic. Though authority everywhere frequently meets with lack of enthusiasm by subordinates, it is not often openly flouted and insulted. Though authori-

ties everywhere have difficulty persuading subordinates to be devoted to the goals of organizations, they only rarely have difficulty carrying on orderly social intercourse. It is consistently problematic whether orderly social intercourse will take place in classrooms.[9]

We take the risk of extending his notion of rebellion, casting our net wider to include aspects of behavior common to the literature on delinquent subcultures and delinquent life styles. We do this for two reasons. First, the study in which this replication is attempted was well in progress when we became aware of Stinchcombe's work, so we could not include many of his empirical indicators of rebellion within the high school. Second, we think that the major issue is adolescent rebellion with a wider referent than the school setting. Stinchcombe does indeed argue that his conception of rebellion should "fit" the problem of delinquency. In a section explicitly rejecting the Cohen hypothesis regarding the development of delinquent behavior, Stinchcombe argues:

> We have to find a formulation of the "facts" of distribution that economically organizes at the same time ethnic, social class, ecological, and sex differences in official delinquency rates. It is our contention that the formulation that can do this refers to the *future* status of the adolescent, rather than to the status of his family of origin. . . . The common element differentiating depressed ethnic groups from other working class populations in their *public* status is the labor market, their occupational life-chances, rather than their patterns of early socialization.[10]

He then goes on to propose:

> In other words, the reformulated "facts" of distribution of official delinquency are that it is concentrated in those sectors of the adolescent population *who will make* up the manual working class in the next labor market cohort (males, of working-class origin, especially in depressed ethnic groups, and especially in slum areas where schools provide few students with the chance to move up).[11]

And he concludes in hypothetical language:

> If future research should not overturn the more speculative of the "facts" of distribution of delinquency (and implicitly, of expressive alienation), we may state the following general "fact" of distribution: Expressive alienation appears to be most common among the *adolescents* of school age who are exposed to *more universalistic labor markets,* and who *will fill* the manual working class positions in those markets.[12]

---

[9]Ibid., p. 1.
[10]Ibid., pp. 52–53.
[11]Ibid., pp. 53–54.
[12]Ibid., p. 57.

What we will do here in testing the hypothesis of differential stress is to examine a range of items which indicate involvement in a pattern of peer rebellion and deviance. One measure will be official delinquency, i.e., appearance before the juvenile court. In order to avoid the implications of being dependent upon this one measure, with its well known biases, we also will include items which assess: (a) the extent to which the young person *actually engages* in other "troublesome" or problematic behavior (fighting, drinking, smoking), (b) the extent to which the young person participates in potentially rebellious peer cultural activities, and (c) the willingness of the adolescent to follow the dictate of his peers when these are in opposition to adult desires. The inclusion of a wide range of deviance and peer orientation items, especially if the findings are consistent across such measures, permits a more plausible test of the hypothesis than is possible with only one or two measures.

Thus, we do recognize at the outset that in some respects this will not be a "fair" test of Stinchcombe. In these few pages, we could not test the totality of what he has stated in his book-length manuscript. Important changes have been made in some indicators. We restrict attention to a key hypothesis, arguing that if Stinchcombe is wrong here, then we may need to reexamine this whole theory. In a limited sense, the test will be fair. He argues that rebellion should be highest among those with the most to lose. However sophisticated and complex is his total theory, this one hypothesis should be relatively accessible for examination within the empirical limits of this brief investigation.

Research Procedures

Data for the present study were drawn from an on-going longitudinal investigation of adolescents in a medium-sized county (1960 population, 120,888) in the Pacific northwest. A 25 percent random sample was drawn from a sample frame consisting of all male sophomores enrolled in the schools of the county in 1964. From the total of 309 subjects selected, 284 usable interviews were obtained, giving a response rate of 91 percent. The one-hour interviews conducted by the project staff members covered a range of demographic, school, family, work, and peer variables. To these data were added grade point average from school transcripts and delinquency reports from juvenile court records.

Specific indicators, two of status prospects and one of status origins, are needed to test the Stinchcombe hypotheses. The first measure of prospects, college plans, is assessed by response to the statement, "I expect to go to college," to which 64 percent responded "yes," and 32 percent responded "no"; with four percent giving uncodable responses. The simple college/noncollege differentiation yields the information necessary to examine the specific hypotheses under question, although the absence of a category to evoke the "ambiguous" response prevents testing some parts of the Stinchcombe analysis with these interview data.

The second measure of school status consists of academic achievement as measured by cumulative grade point average. Since we are especially interested in those persons doing poorly in school, we have used a dichotomy—those earning a GPA below a 2.00 (or "C") being placed in the "low" GPA category; those above this point in the "high" category. With these cutting points, only a small proportion of the *total* sample, 31 percent, fall into the "low" GPA category. This was done to assure some kind of agreement between our measure of "low" grades and the perception of the student that he was doing poorly.

Because of the limited number of cases, the indicator of status origins, i.e., of social class background, must be treated as a dichotomous attribute. Using the father's occupation as the determinant of status origins, occupations ranging from executives and professionals to clerical and sales workers are included together in a "white-collar" category that comprises 50 percent of the population. In the "blue-collar" category are classified such occupations as skilled manual workers, machine operators and unskilled workers; this group comprises 42 percent of the sample. Eight percent of the boys could not be classified by status origins.[13]

Turning now to the empirical indicators of rebellion against which the stress hypothesis is to be tested, we will first examine a group of variables designed to assess involvement in what might be called "rebellious subculture" activities (the terms in parentheses indicate how the variable is identified in the table):

1. A measure of the adolescent's perception of rebellion among his friends, as indicated by response to the statement that his friends "could have gotten in lots of trouble with the police for some of the stuff they pull." ("Friends in Trouble")
2. A measure of willingness to engage in deviant behavior when pressured by friends, as indicated by response to the statement that "If I was out somewhere with my friends and they started drinking, I would join them." ("Drink with Friends")
3. A measure of involvement in a pattern of youthful hedonism, as meas-

---

[13]Stinchcombe, also working with low frequencies, found some important differences between upper-middle and lower-middle-class boys which would cancel out if the groups were combined. We have combined these two categories into a single white-collar group, since even with this simple cutting point we are left with only 13 students in the low grade point average/white-collar group. In our extensive examination of the class variable among the boys of this study, we have found no differences within the white-collar category that suggest any problem in combining, or any significant loss of information by such combination. Putting it another way, extensive analysis has yielded no finding of either curvilinear or problematic complex interaction effects.

ured by response to the statement that "I really enjoy cruising around at night to see what is going on." ("Enjoy Cruising")

4. Three measures of what Cohen has called "group autonomy," or the rejection of adult restraints on peer activities. The questions require a decision in a hypothetical situation posing conflicting demands by peers and by adult authority as represented by (a) school officials, (b) parents, and (c) police. The specific items are:

    (1) the choice made by the respondent when confronted by a conflict between the school principal's request for attendance at a school rally, and friends' invitation to go for a ride in their car; ("Peers versus Principal")

    (2) the choice made by the respondent when pressured by friends to go somewhere parents have forbidden the youth to go; ("Peers versus Parents")

    (3) the choice made by the respondent when he has knowledge of a crime (shoplifting) committed by a friend and is asked for information by police. ("Peers versus Police")

A further group of variables deals more directly with actual engagement in deviant, or "troublesome," behavior, and consists of:

1. Drinking, as measured by response to the question, "Do you drink beer?" ("Drink Beer")

2. Fighting, as measured by agreement or disagreement with the statement, "I like to get into a good fight now and then." ("Like to Fight")

3. Official delinquency, as measured by a review of juvenile court records (traffic offenses excluded). ("Official Delinquency")

For our test of Stinchcombe's strain hypothesis, we have constructed a complex table showing the percentages of "rebellious" responses on the nine rebellion variables, first by social class background and college plans, and second by social class background and grade point average. The assessment of the simultaneous contribution of "status origins" and "status prospects" to rebellion can be found in Table 1. Looking at the "college plans" segment of the table, for example, a comparison of the individual row entries for columns one against two, then three against four, will tell us whether white-collar youth are more rebellious than blue-collar youth with similar college plans; while comparison of row entries in columns one and three, then two and four, will tell us whether noncollege-oriented youth are more rebellious than college-oriented youth at similar levels of economic status. In the grade point average segment of the table, comparisons of row entries for columns five against six, and seven against eight will indicate the "effect" of class on rebellion with grades controlled; while comparing columns five against seven, and six against eight will indicate the "effect" of grade point average on rebellion with social class background controlled.

The findings of the present study, as shown in Table 1, can do little more than add to Stinchcombe's discouragement. Considering the hypothesis

Table 1: Percent of Rebellious Responses to Selected Measures of Rebellion by Class Background, Grade Point Average, and College Plans

| | COLLEGE PLANS | | | | GRADE POINT AVERAGE | | | |
| | Yes | | No | | High | | Low | |
Rebellion Item	(1) White Collar (N = 105)	(2) Blue Collar (N = 63)	(3) White Collar (N = 30)	(4) Blue Collar (N = 53)	(5) White Collar (N = 111)	(6) Blue Collar (N = 77)	(7) White Collar (N = 28)	(8) Blue Collar (N = 44)
"Friends in Trouble"	32	36	57	66	30	43	75	64
"Drink with Friends"	47	48	70	65	46	52	75	61
"Enjoy Cruising"	57	60	80	80	57	61	82	84
"Peers versus Principal"	52	44	67	68	52	48	83	70
"Peers versus Parents"	31	24	44	53	28	31	65	46
"Peers versus Police"	63	52	70	81	59	57	82	79
"Drink Beer"	34	43	57	66	35	44	64	72
"Like to Fight"	18	24	37	36	18	20	43	48
"Official Delinquency"	15	24	30	34	14	21	36	41

Mean Percentage Difference[a]
Between Columns:
1 versus 2 = 0.7%
3 versus 4 = −4.1%
1 versus 3 = 18.1%
2 versus 4 = 21.6%

Mean Percentage Difference[a]
Between Columns:
5 versus 6 = 4.2%
7 versus 8 = 4.4%
5 versus 7 = 29.6%
6 versus 8 = 20.9%

[a]The percentage differences in rebellious responses are computed in the direction expected by the theory, i.e., it is hypothesized that 3 > 4 and 7 > 8, but that 2 > 1 and 6 > 5, while 3 > 1, 4 > 2, 7 > 5, and 8 > 7.

of strain among downwardly mobile youth, which requires a comparison of white-collar and blue-collar youth who are, first, "noncollege" (columns three against four), and second, receiving low grades (column seven against eight), no pattern of greater rebellion among downwardly mobile white-collar boys can be observed in terms of direction of difference. On only two of the nine variables in the case of college plans, and only five of the nine variables in the case of grades, are downwardly mobile white-collar boys more rebellious than nonmobile blue-collar boys.[14] These findings, unlike those of Stinchcombe, do not provide even "fragile" support for the hypothesis. It seems quite clear that downward mobility is not accompanied by higher incidences of rebellion among the middle-class boys in our sample.

A more rigorous quantitative test of this idea can be obtained by examining the magnitude of the differences in the percentage of rebellious responses. By summing (in the direction predicted by the Stinchcombe hypothesis) the differences for the noncollege youth between white- and blue-collar groups (column three by column four, i.e., 57–66, 70–65, 80–80, etc.) and dividing by the number of comparisons, we find a negative mean percentage difference, − 4.1, indicating a slight tendency for any differences to be in the opposite direction predicted by the Stinchcombe theory. This indicates that, if anything, noncollege bound white-collar boys are slightly *less* rebellious than noncollege-bound blue-collar boys. In the case of students earning low grades, while the mean difference between white- and blue-collar youth (4.4) is in the right direction, i.e., white-collar youth being slightly more rebellious, the difference is hardly large enough to claim confirmation of the hypothesis. Downward mobility does not appear to be significantly related to the incidence of rebellion.

There is another aspect of this hypothesis that we can examine. Stinchcombe argues, as part of his general theory, that while upwardly mobile working-class youth should be less rebellious than their nonmobile working-class peers, they can be expected to be more rebellious than stable middle-class boys. When this assertion is tested against the present data by means of comparisons between upwardly mobile blue-collar boys (those headed for college or earning high grades) and stable white-collar boys, it fares no better than its earlier corollary. Among those with bright status prospects, i.e., those planning to attend college or earning top grades, there is no strong tendency of blue-collar boys to be more rebellious than white-collar boys. The mean percentage differences in the extent of rebellion between the class groups is virtually zero in the case of college plans (0.7, comparing columns one and two) and only slightly higher for those earning higher grades (4.2, comparing columns five and six). We conclude, then, that successful blue-

---

[14]Greater rebelliousness is indicated by the direction of the relationships, not by the application of a significance test.

collar youngsters are not more rebellious than their white-collar counterparts.

Apparently something is amiss in Stinchcombe's conception of the adolescent experience, at least if these data can be taken as a test of his hypotheses. We must note that at least part of his argument can be supported: our measures of status prospects do appear to be related to rebellion. Returning to the data in Table 1, relatively large percentage differences can be found in the levels of rebellious responses among noncollege and college bound youth, both among white-collar (a mean percentage difference score of 18.1, comparing columns one and three) and among blue-collar (mean percentage difference of 21.6, comparing columns two and four) boys. Similarly, those earning low grades are more likely to be rebellious, this being true again for white-collar (mean percentage difference of 29.6, comparing columns five and seven) and blue-collar (mean percentage difference of 20.9, comparing columns six and eight) boys. Quite clearly, rebellion does appear to be related to what Stinchcombe calls status prospects. Those boys facing a dim economic future, as indicated by low grades and noncollege orientation, are more likely to rebel. When we find that this holds independent of class level, we question the network of ideas Stinchcombe has woven together to make sense of status origins, status prospects, and adolescent rebellion.

Discussion and Conclusions

These data fail to support the hypothesis of adolescent strain as a product of status origins. Thus we face the same problem that led Stinchcombe to develop his hypothesis in the first place: how to account for the fairly strong relationship between status origins and status prospects, and also between status prospects and rebellion, when little or no relationship obtains between status origins and rebellion. Stinchcombe's solution was to use anomie theory as a basis for positing status origins as a variable which would interact with the response to school experiences, and lead to a differential response for boys of different class origins. Downwardly mobile middle-class boys would feel more stress, and therefore be more rebellious, than stable working-class boys; while upwardly mobile working-class boys would be more rebellious than stable middle-class boys.

Since our data fail to support this hypothesis of differential strain, Stinchcombe's concept of adolescent rebellion is open to question. One major problem may lie in his interpretation of the temporal functioning of the economic variables. This is particularly true of the futuristic emphasis implicit in the designation of adjustment variables as "status prospects."

For Stinchcombe, grades or college plans have an impact in the immediate life of adolescents by virtue of their "articulation" with future labor market position. Wedded to the anomie tradition, the economic "fact" of such a linkage becomes, to Stinchcombe's potentially working-class boy, a psychological fact as well. There is certainly abundant evidence that youth who do not go to college are likely to occupy low positions in the economic order. We may even agree that these boys have some realization of the economic vulnerability that attaches to the noncollege track. Further, our own data support without question that part of the Stinchcombe argument which deals exclusively with status prospects: college plans and grades do emerge as strong correlates of rebellious behavior.

Yet it is possible that Stinchcombe gives too much weight to the future social class and economic ramifications of school experience. An alternative explanation is that the rebellion of failing youngsters is a response to the *immediate* effects of failure, rather than to its implications for future low status in the essentially external economic world. Placement in noncollege tracks of the contemporary high school means consignment to an educational oblivion without apparent purpose or meaning; but the effect of this placement in producing rebellion may stem from the stigma, humiliation, and hostility generated within the school itself, rather than from a reaction to anticipated consignment to a working-class role.

The focus of this paper permits no more than outlining this alternative hypothesis. This investigation has shown that, first, measures of school adjustment, interpreted by Stinchcombe as status prospects, are more powerful in explaining youth rebellion than are social class origins. In fact, class origin appears to have virtually no direct effect on rebellion. Second, Stinchcombe's effort to preserve the logic of anomie theory by hypothesizing greater strain (and thus higher levels of rebellion) among downwardly mobile middle-class boys in comparison with stable working-class boys, is not supported here. And third, we have suggested in the closing paragraphs that the importance of school adjustment in generating patterns of rebellion may lie not so much in the future, as implied by Stinchcombe's concept of "status prospects," as in the immediately experienced stigma of failure as interpreted within the status system of the school. Quite clearly, both an expanded logical argument and additional data are needed if this alternative hypothesis is to receive serious consideration.

Although an examination of recent sociological literature reveals an increasing utilization of such concepts as *youth culture, adolescent subculture,* and *adolescent society,* there is a noticeable absence of these terms in the literature pertaining to adolescent drinking. Those making reference to the notion of a youth culture generally dismiss the concept on the premise that it adds little to our understanding of teen-age drinking.

Maddox and McCall, for example, admit that peer group influence may be related to drinking but argue that this is neither a necessary nor sufficient condition:

> Some observers of the American scene describe adolescence as a time necessarily associated with stress and strain which, in turn, produce a "youth culture" and peer groups antagonistic to adult authority and goals. While this interpretation is certainly plausible, it has not been rigorously tested; the evidence, such as it is, is ambiguous. . . . *Given what we know about the importance of parents as models for behavior, a majority of adolescents in our society would in all probability come to use beverage alcohol eventually even if there were no peer group experience at all since young people tend to perceive some drinking as an integral and legitimate part of adult behavior.* The emphasis of this evidence overwhelmingly favors adolescent identification with adulthood, rather than hostility to adult goals or authority.[1]

Yet, it is not clear that even the data presented by Maddox and McCall support this thesis. First, almost no youth, including the youth who drink, see teen-age drinking as unconditionally "all right," that is, tolerable, for adolescents.[2] If drinking were a function of identification with adult status, one might expect that at least some of the drinking youth would see the behavior as unconditionally acceptable for youth of their own age. Second, according to Maddox and McCall, teen-agers see drinking as being "situationally appropriate." Their data show that most youngsters see distinctively adolescent settings as the locale where teen-age drinking takes place, especially, to use their terms, at " 'wild,' 'unsupervised,' 'beer,' etc., parties." Adolescent drinking is not seen as taking place with adults, or where adults are present, but in places distinctive for the absence of adults and adult controls—for example, in "secret, out of the way places."[3] And third, not only do teen-agers seek settings that are free from adult supervision, they do this in concert with other adolescents in such a way as to preserve secrecy:

"Drinking as Rebellion: A Study of Adolescent Drinking" by Kenneth Polk and Steven R. Burkett. Original material for this book, the article is published with the permission of Steven R. Burkett, co-author.

[1]G. L. Maddox and B. C. McCall, *Drinking Among Teen-agers* (New Brunswick, N. J.: Rutgers Center of Alcohol Studies, 1964), p. 7. © 1964, *Journal of Studies on Alcohol.*
[2]Ibid., p. 67.
[3]Ibid., p. 30–34.

Teen-age drinking is surrounded by an aura of illegality. It is premature from the standpoint of many, if not most adults, especially if it is not done in a context subject to adult supervision and control. Special precautions on the part of teen-agers to avoid detection are therefore required. Consequently, students themselves place less emphasis on the social facilitation accompanying the use of alcohol than on the group-identification potentialities of its use. While the "wild party" is specified as a common occasion for drinking, the importance of this behavior appears to lie in its symbolizing membership in a group more than anything else.[4]

One conclusion derivable from the above is that there are strong subcultural supports for teen-age drinking. Such a subculture provides the secret setting and preserves the secrecy of the activities that take place. The protection of youth from outside sanctions, in this case adult reponse to the illegality of the youthful drinking, is one of the fundamental functions served by a subculture.[5] The reference to "group-identification" and "symbolic membership in a group" appear to be quite consistent with the interpretation of the existence of subcultural support for teen-age drinking.

Why then do Maddox and McCall prefer not to analyze the subcultural aspects of youthful drinking behavior? In part, this decision is the result of their view of the nature of youth culture and how it might relate to drinking behavior. For example, they state:

There is simply no evidence that an abstinent adolescent is inevitably seduced by his peers who drink, or that peer group drinking is typically unrestrained by group norms. . . . The myth of inevitable and irresistible peer group pressure to drink and to drink excessively may tend to become, unfortunately, a kind of self-fulfilling prophecy.[6]

This is a somewhat distorted view of the possible consequences of youth culture. Few would argue, for example, that youngsters are "inevitably seduced" by a peer culture. At the same time, it may be appropriate to examine the subculture of peers which seems to provide important social supports for drinking behavior. A number of studies point to the social nature of youthful drinking and to the importance of peer culture in supporting such behavior.[7] Such a perspective does not in any way assume that

---

[4]Ibid., p. 80.

[5]E. A. Smith, *American Youth Culture* (New York: The Free Press of Glencoe, Inc., 1962).

[6]Maddox and McCall, *Drinking Among Teen-agers*, p. 80.

[7]J. R. Gusfield, "The Structural Context of College Drinking," *Quarterly Journal of Studies on Alcohol* 22 (1961): 428–42.

J. R. MacKay, "Clinical Observations on Adolescent Problem Drinkers," *Quarterly Journal of Studies on Alcohol* 22 (1961): 124–34.

E. M. Rogers, "Reference Group Influences on Student Drinking Behavior," *Quarterly Journal of Studies on Alcohol* 19 (1958): 244–53.

A. D. Slater, "A Study of the Use of Alcoholic Beverages Among High School Students in Utah," *Quarterly Journal of Studies on Alcohol* 13 (1952): 78–86.

C. Sower, "Teenage Drinking as Group Behavior," *Quarterly Journal of Studies on Alcohol* 20 (1959): 655–68.

drinking within the peer culture is "unrestrained." In fact, if the drinking were unrestrained it would not be possible to protect the all important secrecy. Further, focus on the adolescent subculture component does not assume that this "inevitably" leads to excessive drinking. At best a subculture provides the back-drop within which the individual actor behaves.

Perhaps the basic problem with the notion of a "youth culture"—and the resulting failure to utilize the concept in research—is the lack of clarity surrounding the concept itself and particularly the identification of its referent. Coleman, for example, argues that as a result of rapid social change, children and their parents get out of touch with each other, while the school takes on many of the functions previously reserved for the family. This segregation of youth, according to Coleman, forces the adolescent inward toward his peers, creating a distinctive peer culture which in important ways is in opposition to adults and adult expectations.[8]

Critics of this approach have argued against the sweeping generality that all youth are equally caught up in a culture which is opposed to adult society. This is essentially the argument posed by Elkin and Westley on the basis of their study of an upper-class suburb: "In Suburban town and other communities studied the youth culture elements exist, but they are less dominant than are accepted family and authoritarian guidance patterns."[9]

Bealer and Willits have noted that greater participation in the youth culture signifies closer allegiance to parental norms. These same writers, however, suggest that the problems of identifying a pure youth culture stem largely from the nature of adolescent behavior itself: "One might argue that it is more accurate to speak of many youth cultures, and indeed, differentiation of various types of adolescent behavior may provide a more fertile field for research and understanding than efforts to determine and define a more or less common culture pattern.[10]

It is no doubt true that some youth look to adults for guidance and accept their authority quite willingly in preference to that of their peers. It is also true that many youth turn toward their peers or spend more time with their peers than with adults, participating in such activities as school dances, athletics, and student government. However, one can argue as Berger has that these activities involve acquiescence to adult authority and values to a far greater extent than, for example, Coleman would admit:

> Coleman tells us that good grades and concentration on academic work are seen by adolescents as acquiescence and conformity to adult pressures,

[8]J. S. Coleman, *The Adolescent Society* (New York: The Free Press of Glencoe, Inc., 1961), pp. 3–4.

[9]F. Elkin and W. A. Westley, "The Myth of the Adolescent Culture," *American Sociological Review* 20 (December 1955): 680–84.

[10]R. C. Bealer, F. K. Willits, and Peter R. Maida, "The Myth of a Rebellious Adolescent Subculture," *Rural Youth in Crisis*, ed. L. G. Burchinal (Washington, D.C.: U.S. Department of Health, Education and Welfare, 1965).

whereas social affairs, extracurricular activities, and athletics are seen as "their own." But these activities do not "belong" to adolescents nearly so much as Coleman imagines. How could they when they are initiated and supported by the schools, sponsored and run by the faculty advisors, coaches, and local advisory groups, and considered by grown-ups to be organized training grounds for the assumption of adult responsibilities.[11]

A somewhat similar view is taken by Havighurst and Taba. Although admitting the existence of a youth culture, they argue, as we noted earlier, that one youth culture style is very much a part of school success and conventional middle-class morality.[12]

Although many or perhaps most adolescents show either an active or passive acceptance of—or acquiescence to—adult values and norms, some youth show a pattern of noncommitment—or lack of commitment—to those values and norms. These are frequently the youth who do poorly in school, are not planning to attend college, are not preparing for white-collar occupations, and so on. Polk and Halferty, for example, found that these youth are more likely to reject adults as role models and turn to their friends for support. They illustrate, in effect, a pattern of withdrawal or disengagement from the adult sponsored world and from the normal activities of adolescence. These same youth are likely to engage in rebellious and delinquent activities which are opposed to adult expectations.[13] In their study of troublesome youth, Karacki and Toby identified three problematic themes (search for immediate gratification, peer loyalty, use of physical aggression to assert masculinity) which appear to run through the culture of these youth.[14]

Due to their lack of commitment to adult society, these youth do not have what Toby refers to as a "stake in conformity." Because they are already oriented in opposition to adults, they have in effect nothing to lose. At the same time, they can gain status in the eyes of their peers.[15]

Given the above, it is the purpose of this chapter to examine the relationship between drinking and the various dimensions of the adolescent society. In the analysis and discussion which follows, our attention will be focused on two basic propositions. *First, the greater the extent to which some adolescents withdraw from the "success stream" through high school,*

[11]B. M. Berger, "Adolescence and Beyond," *Social Problems*, 10 (Spring 1963): 394–408.

[12]R. J. Havighurst and H. Taba, *Adolescent Character and Personality*, (New York: John Wiley & Sons, Inc., 1949), p. 36.

[13]K. Polk and D. S. Halferty, "Adolescence, Commitment, and Delinquency," *Journal of Research in Crime and Delinquency* 3 (July 1966): 82–95.

[14]L. Karacki and J. Toby, "The Uncommitted Adolescent: Candidate for Gang Socialization," *Sociological Inquiry* 32 (Spring 1962): 203–215.

[15]J. Toby, "Social Disorganization and Stake in Conformity," *Journal of Criminal Law, Criminology, and Police Science* 48 (May-June 1957): 12–17.

the more likely they are to become involved in a pattern of alienation and rebellion. And second, the greater the degree of involvement in a pattern of alienation and rebellion, the more likely an individual will be to engage in regular drinking behavior.

Success is viewed here as a multifaceted phenomenon, consisting of such factors as: academic performance (grades, hours spent on homework, and a view of oneself as a good student); future orientation (college and occupational plans); social activities (participation in the culture of the school); and supportive attitudes (liking school and seeing school as important for success). We expect that drinking will be negatively related to these variables. At the same time, we expect that drinking will be positively related to such indicators of alienation and rebelliousness as delinquency, fighting, and a willingness to follow peer—rather than adult—directives for behavior. Drinking, it must be remembered, is legally reserved for adults. Thus, teen-age drinking may be perceived as an affront to adult expectations and one aspect in a wider pattern of anti-adult behavior. The peer group, on the other hand, plays a supportive role for youth. While drinking may represent an attempt to announce one's approaching adulthood, it is within the peer group that one receives the necessary social supports for current behaviors.

The Data

The data for this investigation are drawn from a larger study of high school adolescents in a medium-sized county (1960 population, 120,888) in the Pacific northwest of the United States. This setting is essentially non-metropolitan, the most recent census showing that 36 percent of the population of the county is found in the small city center (population 50,000) 31 percent in the surrounding smaller cities (population 43,800) and 33 percent in rural areas (population 46,200). Some effects of dominance are exerted by a moderately large metropolitan complex (1960 population, 400,000) which has its center approximately 50 miles up the valley from this area. The county is fundamentally white (less than .2 percent Negro) and the labor force is rather evenly distributed between white-collar and blue-collar work.

The 284 male youth interviewed were selected from the twelfth grade class, so that control is exerted over the age and sex variables through exclusion. The youth were randomly selected from a frame defined by tenth grade rosters. The present group is a sample of all students enrolled in these schools during the sophomore year (those individuals who moved were followed and interviewed). The response rate was 92 percent. The students were interviewed by staff from the research project for a period of one hour. The interview schedule covered a range of demographic, school, family, work, and peer relationship variables.

Review of these interviews shows that most of this group of students said they lived in a town or suburb (69 percent); the rest said they lived either on a farm (21 percent) or "in the country" but not on a farm (9 percent). Using father's occupation as a measure of status origins, 43 percent of the students can be placed in a blue-collar category made up of unskilled, semiskilled, and skilled occupational groups; a slightly larger number, 49 percent, had white-collar backgrounds ranging from professional and executive to clerical and sales occupations. For a relatively small group, eight percent, it was not possible to determine occupational background. Turning to other attributes, a majority of these students indicated that they planned to go to college (58 percent); close to two-thirds were performing at a level of "C" or better (that is, 61 percent had grade point averages above 2.00).

In order to obtain an accurate assessment of youthful drinking, two separate measures are drawn from the interview schedule. The first item is addressed to the simple fact of drinking; this item asks the youngster whether he drinks beer and if so with what frequency. When asked if they drink beer, 32 percent of these adolescents said "no" and an additional 22 percent indicated that they had only once or twice. In the construction of the correlation tables reported later, these two groups are combined to form the "nondrinking" categories. At the same time 40 percent indicated occasional consumption of beer, and six percent indicated regular consumption of beer. These two groups are combined to form the "drinking" category on this item.

A second measure of drinking used here consists of responses to the question: "Do you drink to the point where you feel 'high'?" (No further clarification was added.) This item is deemed relevant because it deals not only with the simple act of drinking but with an important qualitative aspect as well. The response categories are treated in the same manner as the previous item, with the 58 percent "no" and the 16 percent "only once or twice" responses considered as "nondrinkers." The 3 percent indicating this a regular event and the 23 percent for whom drinking to the point where they are high is something that happens occasionally are combined to form a category of adolescent "drinkers." These students were asked if they had experience with other alcoholic beverages. Consistent with other findings, smaller percentages of these students acknowledged regular or occasional usage of hard liquor (32 percent). Preliminary analysis of the response to this item indicated it added little to the present study that cannot be gleaned from investigation of beer drinking.

In testing the hypotheses that have been derived, the relationship between these two measures of adolescent drinking and large clusters of variables are examined. To simplify the interpretation of these relationships, the tables which follow contain coefficients which assess the degree of association between the given variables. Since the two drinking variables have been dichotomized, we have followed a procedure here of dichotomizing the other variables as well. The measure of association selected here is the relatively simple Q coefficient, one of the standard coefficients available for 2 × 2 tables. As is true of the common product-moment correlation coefficient (r), the value of Q can vary from .00 to ±1.00; however, typically the r value for a given relationship between two variables will be somewhat lower than the Q value produced when these same data have been dichotomized. In the present study, Q values of less than .10 will be treated as an indication of no relationship, values between .10 and .30 as weak to moderate, above .30 moderate to strong. For a description of the Q coefficient, see Blalock's *Social Statistics.*[16]

Findings

An examination of the responses of these adolescents provides support for the hypothesis of a linkage between adolescent drinking and withdrawal from the success stream of the high school (see Table 1). The act of drinking beer, and of drinking to the point of becoming high, does seem to be negatively related to some academically relevant activities. These include grade point average (the Q values being − .57 and − .48 respectively when the grade point average is dichotomized at 2.5), time spent on homework (the Q values are − .46 and − .53 when time spent on homework is subdivided with those spending less than six hours per week doing homework in the "low," those spending six hours or more in the "high," category), and seeing oneself as a "good student" (− .55 and − .48). Very significantly, this is accompanied by lowered occupational (− .46 and − .46, dichotomized according to white-collar and blue-collar aspirations) and educational aspirations (− .45 and − .36, dichotomized according to college and non-college aspirations). It is apparent, then, that drinking is an activity that belongs outside the success-oriented and essentially conforming peer culture observed by Havighurst and Taba.[17]

In view of the above, it seems reasonable to assume that, for those who are doing well in school, the school becomes a locus for social as well as academic activities. In this regard, we find some relationship between par-

[16]H. M. Blalock, *Social Statistics* (New York: McGraw-Hill Book Company, Inc., 1960), p. 231.

[17]Havighurst and Taba, *Adolescent Character and Personality.*

Table 1: Relationship Between Adolescent Drinking and Selected Success Stream Attributes (Q Coefficients)

	DRINKING VARIABLES	
SUCCESS VARIABLE	*Beer Drinking*	*Becoming High*
1. Academic attributes		
a. Grade point average	−.57	−.48
b. Time spent on homework	−.46	−.53
c. Seeing self as a good student	−.55	−.48
2. Future orientations		
a. White-collar occupational aspiration	−.46	−.46
b. Plan to attend college	−.45	−.36
3. Social activities		
a. Participation in school activities and organizations	−.34	−.27
b. Perception of self as close to the center of things	−.36	−.44
4. Supportive attitudes and behavior		
a. Disagree that school is dull and boring	−.49	−.41
b. Agree that "I like school"	−.47	−.45
c. Agree that college education is necessary for a good job	−.22	−.15
d. Agree that school is a waste of time for work planned	−.26	−.33
e. Friends college-bound	−.46	−.53

ticipation in school activities (Q values of −.34 and −.27, where participation is dichotomized by creating a nonparticipant category of those who do not participate in any activities, contrasted with a participant category of those participating in one or more such activities), and between the tendency of these respondents to see themselves as close to the "center of things" in the school (Q values of −.36 and −.44). It is important to note that there is an interdependence between youth and adults, especially school officials, in school activities. Thus, given the general adult and legal prohibitions against the use of alcohol by adolescents, it is perhaps this guidance and consent role of adults that leads to the absence of alcohol use among the successful students. "Buying into" this attitude toward alcohol use may become an important component of the actual participation in the social system of the school. Withdrawal from the success stream, on the other hand, reduces the potential cost of alcohol use since the accompanying lack of commitment to the school and its activities gives the threat of suspension of participation less meaning. Furthermore, withdrawal from the system lowers the probability of participation in the kinds of acceptable social activities where alcohol use can be controlled to some degree if not prohibited, by adults.

In view of the above, it is of interest to note that for the drinker, school is not as likely to be an interesting or agreeable experience. The data show, for example, a greater probability of agreement that school is "dull and boring" $(-.29$ and $-.41)$, and a lowered probability of agreement that the students like school. Despite this, however, it is significant that this pattern of withdrawal is not accompanied by a complete negation of the importance and legitimacy of education, either generally or in their own instance. Although in the appropriate direction, nonetheless less powerful relationships are observed when these youth respond to the questions asking if a college education is necessary for a good job $(-.22$ and $-.15)$ or when asked if school is a waste of time for the work they plan to enter $(-.26$ and $-.33)$. These findings suggest, then, that at least an initial or partial commitment to the success theme, combined with poor performance and lack of social involvement, may contribute to the total pattern of withdrawal from the system. As a final example of the web-like character of success flow involvement, we note that high school students who drink are less likely to have friends who are college-bound, that is, also in the success stream $(-.42$ and $-.38)$.

When we turn to the second aspect of this study, we find similar support for the hypotheses regarding an association between drinking behavior and involvement in a pattern of alienation and peer rebellion (see Table 2).

Looking first at the domain of "trouble," relationships do emerge between drinking and official delinquency—referral of the adolescent to the juvenile court for a delinquency offense (.45 and .44), a tendency to enjoy fighting (.48 and .35), and a general orientation to norm violation as indicated by agreement with the statement "sometimes I like to try to get away with doing things I know I am not supposed to" (.47 and .37). It is also clear that peers and peer involvements play an important role in teen-age drinking. Not only are the students who drink more likely to spend their leisure time with friends (.35 and .36, when the variable is dichotomized with those spending six hours or less per week with their friends constituting the "noninvolved" group, those spending seven hours or more the "involved" group), but the quality of these friendships differ. This can be seen in the high probability of agreement that friends could be in trouble for the "stuff they pull" (.54 and .66), and the very high probability that their friends, like them, are likely to drink (.87 and .90).

A central issue of this general alienation hpyothesis concerns the influence peers have over the behavior of individual adolescents, especially influence directing youth to reject the attempts of adults to guide and control behavior. If our hypothesis is correct, drinking adolescents are caught up in such a pattern of rebellion to a greater extent than are nondrinkers. To determine if this is the case, three situations have been selected to assess the range of rejection. These situations analyze how peer pressures compare

Table 2: Relationship Between Adolescent Drinking and Selected "Trouble" and Peer-Rebellion Attributes (Q Coefficients)

	DRINKING VARIABLES	
REBELLION ATTRIBUTES	*Beer Drinking*	*Becoming High*
1. *"Trouble" domain*		
a. Official delinquency	.45	.44
b. Agreement with "I like to get in a good fight now and then."	.48	.35
c. Agreement with "Sometimes I like to try to get away with doing things I know I am not supposed to."	.47	.37
2. *Peer Involvement*		
a. Time spent with peers	.35	.36
b. Agreement with "My friends could have gotten in lots of trouble with the police for some of the stuff they pull."	.54	.66
c. Agreement with statement that friends are likely to drink	.87	.90
3. *Peer Autonomy Against;*		
a. Parents, as indicated by response when a situation posed forcing a choice between going someplace forbidden by parents but pressured by peers.	.63	.59
b. School authority, as indicated by a forced choice between going to a rally as directed by principal or going riding with friends.	.56	.60
c. Community authority, as indicated by response to a hypothetical situation where subject has knowledge of a crime (shop-lifting) committed by a friend and is asked what he would tell if questioned by police.	.46	.58

with the expectations of parents, school authorities, and community authorities such as police. Significantly, in all three situations the teen-age drinker is more likely to reject adult authority and to turn toward his peers. These responses indicate a greater willingness to go out with peers when forbidden to do so by parents, to follow peers when requested to do something else by a school official, and a lowered willingness to divulge information to police regarding the criminal activities of a friend (see Table 2).

These findings can contribute to an understanding of the nature of adolescent experience as it relates to adolescent drinking. Once the specific components of the referent are understood, it seems that drinking does play a role in the admittedly different dimensions of youth culture. We have found that drinking is characteristically an aspect of a pattern defined by youth standing outside the conforming species of the adolescent peer culture suggested by Havighurst and Taba, with its emphasis on successful participation in the academic and social activities of the school. At the same time, successful engagement in the prohibited, and in fact, illegal act of drinking does rely on secrecy and the development of a set of norms by which a united subcultural front can be presented against adult authority. Equally important is the "trouble" aspect of youth culture that we have observed. The finding that drinking is related to delinquency and to involvement, both behaviorally and attitudinally with peers, adds to our understanding of how and where delinquency fits into the adolescent experience.

It might be argued that these findings are a simple function of the social class variable: If a lower class position is closely associated with success stream activities, and if drinking is closely associated with class position, then any relationship between success stream activities and drinking might be a spurious by-product of the stronger effects of social class. This is clearly not the case here, however. Among these adolescents, the relationship between social class and success stream variables are generally modest at best. For example, while the relationships between social class backgrounds and some success stream variables are moderately strong, as is true in the case of college plans ($-.46$) and time spent on homework ($-.34$), they are less strong in the case of grades ($-.28$) and seeing oneself as a good student ($-.12$). Most important for the argument are the lower level relationships between social class and the measures of drinking. The logic of the conditions of spuriousness would require these last relationships to be much higher if the earlier observations were to be explained away by social class background.

The ultimate test of the hypothesis, of course, calls for an examination of the original relationships when social class is controlled. Two illustrations will suffice to make the point that the findings noted here are not negated by the social class variable. Taking academic performance first as a measure of "success," we observe that beer drinkers are likely to earn low grades both among white-collar (32 percent versus 12 percent showing a grade point average of 1.99 or less) and among blue-collar (48 percent versus 22 percent) adolescents (see Table 3).

Looking second at the trouble dimension, drinking boys are more likely to be delinquent, whether they are white-collar (30 percent versus 12 percent being delinquent) or blue-collar (42 percent versus 13 percent). Similar findings obtain on the other variables, indicating that one cannot explain away the relationships between drinking and success or trouble by assuming that all are a function of the social class variable.

**Table 3: Percentage of Drinking and Nondrinking Youth
Who Earn Low Grades and Who Are Officially Delinquent,
by Social Class**

	WHITE-COLLAR		BLUE-COLLAR	
Item	*Drink Beer* $N = (148)$	*Non-Drinkers* $N = (53)$	*Drink Beer* $N = (169)$	*Non-Drinkers* $N = (53)$
Percentage earning less than 2.00	32	12	48	22
Percentage officially delinquent	30	12	42	13

Conclusions

There are at least two clear implications of these findings. First, the pattern of logic used suggests that if one wishes to understand, or perhaps deal with, the problem of teen-age drinking, attention may have to be directed at the wider pattern of withdrawal, alienation, and rebellion. While nothing here conclusively demonstrates this conclusion, it can be urged that drinking might be viewed usefully as merely one of many symptoms of alienation, rather than as a separate and distinct phenomenon of and by itself. Certainly a number of qualitative descriptions of delinquent and problem youth have emphasized drinking as one of many kinds of deviant acts engaged in by such youth, thus providing support for the assertion that we can understand drinking specifically if and when the more general deviant role has been accounted for.

A second implication of these findings has to do with the development of strategies and tactics of alcohol education in schools. Our findings suggest that the adolescents most likely to drink are those who have withdrawn psychologically from the school and have developed elaborate peer defenses against adult attempts to guide and control their behavior. From this we can conclude that the typical lecture, film, and pamphlet approach to alcohol education runs the risk of missing the group for whom its message is most appropriate. Approaches through the classroom are likely to find an attentive audience of eager and cooperative youth who will do little drinking anyway, along with a bored, apathetic—if not antagonistic—tuned-out group who probably will be little affected by the experience.

The concept *youth culture,* when its empirical and logical referents are made explicit, appears to add something to a portrait of teen-age drinking. In coming to this conclusion we have taken a different approach than that which led Maddox and McCall to a much different conclusion. We have not argued that the culture emerges from the storm and stress of adolescence.

Rather, we have argued that there is a limited sector of experience, centering especially in successful school adjustment, that contributes a variable stress factor which is an important aspect of a particular kind of rebellious youth culture. This narrow definition allows us to see that there exists not one but many kinds of youth culture, and that the social context of withdrawal and rebellion may be fundamental to our understanding of teenage drinking as a social phenomenon.

school pressures
toward deviance

As a means of gaining further support for the notion that a characteristic pattern of youth culture and rebellion is generated from the structure and process of the school, we were quite naturally led to an examination of school systems other than our own. In the belief that there should be great similarities between the youth cultures of countries with similar educational practices, our attention came to rest on the British system. While the specific character of the British system of education is undergoing considerable change, the task of selecting a few academic elites for university preparation and entrance remains relatively intact. Attempts have been made to liberalize the educational process through: (a) elimination of the controversial "11-plus" examination used to sort adolescents into appropriate secondary schools, and (b) the creation of comprehensive secondary schools which results in the elimination of the distinction between *secondary modern* and *grammar* schools. However, a low age of virtually automatic school departure (steps have been taken to raise the level from 15 to 16) still remains, assuring that only a minority will go all the way through the secondary school with an even smaller proportion going on the university.

Tracking, or *streaming* as it is known in Great Britain, is very much a part of the British educational process. It becomes significant and relevant to ask if the observations we have made on the impact of tracking in the development of deviant careers applies to this situation. While we do not have original data ourselves, a study made in England by Barry Sugarman[1] closely parallels our own work. (That is, his data base is similar to ours. His conclusions are somewhat different from the ones we draw). Sugarman sees adolescence as a time of stress and educational decision making. He argues that two dominant adolescent life styles are available to the student: (1) the official *pupil* role, involving acceptance of the values and norms held by the school; and (2) the *teen-ager* role, which he identifies as "roughly an inversion of the 'pupil' role." Sugarman suggests that because the school has nothing to offer many students, the pupil role lacks appeal for those students. Those disinterested students subsequently seek, through the teen culture, another means of gratification and status reward. The pupil role, then, is representative of the adult society, and the teen-ager role represents

"School Pressures Toward Deviance: A Cross-Cultural Comparison" by Kenneth Polk and William Pink. This is a revised version of a paper, "Youth Culture and The School: A Replication," published in the British Journal of Sociology, Vol. XXII, No. 2, June, 1971. It is published here with permission of William Pink and of the British Journal of Sociology.

[1]Barry Sugarman, "Involvement in Youth Culture, Academic Achievement, and Conformity in School," *British Journal of Sociology* 18 (June 1967): 151–64.

a youth culture that holds values and norms that are in important ways opposite to those of the adult society.[2]

Much of Sugarman's work is concerned with the teen-ager role and related features of the youth culture, and with how these derive from lack of adjustment within the school system. He contends that adolescents involved in the youth culture will demonstrate their membership in distinctly characteristic ways:

> By dressing and adorning themselves in styles not shared by their parents and perhaps abhorred by them, they are saying in effect that they are not dependent on parental approval. There are two different attitudes that young people may show in their choice of styles: one is to strive for real individuality in dress and manner, the other is to express solidarity with fellow teenagers by wearing what serves as their uniform. Both involve the repudiation of parental and adult standards.
>
> This repudiation, so I hypothesize, extends beyond matters of taste and fashion to a repudiation of other adult standards, so affecting the behavior of the young over a wide area.[3]

Deriving an empirical index of commitment to this role of teen-ager, Sugarman presents data in support of his assumption that those most highly committed do demonstrate a repudiation of the traditional values and norms espoused by the school.

From these same data he further contends that the youth cultures of Britain and America are different. To support this assertion, Sugarman offers justifications which require that he go far beyond the limits of his data (since he has findings only for British boys). It is his major contention that the British youth culture flourishes outside of the school setting, while the American youth culture is centered inside the school:

> There is one point of comparison with some of the American studies that should be considered. Whereas this study found youth culture to be linked to a thoroughgoing alienation from school, the studies of Coleman and Gordon in the United States have found something different. They found that although the basic values of youth culture conflict with those of the academic world, the institutional focus of youth culture is, nevertheless, at the high school.[4]

---

[2]This is reminiscent of Albert Cohen in *Delinquent Boys*, where he says "The delinquent subculture is not only a set of rules, a design for living which is different from or indifferent to or even in conflict with the norms of the "respectable" adult society. It would appear at least plausible that it is defined by its negative polarity to these norms. That is, the delinquent subculture takes its norms from the larger culture but turns them upside down." Albert K. Cohen, *Delinquent Boys* (New York: The Free Press of Glencoe, Inc., 1955), p. 28. There is obviously much of the same spirit of opposition in the formulation of values and norms of the "teen-ager" youth culture.

[3]Sugarman, "Involvement in Youth Culture," p. 153.

[4]Ibid., p. 160.

It is at this point we must take exception to the conclusions drawn by Sugarman. His assertion that the youth culture he describes holds values and norms opposed to those of the adult society does not arouse our concern, because that is consistent both with his data and our expectation. What we do find wanting is his notion that the youth cultures of Britain and America are distinctly different. Neither theoretically nor methodologically is he able to draw such an inference, because he does not present data contrasting the responses of adolescents in the two countries.

If such comparative data had been available, Sugarman might have been led to quite different conclusions. It is our hypothesis, for example, that in America the same categories of students comprise the youth culture as Sugarman identifies as comprising the British youth culture, namely the nonmobile working class, the downwardly mobile middle class, and those who cherish hopes of mobility along channels where the criteria of the school do not apply. We expect to find among American youth patterns of responses virtually identical to those found in Britain by Sugarman. If we do find such similarities, we shall be in a position to support Sugarman's general hypothesis about adolescent culture, while at the same time requiring some revision of his ideas about British-American differences.

Data for the present study were drawn from the Marion County Study. In describing these data, we occasionally use the term *American* adolescents when contrasts are made with Sugarman's *British* students. The intent of the present analysis is to make comparisons of adolescents between the two countries—thus the use of these terms. While our data may be suggestive, there are obvious limitations in viewing these adolescents as representative of American teen-agers, just as Sugarman's data drawn from four London secondary schools hardly can be presumed necessarily to provide a portrait of typical British teen-agers. The question to be examined is whether Sugarman's hypotheses about differences in adolescent behavior between British and American students fit the present data on admittedly restricted samples. It is only in a limited sense, then, that the terms British and American are used in the present study, and we assume that only extensive work on wider samples will establish the wider applicability of any observations made in this investigation.

As we proceed step by step through Sugarman's analysis, we find that the present study does not constitute an exact replication. There are many instances where the specific empirical indices must differ. At times this is because the instruments are not the same (the present report is derived from a larger study that was well underway when Sugarman's work appeared, precluding the development of exactly comparable items). At other times it is because the situational differences of British and American secondary schools demand different approaches—simply in order to ensure addressing the same problem.

Sugarman's first task was to make up an index of commitment to the role of teen-ager, which he did by combining three self-report behavioral indicators:

1. Making the teen scene—an indication of spontaneous hedonism, listening to pop radio stations, wearing teen-ager fashions
2. Smoking
3. Dating

Theoretically this index is a mix of the pull of the norms and values of the youth culture and of the degree of assertion of adult status within a situation in which adult status is systematically withheld:

> The three component indicators of teenage commitment (making the teen scene, dating, and smoking) are quite highly and significantly intercorrelated and therefore are combined together to give a more powerful measure of the degree of teen-age commitment or involvement in British youth culture.[5]

In constructing our comparable index of teen-age commitment we were faced only with the selection of an indicator that was logically consistent with "making the teen scene," since we had ready access to identical data for smoking and dating. We do not have any of the three kinds of measures of "making the teen scene" used by Sugarman in our interview schedule. What we do have is one item that does approximate the central idea, the indicator referring to *cruising*—the driving of cars repetitiously up and down virtually ritualistic defined streets, occasionally parking at similarly ritualistically designated spots. The specific item is: "I really enjoy cruising around at night to see what is going on." Using a procedure similar to Sugarman's, these three items (cruising, smoking, and dating) have been scored and combined, creating a dichotomous Index of Commitment to Teen-age Role.

For purposes of the present discussion we have modified Sugarman's presentation format. The data for his study were presented in 3 × 3 tables. Since some of the variables we use are inherently dichotomous, we could not present a uniform array of 3 × 3 comparisons. Instead, we have reduced all arrays (including Sugarman's) to 2 × 2 tables, because (a) all tables then can be compared both across items and between countries, and (b) there is no evidence that any information whatsoever is lost, since we are interested primarily in the direction of the relationship. No curvilinear trends appear in the higher order arrays which would confound the examination of the directional hypotheses in the 2 × 2 tables. Also, this procedure obviously simplifies data presentation, since only one half of

---

[5]Ibid., pp. 154–55.

the distribution of the dependent variable needs to be presented, that is, the proportion of individuals with high scores of teen-age commitment.

Given the development of this index, we can now proceed to follow the elaboration of Sugarman's hypothesis. His first contention was that "On the assumption that youth culture involves a repudiation of the values and norms of the school, we hypothesize that high teen-age commitment tends to go along with unfavorable attitudes to school."[6]

From his statements, it is not clear how Sugarman measured attitude toward school. We utilize the response of our group of adolescents to the following question: "School is dull and boring." When we examine the resulting data, we find support for the general hypothesis in the comparable pattern of response among the American and British students (see Table 1).

Table 1: Percentage of Students with High Teen-age Commitment, by Attitude to School

	BRITISH SAMPLE ATTITUDE TOWARD SCHOOL[a]		AMERICAN SAMPLE ATTITUDE TOWARD SCHOOL[a]	
	Favorable	*Unfavorable*	*Favorable*	*Unfavorable*
Percentage with high teenage commitment	14	31	18	34

[a]British responses drawn from Sugarman, "Involvement in Youth Culture, Academic Achievement, and Conformity in School"; American data derived from responses indicating agreement or disagreement of Valley County adolescents with the item: "School is dull and boring."

In both cases, the level of teen-age commitment was higher among those students with the more unfavorable attitudes toward school. In the American sample, 34 percent of those with unfavorable attitudes toward school display high levels of teen-age commitment, in contrast to 18 percent of those with favorable attitudes to school (the comparable figures for the British students being 31 and 14 percent, respectively).

In his second hypothesis, Sugarman draws a connection between teen-age involvement and orientation to the future: "One of the key value conflicts hypothesized here concerns the value of deferred gratification or future orientation. We are hypothesizing that high teen-age commitment goes along with low scores on future orientation."[7]

The American scene creates an excellent measure of future orientation —the student's plans for going on to college. Using this, we find, again, results directly comparable to those observed by Sugarman. (see Table 2).

[6]Ibid., p. 155.
[7]Ibid.

Table 2: Percentage of Students with High Teen-age Commitment, by Future Orientation

	BRITISH SAMPLE FUTURE ORIENTATION[a]		AMERICAN SAMPLE FUTURE ORIENTATION[a]	
	High	*Low*	*High*	*Low*
Percentage with high teenage commitment	16	29	18	35

[a]British responses drawn from Sugarman, "Involvement in Youth Culture, Academic Achievement, and Conformity in School"; American data derived from responses concerning college plans of Valley County adolescents.

In both countries the higher levels of teen-age commitment are found among those scoring lowest on future orientation. (The differentials are 35 versus 18 percent in the American sample, 29 versus 16 percent in the British study.) At this point we enter a slight demurer to Sugarman. In developing this second hypothesis, he draws upon the literature dealing with future orientation and the concept *deferred gratification*. In this literature it is assumed that by working hard in school the committed young person is deferring the immediate satisfactions available to those who are lazy and "mess around." This perspective ignores the intrinsic rewards which are a part of being successful in school, and many of these have to do with fun and very immediate gratifications. In the comprehensive high school in the United States, academic achievement is closely related to future orientation, and so is participation in the many school activities such as clubs, interest organizations, rally and pep squads, and even athletics.

High levels of future orientation do not mean a deferral of gratification in the sense often implied by the term. What actually happens is that alternative mechanisms for "having fun" are created. Those who are part of the success stream of the high school—those with high levels of academic achievement—are more likely to be able to find their fun tied up with the sanctioned activities of the schools. The others—those with low achievement—in some respects resemble social outcasts and in fact encounter a number of official bureaucratic devices (such as rules that prohibit those with very low academic performance from participating in school activities) which virtually assure that they *must* seek their fun outside the school setting. A stroll through most secondary school yards or campuses should dispel the dour, even puritanical, overtones to the concept of deferred gratification. The warm and easy laughter and patter that bespeaks of ease and comfort is most likely to come from those pupils who are doing well, who know it, feel it, and are enjoying themselves. If the academically unsuccessful students seek their pleasure elsewhere, as in what we are calling the teen-age culture, it may be because the official structure of the school holds out precious few options within the school for finding enjoyment, let alone meaning. Indeed, in his recent study of a British secondary school, Hargreaves observes:

> For boys in high streams life at school will be a pleasant and rewarding experience, since the school system confers status upon them. This status is derived from membership of a high stream, where boys are considered to be academically successful, and are granted privileges and responsibility in appointment as prefects and in their selection for school visits and holidays. The peer group values reflect the status bestowed on such boys by the school in being consonant with teachers' values. Conformity to peer group and school values is thus consistent and rewarding.[8]

Certainly, in both countries there do appear to be characteristic responses to academic achievement. Sugarman expected to find a close relationship between academic achievement and teen-age commitment:

> On the assumption that involvement in youth culture, with its rejection of school values, will tend to correlate with a low level of effort in relation to the goals of the school, we hypothesized that underachievement tends to be associated with high commitment to the teen-age role.[9]

The procedure of routine term examinations graded on an "A" through "F" for each course in the American high school provides us with a more direct measure of academic achievement than Sugarman's complicated method of assessing this same variable in the British secondary school. Despite the different measures in the two countries, however, the results run in the same direction and are remarkably parallel. Those who do poorly in school, in both the British and the American samples, are more likely to exhibit high levels of commitment to the teen-age culture (36 percent of the low achievers, compared with 7 percent of the high achievers in the United States group falling into the category of high teen-age commitment, the comparative British figures being 28 and 14 percent) (see Table 3).

One of Sugarman's more interesting observations was the connection between misbehavior and teen-age culture: "On the assumption that youth culture involves a rejection of the teen-ager's subordination to adults, we hypothesized that poor conduct ratings would go along with high commitment to the teen-age role."[10]

Sugarman's measurement of conduct was based on a rating by school personnel. Lacking such information, we have decided in this instance

---

[8]David H. Hargreaves, *Social Relations in a Secondary School* (London: Routledge and Kegan Paul, 1967), pp. 168–69.

[9]Sugarman, "Involvement in Youth Culture," p. 156.

[10]Ibid., p. 157.

Table 3: Percentage of Students with High Teen-age Commitment, by Academic Achievement

	BRITISH SAMPLE ACADEMIC ACHIEVEMENT[a]		AMERICAN SAMPLE ACADEMIC ACHIEVEMENT[a]	
	High	*Low*	*High*	*Low*
Percentage with high teenage commitment	14	28	7	36

[a]British responses drawn from Sugarman, "Involvement in Youth Culture, Academic Achievement, and Conformity in School"; American data derived from school records of grade point averages of Valley County adolescents.

to utilize two measures of misconduct. The first of these is juvenile delinquency, based on data drawn from official juvenile court records. As was true among British youngsters, in our sample trouble and teen-age commitment bear some relationship to each other. Those with records of delinquency show a higher incidence of teen-age commitment (41 percent) than those without such records (19 percent) (see Table 4).

Table 4: Percentage of Students with High Levels of Teen-age Commitment by Conduct Rating

	BRITISH SAMPLE CONDUCT RATING[a]		AMERICAN SAMPLE CONDUCT RATING[a]	
	Favorable	*Unfavorable*	*Favorable*	*Unfavorable*
			(Case I: Delinquency)	
Percentage with high teenage commitment	12	36	19	41
			(Case II: Fighting)	
			16	46

[a]British responses drawn from Sugarman, "Involvement in Youth Culture, Academic Achievement, and Conformity in School"; American data from responses of Valley County adolescents in Case I according to reports of official delinquency obtained by a survey of records maintained by the county juvenile court (traffic offenses were excluded); Case II according to agreement or disagreement with the item: "I like to fight."

A second measure was carried here to protect against the well-known biases influencing official delinquency. Included in the interview schedule was an item asking the response to the question: "I like to fight." Assuming that those who agree to this statement are likely to be viewed as troublesome characters and thus to resemble the intent of Sugarman's item of conduct, we find, in fact, that teen-age commitment is higher among those who agree (46 percent) than among those who disagree (16 percent—the comparable British figures being 36 and 12 percent) (see Table 4).

Sugarman's final hypothesis was that an important explanatory variable to teen-age commitment was the "intellectual quality" of the pupil's home background. It is unfortunate that our present data are probably weakest in matching up with Sugarman's on this dimension, which Sugarman sees as fundamental in the generation of different patterns of adolescent involvements. We have no direct way of assessing the intellectual quality of the family life from our interview schedule. We must instead resort to two indirect measures. One of these is parental social class, as measured by father's occupational background. The second is the parental emphasis placed on education, as indicated by whether the adolescent sees his parents as expecting him to go on to college.

Present data are somewhat less kind to this final hypothesis. The differences we find on these two measures are the lowest observed, and in the case of occupational background, the level of teen-age commitment is virtually identical among white-collar and blue-collar students (23 percent of the white-collar and 26 percent of the blue-collar boys showing high levels of teen-age commitment) (see Table 5). Some differentials in youth

Table 5: Percentages of Students with High Teen-age Commitment by Variables Assessing the Quality of Home Environment

	BRITISH SAMPLE QUALITY OF HOME ENVIRONMENT[a]		AMERICAN SAMPLE QUALITY OF HOME ENVIRONMENT[a]	
	Favorable	*Unfavorable*	*Favorable*	*Unfavorable*
			Case I: Parental occupational status)	
			23	26
Percentage with high teenage commitment	16	24	(Case II: Parental college expectations)	
			18	33

[a]British responses drawn from Sugarman, "Involvement in Youth Culture, Academic Achievement, and Conformity in School"; American data from responses of Valley County adolescents in Case I to an item asking for the occupational status of father (those with white-collar parents being considered "favorable" for comparative purposes, those from blue-collar homes "unfavorable," drawing upon the assumption current in sociological literature that middle-class homes are more likely to place a high value on education. See, for instance, Albert K. Cohen, *Delinquent Boys*, pp. 73–120); in Case II it is based on the adolescent's perception of whether the parents expect him to go on to college after high school.

culture commitment on these indirect measures of family background are found (the differentials in the case of parental support for college being

33 versus 18 percent), however, so that we cannot reject the notion that the quality of the intellectual style of the family serves at least to mediate other factors which lead to the development of diverse student careers.

The findings of the present study, then, provide consistent verification for Sugarman's results among British adolescents. The description Sugarman provides for British boys involved in the teen-age culture consequently would appear to apply just as well to these American boys:

> We have seen that these boys are on the whole rebelling against the norms imposed by the school and performing academically below expectations; they have unfavorable attitudes toward school and score low on deferred gratification. To the extent that performance in school and the recommendations of teachers count in later life, either in getting jobs or places in further education, these young people have very poor chances of career success. Youth culture, defined and measured this way, is in this sense the culture of the nonmobile working class, the downwardly-mobile and of those who cherish hopes of mobility along channels where the criteria of school do not apply.[11]

What we must question, then, is Sugarman's contention that the most visible youth culture in Britain is different than the one most visible in the United States. The comparability of our findings would suggest that in both countries a species of youth culture may spring up as a reaction to failure within the school setting. Coleman[12] and Gordon[13] isolated a different youth culture than observed here, perhaps because they asked different questions. As Sugarman himself observed, Coleman was concerned not with involvement in a youth culture, but with involvement and status ". . . . in the teen-age *social system* at high school, specifically that of the 'leading crowd' of the high school."[14] This "leading crowd" of individuals were those who, by and large, showed high levels of academic achievement and were involved in (and leaders of) organized activities. In short, they were the stars of the official school oriented pupil culture. As others, notably Berger,[15] have commented, if the American adolescent emphasizes an active social life and athletics at the expense of intellectual enterprises, it is not because he is rebelling from American adult culture; he may in fact, be providing an accurate reflection of it.

---

[11]Ibid., p. 160.

[12]James S. Coleman, *The Adolescent Society* (New York: Free Press of Glencoe, Inc., 1961).

[13]C. Wayne Gordon, *The Social System of the High School* (New York: The Free Press of Glencoe, Inc., 1957).

[14]Sugarman, "Involvement in Youth Culture," p. 161.

[15]Bennett Berger, "Adolescence and Beyond," *Social Problems*, 10 (Spring 1963) 394–408.

We now have a minor puzzle. Sugarman is certainly accurate in point-
ing out the differences between British and American secondary schools.
The extracurricular life, as officially sanctioned, is more elaborate in the
United States high school and contains elements "rigidly excluded" from
British schools.[16] Yet we must question his conception of greater focus of
the teen-age social system outside the school in Britain than in the United
States. In both countries, for some adolescents a significant aspect of the
social life centers in a culture with its roots explicitly outside of the school—
the coffee bar and the drive-in appear to serve comparable functions, to give
one illustration.

What is curious is that the 'outsiders"—the official rejects—of these two
different systems display very similar patterns of adaptation. If the systems
are so different, should not these patterns among the outsiders be more dis-
parate? An alternative conception is that the manifest differences between
British and American secondary schools blur the essential similarity of
choice faced by the adolescent, the choice posed by Sugarman himself:

> We may picture the teenager as being placed between the rival appeals
> of two cultures or sets of assumptions and standards: the youth culture
> and the "official," middle-class, adult culture represented by the schools
> and, for some, by their parents too. Below a certain age the young are
> obliged by law to attend school. There they find that teachers and others
> have constructed a complex set of rules and unstated expectations for
> them to conform to, with rewards and punishments of very limited kinds
> to back them up. These schools only work really successfully to the extent
> that they can elicit from their pupils a commitment to their role as pupil;
> to the extent that pupils *care* about doing well and being well thought of by
> their teachers.[17]

In both Britain and America the young person who rejects the official
world of the school has a problem, a problem which extends beyond the fact
that the law compels him to remain in school. In contemporary industrial
society, the school serves a gatekeeper function for adult occupational
attainment. Once the adolescent is directed into a flow leading to a low
status future, the compelling logic of the substance and process of education
is no longer resonate. Many no longer *care,* precisely because it makes little
difference whether they care or not. The evidence is clear, both in Britain
and in the United States. Youngsters in the lower streams feel the sting of
poor teaching, inadequate resources, and lack of educational concern or
commitment. Hargreaves, in developing his hypothesis that within the
school there exist two model cultures (the "academic' and the "delinques-
cent"), has pointed out that once the adolescents have been "streamed,"

---

[16]Sugarman, "Involvement in Youth Culture," p. 162.
[17]Ibid., p. 153.

aspects other than the mere organization of the school arise to contribute of the process of alienation for those on the bottom:

> The effect of this separation of the upper from the lower streams for Handicraft and Games is that they have differential opportunities for interaction. A boy of either the two upper or the two lower streams will, in these two subjects which enjoy six periods a week, be brought into immediate contact with the members of the other stream in his subculture, but not with members of the other subculture. In this way the structure of the timetable divides the streams into two halves and helps to account for the division in the friendship choices we observed at the beginning of the chapter, and for the normative differentiation, since this differential opportunity for interaction creates an artificial barrier to communication. When we add to this the fact that members of upper streams have common teachers, common homework, and common school visits, we can see that these organizational elements may have far reaching effects on the pupils.[18]

Sugarman, in his closing sentence, suggests that the study of youth culture is just beginning. In echoing his comment, we urge more complete comparative studies of adolescent behavior. The findings of Sugarman, Hargreaves, Stinchcombe,[19] and Polk[20] all suggest that in both Britain and the United States the pattern of youthful rebellion called the delinquent subculture may find its source in the organizational structure and process of the school. The present study adds to these observations by advancing some findings of similar response among groups of adolescents in British and the United States to withdrawal from the official pupil role of the school. If these findings are at all suggestive, one might hope for further studies done within a more exacting comparative framework.

---

[18]Hargreaves, *Social Relations in a Secondary School*, pp. 170–71.

[19]Arthur Stinchcombe, *Rebellion in a High School* (Chicago: Quadrangle Books, 1964).

[20]Kenneth Polk, "Class, Strain, and Rebellion Among Adolescents," *Social Problems* 17 (Fall 1969): 214–24. Also reprinted in this volume.

3

ways that the school contributes to delinquency

deviance
in the public
school

The past decade has seen an increasing amount of attention being given by social scientists, educational decision makers and administrators, classroom teachers, and others to problems centering around the failure of the school to educate and train effectively a sufficiently large proportion of youth. These problems include, first, the tendency of some students to drop out before graduation from high school. But, second, they include the closely related—and frequently antecedent—problems of underachievement and academic failure among students believed to be intellectually capable, students whose misconduct disrupts classroom procedure and school discipline.

It is the main contention of this paper that the answers and solutions which are found and, indeed, the very questions which are posed about these problems, depend on the conception held—explicitly or implicitly—of these forms of deviant behavior. It is our thesis that *underachievement, misbehavior, and early school-leaving are properly and most usefully to be seen as adverse school-pupil interactions* and not simply as individual acts, carried out by students as natural responses to damaged psyches or defective homes. The distinct advantage of this view is that attention—of the educator as well as of the investigator—is directed toward rather than away from one of the partners in the interaction, namely the school itself.

Deviance As Interaction

The starting point of an interactional approach to deviance is the observation that there is nothing inherent in an act making it deviant. It becomes so only as a label is applied to it by others. This in turn happens when that act is defined as in violation of some social norm.[1] Thus ". . . . deviance is not a property inherent in certain forms of behavior; it is a property conferred upon these forms by the audiences which directly or indirectly wit-

"Deviance in the Public School: An Interactional View" by Walter E. Schafer. A shorter version of this chapter was previously published in Edwin J. Thomas (ed.), Behavioral Science for Social Workers, (New York: The Free Press of Glencoe, Inc., 1967). Reprinted by permission of The Macmillan Company, Inc.

[1]Our use of the term *norm* follows the definition set forth by Muzafer Sherif in "Integrating Field Work and Laboratory in Small Group Research," *American Sociological Review* 19 (December 1954): 759–71: "The term 'social norm' is a sociological designation referring to . . . all products of group interaction which regulate members' behavior in terms of the expected or even the ideal behavior. A norm denotes not only expected behavior but a *range of tolerable behavior*, the limits of which define deviate acts." (His italics.)

ness them."[2] Howard S. Becker, perhaps the most persuasive exponent of this view, has alternatively put it this way: "Social groups create deviance by making the rules whose infraction constitutes deviance and by applying those rules to particular people and labeling them as outsiders. . . . The deviant is one to whom that label has been successfully applied."[3] According to Talcott Parsons, "It is, therefore, not possible to make a judgment of deviance or lack of it without specific reference to the system or subsystem to which it applies."[4] And further, "It must not be forgotten that (deviant tendencies) are always relative to a particular set of complementary role-expectations, to a particular alter or class of alters, and to a particular normative pattern or subsystem of them."[5]

Deviance, then, is an exchange between an individual and some other individuals, who represent or claim to represent the interests and standards of a particular group. It is not properly to be seen as simply an action engaged in by an individual but rather as a characteristic of an interaction between persons. "The full analysis of the problem (of deviance) can only be attained on the level of treatment of the interactive system *as a system*, not by isolating any one personality. This is the fundamental difference between the sociological and the 'clinical' point of view."[6] In short, the *interaction*, rather than only one of the partners in the exchange, must be the target of attention. Both parties—their orientations, actions, and responses to each other—must be included in any adequae conceptualization of deviance.

Deviance is a process and not simply an event or series of events at single points in time. In the words of Albert Cohen:

> The history of a deviant act is the history of an interaction process. The antecedent of the act is an unfolding sequence of acts contributed to by a set of actors. A makes a move, possibly in a deviant direction; B responds, A responds to B's responses, etc. In the course of this interaction, movement in a deviant direction becomes more explicit, elaborated, definitive— or it may not. Although the act may be socially ascribed to only one of them, both ego and alter help to shape it.[7]

---

[2]Kai Erikson, "Notes on the Sociology of Deviant Behavior," in *The Other Side*, ed. Howard S. Becker (New York: The Free Press of Glencoe, Inc., 1964), p. 11.

[3]Howard S. Becker, *Outsiders* (New York: The Free Press of Glencoe, Inc., 1963), p. 8.

[4]Talcott Parsons, *The Social System* (New York: The Free Press of Glencoe, Inc., 1951), p. 250.

[5]Ibid.

[6]Ibid.

[7]Albert Cohen, "The Sociology of the Deviant Act," *American Sociological Review* 29 (February 1965): 9.

There are a number of elements of this interaction process which call for attention, both in action and in research.

This paper is an attempt to show some of the consequences of viewing deviance in the school from an interactional perspective. It is our thesis that new light can be shed on the dropout problem when the events which usually lead up to early departure are viewed in this way. Perhaps the major insight is that the so-called dropout problem quickly becomes at least in part a force-out problem.

Deviance in the School: Problematic Issues

If underachievement and misconduct in the school are seen as fundamentally interactional, a number of issues become problematic, both for practice and for research. The next two sections discuss issues involving the organizational process of judgment of pupil deviance: the varying nature of school norms and the conditions under which norms may be differentially enforced. The discussion then turns to a series of issues centering around the nature of the deviant role: differential effects of public versus private, and early versus late identification of the deviant; factors influencing the kinds of responses made to pupils judged as deviant; effects of school responses on such pupils; and difficulties in shedding the deviant label—difficulties brought on by organizational practices as much as by deviant motivation.

Underachievement and Misconduct as School-Defined

Behavior becomes deviant, we have said, only when it is defined as unacceptable by other members of a group. This implies that whether a person is deviant or not depends in part on his engaging in a particular act and in part on that act being judged as unacceptable. Thus, a behavior in the classroom may or may not be deviant, depending on whether it is or is not judged to be in violation of normative prescriptions.

Perhaps the first issue which becomes problematic, then, is this: what are the norms which regulate pupil conduct and performance and by which pupils are judged? Some norms are universally found. All schools, for instance, are legally bound to require attendance until some specified age is reached, usually 16 or 17. And once in attendance, pupils are expected to perform at their highest possible levels in their schoolwork. This means that academic success goals are to be internalized and pursued by all youngsters, the height of those goals to be limited only by the innate capability of the student.

In addition, and partly to ensure maximum achievement, all students must achieve above a minimum academic level. It is clear that this norm is somewhat of a different character than that of achieving up to potential. This is an absolute, not a relative standard. It applies generally, irrespective of ability (although, as we shall see, the minimum standard may be scaled down with low ability of students). Performing below this level constitutes receiving a different, usually more severe, label as being deviant. Academic failure, in short, is no longer simply "non-A" in the absence of high achievement; rather, it becomes "F" for failure, "F" being qualitatively different from all grades above, regardless of the capability of the student.

"Associated with the expectation that the student will learn is the further anticipation that he will do nothing to interfere with his learning. This is the common-sense concept of school discipline."[8] The particular nature of norms regulating pupil conduct may vary a good deal from school to school, although students generally are subject to norms which refer to these points:

> work and punctuality; care of building and grounds; self-control; self-direction and individual responsibility; safety and welfare of the children; respect, deference, and obedience to the teacher; ordering relations among pupils, limiting of conflict and aggressiveness, facilitating sharing, cooperation, considerateness, and politeness; general standards of morality, such as prohibitions of swearing, smoking, and stealing."[9]

Thus, a sample high school teacher's handbook makes explicit reference to specific regulations having to do with truancy, tardiness, classroom and homeroom misbehavior, misbehavior on the campus and school area other than classroom or homeroom, smoking, running in the corridors, driving cars and motor bikes, defacing or damaging school property, undue familiarity (necking), false fire alarm, loitering on streets in the area, smoking across from school, stealing, snowballing, and fighting or scuffling in the school or on the campus.

This list does not, of course, exhaust the norms by which students in this particular school are judged. Moreover, we would expect lists from other schools to look quite different. This does, however, indicate something of the range of prescriptions and proscriptions which, when violated, may lead to labeling of students as deviants.[10]

---

[8]Wilbur Brookover and David Gottlieb, *A Sociology of Education*, 2nd ed. (New York: American Book Company, 1964), p. 462.

[9]H. Otto Dahlke, *Values in Culture and Classroom* (New York: Harper & Row, Publishers, 1958), p. 251.

[10]For a discussion of some of the societal functions of classroom norms, see Talcott Parsons, "The School Class as a Social System: Some of Its Functions in American Society," *Harvard Educational Review* 24 (Fall 1959): 297–318.

But in order for deviance to occur, not only must a certain act be engaged in and a norm exist prohibiting such action—that norm must be enforced. Neither the mere existence of a norm pertaining to smoking nor the violation of that norm by a pupil need necessarily result in that act being deviant. The norm must also be enforced and the act judged as intolerable.

Conditions Under Which Norms Are Enforced

Given that there are norms in a school pertaining to student behavior and academic performance and given that behavior has occurred which could be in violation of those norms, the following issues become problematic: What are the conditions under which norms are in fact enforced? Put another way, what are the conditions under which adverse judgment is passed and a label applied to an act indicating it is deviant and to the student who commits it indicating he is a deviant person? And, in a more general sense, what are the conditions under which norm enforcement is rigid, on the one hand, and permissive on the other?

In a certain sense, it is useful to regard each norm as having "tolerance limits." Behavior which is acceptable to the group falls inside those limits, and behavior which is unacceptable and produces sanctions falls outside.[11] Yet ". . . . the concept of 'tolerance limit' (is) misleading for it implies that there is a definite and absolute point at which norm violations will involve a reaction. Actually the relation between norm violation and the (group's) reaction is not as simple as this and may depend on the nature of the situation or on the social status of the deviant."[12] In short, there are factors and conditions extraneous to the particular nature of an act—a behavior or level of academic performance in this case—which have important bearing on whether it is placed inside or outside tolerance limits by those who do the judging.

First, the value orientations and goals of a school affect not only what its norms are, but when and how frequently it enforces those which do exist. Progressive schools, for instance, tend to be more lenient in enforcing norms relating to student conduct in the classroom than are traditional schools. Second, the nature of the pupil population affects what the tolerance limits are in a particular situation. A middle-class school, for instance, will prob-

---

[11]For a systematic analysis of social norms, see Jay M. Jackson, "Structural Characteristics of Norms," in *The Dynamics of Instructional Groups*, the Fifty-Ninth Yearbook of the National Society for the Study of Education (Chicago: University of Chicago Press, 1960), Chap. 7.

[12]Marshall B. Clinard, *Sociology of Deviant Behavior*, 2nd ed. (New York: Holt, Rinehart & Winston, Inc., 1963), p. 20.

ably be characterized by a high level of objective academic performance (that is, when looked at independently of judgments made about it). A lower-class, less able, or less motivated pupil performing at a particular level may be judged as failing in such a school, whereas he might not be in a different setting. Moreover, as a student moves from one level to another (for example, junior to senior high), he may find himself subject to differing standards, not only in terms of schoolwork but also in terms of behavior—partly because the value orientations and goals may vary between levels and partly because the new school may include different types of students than the former school.

Third, tolerance limits depend also on situational factors: the nature of the functional tasks (gym versus English versus homemaking classes), the behavior or performance of other students, and the personality and social characteristics (sex, race, class background) of the teacher. With regard to the last factor, for instance, David Gottlieb has recently reported substantial difference by race or teacher in perceptions of students. "The Negro teachers tended to see the (predominantly Negro) children as 'happy,' 'energetic,' and 'fun-loving,' while the white teachers were likely to see the same children as 'talkative,' 'lazy,' and 'rebellious.' "[13]

Fourth and finally, characteristics of the pupil himself may have an important effect on the nature of tolerance limits and, hence, on whether he receives the label of deviant. These may include his manifest status and identity in the school (college prep, athlete, club leader, good behavioral reputation), as well as his latent identity (sex, race, social class). It is likely, in short, that a teacher's judgment of an act will be shaped by how she sees the actor. For example, a pupil may be less likely to be adversely judged if he is a college prep student leader who also happens to be white and middle-class and has no history (to the teacher's knowledge) of violative behavior or failing work. Additional reference will be made below to some of the issues centering around the effect of reputation on labeling.

Factors such as the above, then, enter into the labeling of student conduct or performance as deviant. It should be clear that the fact that a student is identified and labeled as deviant implies as much about the situations in which he finds himself and, particularly about those who judge him, as about himself and his own actions.

As noted, deviance in the school—as anywhere—is not to be seen as a unitary phenomenon. As Becker puts it:

> Since deviance is, among other things, a consequence of the response of others to a person's act, students of deviance cannot assume that they are dealing with a homogeneous category when they study people who have

---

[13]David Gottlieb, "Teaching and Students: The Views of Negro and White Teachers," *Sociology of Education* 37 (Summer 1964): 345.

been labeled deviant. . . . What, then, do people who have been labeled deviant have in common? At the least, they share the label and the experience of being labeled as outsiders.[14]

Beyond that, however, they may have little in common: Underachievement or misconduct in one school or classroom or for one type of student may not be at all in another setting or for another type of youngster.

There are important implications of these observations. Since the *school* defines the conditions under which particular behavior becomes deviant and particular students take on the label of deviant, a proper understanding of deviance requires that attention be given that definition. This applies, on the one hand, to the researcher who is looking at rates of deviance. It is imperative in comparing rates of underachievement or misbehavior to recognize that there may be qualitative differences among the kinds of behavior which are considered.

On the other hand, these observations apply to the change agent who seeks to decrease deviant behavior (the counselor, social worker, or psychologist). The setting of change targets for ameliorative or corrective efforts requires an awareness of what expectations are being violated. Attempts to change internal, psychological conditions or even overt behavior may lose their effectiveness unless simultaneous efforts are made to articulate behavioral change with the expectations and standards with which the student must conform.

Nature of the Deviant Role

We have contended throughout that as ". . . . a consequence of viewing deviance in a context of interaction, we focus attention on the other people involved in the process."[15] Given that certain behavior has been engaged in or that a particular objective level of academic performance has been attained and that this behavior or performance has been defined as unacceptable by representatives of the school (teachers, disciplinarians), another set of issues, also having to do with "the other people," are these: First, what is the nature of the labeling process itself? That is, by what means are pupils who have been defined as deviant identified and set apart as deserving of some kind of "special treatment"? Second, what happens to them once they are identified and placed? That is, what is the nature of the school's responses to the deviant? Third, what effects do school responses have on future behavior of the deviant? Fourth, how do school reactions to the

---

[14]Howard S. Becker, *Outsiders*, p. 9.
[15]Howard S. Becker, *The Other Side*, p. 4.

deviant make it difficult for him to escape the deviant role, given changes in his motivation and behavior?

ROLE-ENTRY: The deviant individual is one to whom a label has been applied indicating he is somehow different and thus deserving of special treatment. Upon receiving such a label, the individual in essence enters a new role—the role of deviant. This fact has consequences at at least three levels. First, the individual takes on a new public *identity*. Henceforth, he is not just a pupil, but a pupil slightly—or greatly—different from most pupils: he is a poor student, a trouble-maker, or a potential dropout. Second, the formal *status* of the student may change: he is now a student who is on probation, who is ineligible for the football team or who is placed on a remedial or personalized academic program. Third, there are consequences for the *career* and career chances of the pupil of having been labeled as one kind of deviant or another. Thus, for instance, the probabilities increase that such a pupil will be seen and judged in the future as a deviant "should" be seen and judged—as a trouble-maker, a hood, a disrupter. Further, opportunities for achievement and success are likely to become constricted: he is dropped to a less prestigious, rewarding, and useful curriculum or is deprived the chance of participating in student government or sports.

More is said later about the effects on the deviant's career once he is in the role. The point to be underscored here, however, is that differences in the very process of entering the role may have differential effects on the student's identity, status, and career chances. The school in essence finds itself in at least two dilemmas with respect to the identification and labeling of underachievers and pupils who experience behavioral difficulties of one sort or another. On the one hand, it is to its advantage to label and publicly identify those pupils who violate school regulations, inasmuch as norms thereby receive continual reinforcement. The school in essence says, "Look, the rest of you, this is the way *not* to be." Thus, we find that probationary lists are sometimes made public in the school, one consequence of which is the constant reminder that the norms exist and are enforced. But on the other hand, *public* identification has the outcome, for pupils, of establishing them in the eyes of teachers and other adults, as well as of other pupils, as confirmed outsiders or deviants. It seems only realistic to expect that this fact will result in an increased likelihood of being judged as a deviant in the future—for the same objective act that would be judged differently if committed by a student who had never been publicly labeled before. Hence, the likelihood that any existing positive motivation will be further undermined is increased.

A second, similar dilemma has to do with so-called early identification. John Porter argued that the heart of the dropout problem is lack of early identification of deviants and potential deviants.[16] At the same time, however, it is not often recognized that early identification also has the consequence of early and continuing confirmation of the deviant identity, with all that means in terms of how the pupil is perceived and how he perceives himself. Thus,

> Being caught and branded as deviant has important consequences for one's further social position and self-image. The most important consequence is a drastic change in the individual's public identity. Committing the improper act and being publicly caught at it place him in a new status. He has been revealed as a different kind of person from the kind he was supposed to be.[17]

It is not suggested that public or early identification of malperformers or difficult students necessarily be halted. It is simply pointed out that, along with the advantages of these practices there are some important disadvantages, all centering about the fact that a self-fulfilling prophecy may be set in motion whereby a pupil is defined as being somehow different, inferior or bad, he is treated as such pupils "should" be treated, he increasingly sees himself as this kind of person, and sure enough, the likelihood is great that his future behavior will substantiate the label he wears. Particularly in the case of the marginal deviant, the public label may be all that is needed to swing the student away from a conforming orientation and to entrench deeply his deviant motivation. "One of the most crucial steps in the process of building a stable pattern of deviant behavior is likely to be the experience of having been caught and publicly labeled as a deviant. Whether a person takes this step or not depends not so much on what he does as what other people do. . . ."[18] If the very fact of taking on and publicly wearing a label has such vital importance for pupils' careers, another problem, to be treated in a later section, emerges: How can deviants be successfully unlabeled or restored?

SCHOOL RESPONSES TO DEVIANTS: We have contended that one set of issues regarding the deviant role involve the nature of the entry into that role, or in other words, the nature of the labeling process. Another equally important set of issues relates to the nature of the school responses to the deviant once identification and labeling have occurred. What sanctions or other responses are evoked when misbehavior occurs or when academic performance is labeled as too low?

---

[16]John W. Porter, "The Heart of the Dropout Problem: Early Identification," *Michigan Educational Journal* 30 (January 1, 1963): 362–65.

[17]Howard S. Becker, *Outsiders*, p. 31.

[18]Ibid.

There are, of course, a wide variety of sanctions open to a school. In terms of *academic underachievement*, responses range from punitiveness to helping efforts inside the classroom to referral to someone outside the classroom for special assistance (remedial reading teacher, social worker, speech correctionist, counselor), to referral to a disciplinarian for a talk, placement on probation, or suspension. When responses are made inside the classroom to *behavioral deviance*, they may be in the form of corporal punishment, persuasion, moving the pupil's seat, or referral to someone outside the classroom (to a disciplinarian or to someone such as a counselor or a social worker who presumably will attempt to change the behavior by means other than negative sanctions).

Neither the frequency nor the nature of responses to deviant behavior are likely to be random but rather tend to be patterned according to the patterning of a number of other variables: assumptions about the nature and source of the act itself, characteristics of the student (sex, race, social class, curriculum, reputation), characteristics of the teacher or other staff member (sex, race, age, experience, goals), situational factors (type of classroom situation—gym and shop as compared to English and physics; characteristics and behavior of others in the classroom), available resources, and administrative style. In short, what happens to a student once he is defined as deviant depends not only on what he did, but also on who he is, what his past record is, who saw and judged him, and where the deviant behavior occurred.[19]

EFFECTS OF SCHOOL RESPONSES: The observation that there *are* such patterned differences in responses is interesting in itself. It becomes not only interesting but highly important, however, inasmuch as it leads into another set of concerns: what are the effects of school responses to deviant inclinations at time one on the behavior of the same individual at time two? This is perhaps the most critical problem which emerges from an interactional conception of deviance. For it points up the fact that deviant behavior at any point in time is not *solely* the result of some psychological predisposition which is manifesting itself, nor of the attributes and orientations of students when they entered school ("it's the fault of the home"). Rather the school itself vitally affects whether deviance is maintained or

---

[19]In Aaron Cicourel and John I. Kitsuse, *The Educational Decision-Makers* (Indianapolis: The Bobbs-Merrill Co., Inc., 1963), a study is reported which emphasizes the importance for pupils' careers of the decision-making and routing criteria and procedures of the school and especially of counselors. Their findings point to the fact that not only is it consequential whether a pupil is or is not judged as deviant; of equal importance for his career is the particular category of deviants in which he is placed, because different types of deviants may meet with quite different types of responses.

even generated by the way in which it responded to tendencies of students toward deviance at earlier points in time.

This facet of the interactional process of deviance has been highlighted by a number of students of deviant behavior in recent years.

> Even if we focus on the deviant himself, studies carried on in this style (following an interactional approach) are likely to be exceptionally alive to the effect of the reactions of other people on the behavior of the deviant.[20]

> (An) important consideration . . . is the effect . . . of sanctions on the tendency of ambivalent motivations in the interaction process to lead to a cumulatively deepening vicious cycle of intensification of the (tendency toward deviance).[21]

> Whether incipient deviance is checked before it becomes fully conscious, or becomes explicit and the actors more fully committed in a vicious circle of progressively deviant behavior, accompanied by realignments and coalitions within the system, alter contributes as much to the outcome as ego. In short, the outcome is a cumulative and collective product, and the history of the deviant act is the history of an interactional system, not of the actor who happened to author the act.[22]

It is in these respects, perhaps more than any other that deviance in the school is most profitably to be seen as a process over time, involving a series of exchanges between a pupil and teachers, counselors, or others. The youth acts, he is responded to—in ways which may more deeply entrench him in a deviant direction or which may nip deviant tendencies in the bud—he reacts to those responses, and so on.

In order to understand the question of how school responses differentially affect deviant tendencies, it is necessary to understand why students engage in behavior which may be defined as deviant. What is there about some students leading them to engage in behavior or to perform at a level which might result in their being judged as deviant? This question in essence relates to the ego end of the ego-alter exchange and is raised in order to better understand how alter's (that is, the school's) responses bear on these individual sources of deviance. It is our contention that there are three individual or internal factors which may result in behavior or performance likely to be defined as unacceptable by the school: low innate capability, low commitment to school goals, and low acquired capabilities.

Except under unusual circumstances, the school is obliged to take on

---

[20]Howard S. Becker, *The Other Side*, p. 4.

[21]Talcott Parsons, *The Social System*, pp. 273–74.

[22]Albert Cohen, "The Study of Deviant Behavior and Disorganization," in *Sociology Today*, eds. Robert K. Merton, Leonard Broom, and Leonard S. Cottrell, Jr. (New York: Basic Books, Inc., Publishers, 1959), p. 467.

all comers, regardless of capability, skill, or orientation. As a consequence, a wide range of innate capabilities of pupils to perform academic and other school tasks is usually found. Although most youngsters have the intellectual equipment to meet school standards, some do not. Deviance may, then, be the outcome of a simple lack of equipment, particularly when the academic standards against which the work of such pupils is measured are the same or only slightly lower than those against which more able pupils are judged.

Second, if students lack positive commitment to school goals and norms, either academic or behavioral deviance may occur, even if innate capability is adequate. Again, partly because of the enrollment of youngsters of all backgrounds and aspirations, some are found who simply are not very much concerned with whether they do well academically or conform to school standards of conduct. But let it be stressed that low commitment is not entirely a consequence of internalization of values from the home which are not supportive of educational objectives or means. It is crucial, as we shall see, to recognize that commitment is vitally affected by the school's encounter with the child, which includes its responses to his deviant tendencies.

Third, deviance may result from a lack of what we may term acquired capabilities, which consist of academic and social skills necessary for successfully completing academic and other required tasks and for sustaining adequate relationships. Academic skills can be broken down into two components; first, cognitive, and second, study and classroom habits. On the one hand, in order to master course material at any particular grade level, it is necessary that a pupil have assimilated some amount of earlier subject matter. Thus, for instance, to succeed in tenth grade algebra the pupil must have incorporated at least the basic elements of junior high school arithmetic. Particularly vital as a cognitive skill is reading ability, since success in almost any academic course depends on the ability to read at a minimum speed and level of difficulty. On the other hand, as a second type of academic skill, a pupil must know how to study. He must know how to allot his time efficiently, to turn in a neat assignment according to instructions, and so on.

Social skills may similarly be divided into two subareas. The first has to do with relations with school personnel. In order to succeed in the classroom, the pupil must be capable of relating adequately with the teacher in a group setting, as well as on a one-to-one basis. He must be able to ask and respond to questions as well as to discuss such matters as regular assignments, special problems, or special assistance. In the course of a day a pupil also must relate to school staff in nonclassroom situations. This is especially true if he is frequently absent or if he has been identified as having broken school regulations. He may have to relate to the counselor, the assistant principal, the nurse, the custodian, the teacher acting as manager in the hall, and the bus driver.

The second set of social skills has to do with peer relations. The pupil must be able to interact with others in a way that does not disrupt the learning process or otherwise to attract the teacher's attention unduly. At the same time, he must be capable of interacting with other pupils with sufficient frequency to avoid being seen as an isolate or as withdrawn.

If any of these three sets of factors—innate capability, commitment, acquired capabilities—is low, there is a high likelihood of deviance resulting, although the actual occurrence of deviance depends not only on the motivation and behavior of the student but also on the existence and enforcement of norms. Our purpose for making these distinctions has been to shed light on the effects of school responses. In order to be maximally effective in alleviating or heading off future deviant behavior, reponses must not only control, contain, or cut off immediate deviant behavior, but must have the outcome of switching existing lows to highs in terms of sources—that is, of increasing commitment, acquired capabilities, or both, as the case may be.

Little research has been done on the actual effects of various kinds of sanctions on students' future behavior.[23] Common sense does, however, furnish us with certain guidelines. For instance, while sanctions which are highly coercive or degrading (suspension, corporal punishment, excessive long stays after school) may have the immediate outcome of curbing deviant behavior, in the long run it is likely that their result will be further deterioration of the student's educational commitment—further alienation from school personnel, ideals, and norms. Such unintended by-products of sanctioning practices may in fact contribute to the very problems which the sanctions are designed to alleviate. Thus, the school itself may, through its own activities, sustain or even generate the deviance it seeks so hard to reduce.

These unwitting outcomes may be intensified even further by the fact that considerably fewer deviants are deviants because of low commitment than because of low acquired capabilities. Our research has repeatedly made clear that more often than not students in difficulty differ little if any from nondeviants in the extent to which they are concerned about succeeding in school as well as in later life. At the same time, however, we have continually observed that teachers, disciplinarians, and others frequently proceed on the false assumption that it is low commitment which lies at the

---

[23]See Harold W. Massey and Edwin E. Vineyard, *The Profession of Teaching* (New York: The Odyssey Press, Inc., 1961) for an evaluation of classroom sanctioning practices. Amitai Etzioni, in *A Comparative Analysis of Complex Organizations* (New York: The Free Press of Glencoe, Inc., 1961), suggests general directions in his discussion of compliance and control.

base of the problem and thus gear their responses toward increasing motivation and concern about success.

Since it is acquired capabilities rather than commitment which is lacking, deviance persists despite genuine efforts to reduce it. No only does it continue but it frequently increases as continued failure, deprivation, and criticism result in a deterioration of existing commitments. In ways such as these, then, ". . . deviant activities often seem to derive support from the very agencies designed to suppress them." [24]

We are not suggesting only that there be increased remedial, corrective, counseling, and other special services (though these, of course, are greatly needed to facilitate skill and motivational development). What we are stressing is the importance of recognition by those on the firing line that probably more of their students care than they realize and that wise use of responses—those which support manifestations of existing commitment and which serve to develop necessary means or skills—can vitally affect the student's orientation toward school and thus his likelihood of success.

DIFFICULTIES IN SHEDDING THE LABEL: An additional set of problems which emerge from an interactional conception of deviance relate to the fact that once acquired, the label of deviant may be extremely difficult to shed. A pupil is not just a temporary, passing occupant of the role of deviant. Regardless of how drastic the behavior of a deviant may shift, there are mechanisms over which he has no control which may serve to block the road back to full acceptance in the conventional world. [25] As well known by the exconvict, the discharged mental patient, the reformed delinquent or, in the school, the former goof-off, the ceremony of entry into the role of deviant is substantially more public and as a consequence more long lasting in its effects on identity, status, and career chances than the transition out of the role. Erikson has pointed out, in this connection that the

> decision to bring deviant sanctions against an individual is not a simple act of censure. It is a sharp rite of transition, at once moving him out of his normal position in society and transferring him into a distinct deviant role . . . Now an important feature of these ceremonies in our own culture is that they are almost irreversible. Most proscribed roles conferred by society —like those of student or conscripted soldiers, for example—include some kind of terminal ceremony to mark the individual's movement back out of the role once its temporary advantages have been exhausted. But the roles allotted to the deviant seldom make allowance for this type of passage. He is ushered into the deviant position by a decisive and often dramatic ceremony, yet is retired from it with hardly a word of public noise. Nothing has happened to cancel out the stigmas imposed upon him by earlier

---

[24]Kai Erikson, "Notes on the Sociology of Deviant Behavior," p. 15.
[25]Talcott Parsons, *The Social System*, p. 275.

commitment ceremonies; from a formal point of view, the original verdict
or diagnosis is still in effect.[26]

Thus it is that although a student may show quite improved tendencies in
motivation, behavior, and performance, he may continue to find himself
perceived, addressed, and treated as a deviant because of a label once
received, an identity once acquired as a hood, a dumb kid, a troublemaker,
or a sick child. The problem of being locked in to the deviant role, is, we
contend, perhaps the greatest difficulty facing the deviant on his way back—
just as great, perhaps, as changing his own motivation.

Once again, then, our attention is drawn to the school's role in the
deviant behavior of its students. We are at once led to ask, what *are* some
of the processes affecting the permanence and irrevocability of the deviant
label? In what ways, in other words, is the individual student locked in
once he has been placed in the role of deviant?

First, there are certain formal, official means by which students' deviant identities may be confirmed and, in fact, transmitted and diffused.
Perhaps the most important means is the official record keeping or informa-
tional system. A student's current reputation (and, as a result, how he is
seen and judged) may be as often founded on what he has done in the past
as on how he is currently behaving or performing, in part because his biog-
raphy trails him like the proverbial shadow.

> Records accumulate and pass along through channels as the student moves
> up through the grades. . . . The student is "known" and judged through the
> dossier which shadows him, often precedes him. A student entering high
> school may be studied by means of the achievement history and the scores
> made on aptitude and achievement tests, and typed as underachiever, over-
> achiever, bright, hoody, normal, or problem child before he begins his
> high school work.[27]

Once again the school is in a mild dilemma: On the one hand, it must identify students with unusual talent and those needing special attention. On the
other hand, however, a consequence of this practice for the latter type of
student is that career chances may be unalterably hampered. Vinter and
Sarri report that

> Interviews with pupils who are having difficulty illustrate their belief that
> past events will shape future chances:
>
> > "When you get in trouble they never let up on you. They keep calling
> > you in. Like you get caught for smoking and they suspend you. Then
> > they watch out for you so they could catch you again."

---

[26]Kai Erikson, "Notes on the Sociology of Deviant Behavior," p. 16.
[27]Burton Clark, *Educating the Expert Society* (San Francisco: Chandler Publishing Company, 1962), p. 180.

"I have a bad reputation here. Last year in junior high I gave teachers a lot of trouble and I guess the record follows everywhere I go. Teachers here (in high school) have the record. They have to find out about all the kids."[28]

Perhaps the answer is more limited access to such records, if not a decrease altogether in their use. But whatever the *extent* of their use, modification of their contents should be made. *Positive* entries should be more frequent, denoting official exit from the role, in order to counteract the frequency of negative entries which indicate entry into and continuing occupation of the role of deviant.

Second, there are less formal means by which deviant identities are confirmed and transmitted. All too frequently, the teacher's coffee lounge is the burying ground of students' career chances. For, it is here—or wherever teachers meet informally—that reputations are often confirmed and spread: "Do you have that little so-and-so too?" "What about that John Jones. He's been giving me a bad time since the first of the year. You too?" Awareness of this danger prompts some schools to adopt a deliberate and formal policy of communicating nothing about students' reputations or behavior. Often, however, perceptions and judgments of students are founded on what has been heard about reputations or current behavior in other settings.

What has been said refers to the problem of generalization of the deviant label from one time period to another or from one judge or set of judges to others. There are both formal and informal means by which this occurs, as we have seen. At the same time, labels tend to generalize from one area of behavior to another. Here too, the deviant may find himself increasingly locked into the role.

Let us assume that a student has performed in his schoolwork at a level which results in a lower than passing grade. Such grades, of course, may have the consequence, at one level, of reinforcing academic standards and, at another, of mobilizing the student to work harder. As failing grades accumulate on a student's record, however, he is gradually given the label *underachiever* or unmotivated. However, any particular failing grade, and particularly an accumulation of them, may have consequences for the student beyond being a negative judgment itself.

Students are frequently exposed to a kind of double—or even triple—penalty. Those who perform below a certain standard receive adverse grades, and may *also* be denied, as a direct consequence, a wide variety of privileges and opportunities within the school. They lose esteem among their class-

---

[28]Robert D. Vinter and Rosemary C. Sarri, "Malperformance in the Public School: A Group Work Approach," *Social Work* 10 (January 1965): 3–13.

mates, they are seldom chosen for minor but prestigeful classroom or school assignments, and they may be excluded from participation in extracurricular activities. This process, in turn, often subjects such pupils to negative parental responses, representing a third penalty.

The linking of secondary rewards and sanctions to grades may result in far more than reinforcement of academic criteria, since it denies the poor performer legitimate alternative opportunities for recognition and success. His motivation to continue trying and his commitment to educational objectives is thereby jeopardized at the very time when additional supports may be needed to stimulate effort. In these situations the underachieving pupil receives little support for his efforts to improve, as continued failure subjects him to new deprivations.[29]

The same process frequently occurs in the other direction as well—that is, marks are frequently lowered because of misconduct, even when other sanctions have been given. This process of role or label generalization, effected through the application of secondary sanctions, may be an important if seldom recognized means by which the way back is made increasingly difficult for the malperforming or misbehaving student.

Summary and Implications

It has been the main theme of this chapter that the way one conceives of underachievement, misconduct, and early school-leaving has consequences for the issues toward which one is directed. We have seen that viewing pupil deviance as a consequence—or, more accurately, as a facet—of adverse pupil-school interaction points us toward rather than away from the arrangements and practices of one of the partners in the exchange, the school itself. For the school is as much involved in the adverse interaction as the student. It defines what is or is not deviant, it sets the conditions under which success is more or less possible for particular types of students, it contributes to the alleviation—or to the maintenance—of deviance as it responds to behavior defined as unacceptable.

Two major sets of implications follow from what has been said. First, there are important implications for educational practice. "If we view deviance as something that arises in interaction with others, we realize that changes in interactions may produce significant changes in behavior."[30] We have tried to make clear that the school itself may, in one degree or another, maintain or even generate the very malperformance it seeks to eliminate by offering limited opportunity for educational attainment for some

---

[29]Ibid., p. 9.
[30]Howard S. Becker, *The Other Side,* p. 3.

students, by judging students adversely because of characteristics which are independent of their actions, by undermining existing motivation through unwise use of discipline practices, and by making it exceedingly difficult for the student to find his way back once he has been defined as deviant. Thus, "deviant activities often seem to derive support from the very agencies designed to suppress them."[31] To the extent that this is in fact the case, efforts to decrease underachievement and misconduct must be directed toward the school as well as toward the student. Since student orientations, skills, and aptitudes are inseparably tied up with school goals, patterns, activities, and belief systems, both must be simultaneous targets of change.[32]

The second major implication relates to research. In order for educators to design their operations in such a way as to cope effectively with problems of malperformance, much greater understanding must be gained of the nature of student-school interaction. Examples of questions which must be systematically and intensively explored in research are these: What are the variable effects of school structural arrangements, belief systems, discipline, and other coping practices on the orientations and success-chances of students? What are the organizational conditions under which the most effective school responses to deviance can be made? Answers to questions such as these will, we believe, contribute greatly to effective modification of student-school interactions and, hence, to more efficient and complete development of human resources.

---

[31]Kai Erikson, "Notes on the Sociology of Deviant Behavior," p. 15.

[32]For a report on an ameliorative strategy based on this conception of deviance, see Robert D. Vinter and Rosemary C. Sarri, "Malperformance in the Public School."

school career
and delinquency

In order to make understandable the argument that connects the shortcomings of public education with heightened delinquency, we are compelled to provide answers to the following kinds of questions: According to the best evidence, what particular school experiences contribute to delinquency? What specific practices and conditions in the schools contribute to the development of rebellious life styles that become reflected in delinquent behavior?

In reviewing the theories of delinquency earlier, it was noted that the "blocked goal attainment" perspective suggests that school failure when coupled with an emphasis on success creates strain which can lead to delinquency. Such theories suggest, further, that when school demands and rewards are not coupled to adult occupational rewards, additional strain is introduced which also may contribute to the development of delinquency. Available evidence indicates that both of these factors, goal frustration and perceived irrelevancy, can be observed in the behavior of delinquent youth.

Accumulation of Educational Failure, Combined with a Desire for Success

Considerable research shows that most children and youth are exposed to strong pressures to seek after middle or high ranking occupations and to obtain at least a high school if not a college education as a means to that end. Moreover, most parents place considerable importance on their children obtaining middle or high levels of academic achievement.

Widespread stress among parents on educational attainment has been reported in numerous studies in the past, as well as in the recently released national study of *Equality of Educational Opportunity,* which was commissioned by Congress in the Civil Rights Act of 1964, and was directed by James S. Coleman in conjunction with the U.S. Office of Education. This study of over 645,000 students found that in general parents were . . . "highly interested in their [children's] educational success. . ."[1]

Although there are differences in the degree to which education is stressed by parents, several studies show that even most lower status and

---

This chapter was previously published as part of "Delinquency and the Schools"
by Walter E. Schafer and Kenneth Polk in Task Force Report: Juvenile Delinquency and Youth Crime, *The President's Commission on Law Enforcement and the Administration of Justice (Washington, D.C.: U.S. Government Printing Office, 1967), pp. 228–34.*

---

[1]James S. Coleman and others, *Equality of Educational Opportunity.* Washington, D.C.: United States Government Printing Office, 1966, p. 192. In subsequent references, we will refer to this document as the *Coleman Report.*

minority group parents place a high value on school achievement for their children. Riessman reported, for instance, that when . . .

> . . . interviewees were asked the question, "what do you miss most in life that you would like your children to have," over 50 percent of the white lower socioeconomic group (and 70 percent of the Negro group) said "education." Even more significant is the fact that the respondents supplied the word education: they did not select it from a list of possible choices provided by the interviewer . . . This would seem to mean that education, at some level, not only is important to this group but also is in the forefront of their minds.[2]

More recently, Cloward and Jones reported that in a study in the Lower East Side of Manhattan, as many parents from the "lower" as from the "middle" class said education came to mind when thinking of the good life for their sons or daughters.[3] In fact, more from the inbetween "working" class than from the "middle" class gave this response. Finally, the Coleman Report found that, according to student responses, non-white parents placed just as much emphasis as white parents on educational attainment.[4] At the secondary level, in fact, higher percentages of non-white than white fathers wanted their children "to be one of the best students in the class." These and other studies, then, suggest the conclusion that educational attainment and success are stressed to a considerable extent by most parents, whatever their economic position or race.

Parental emphasis on education is continually enforced and supplemented by the mass media and, to an even greater extent, by the schools themselves. When all of these influences are combined, there is little doubt that most children and youth live in a world in which educational success and attainment are strongly stressed and that, while there are differences in degree, this is true of the slum as well as the suburb.

Of even greater importance is that this emphasis is learned by most youngsters, regardless of social or economic background. For example, in a study of Michigan students, Vinter and Sarri found that almost all the youngsters placed a high value on passing courses.[5]

Similarly, in a study of Los Angeles area high school students, Ralph Turner found that all boys and girls in his sample aspired to at least finish

---

[2]Frank Riessman, *The Culturally Deprived Child*. New York: Harper and Row, Publishers, 1962, p. 10.

[3]Richard A. Cloward and James A. Jones, "Social Class: Educational Attitudes and Participation," in A. Harry Passow, editor, *Education in Depressed Areas*. New York: Teachers College Press, Columbia University, 1963, p. 203.

[4]*Coleman Report, op. cit.*, p. 192.

[5]Robert D. Vinter and Rosemary S. Sarri, "Malperformance in the Public School: A Group Work Approach," *Social Work,* Vol. 10 (January, 1965), pp. 3–13.

high school and 85 percent of the boys and 75 percent of the girls hoped to acquire some post-high school training.[6] Albert J. Reiss, Jr., after studying all youth enrolled in junior and senior high schools in and around Nashville, Tennessee, concluded, "adolescents on the whole accept the success goals of education in our society."[7] His research showed that not all youth accept educational goals to the same degree, but contrary to usual belief, Negro and lower income students place a higher value on education than do white and higher income pupils.[8] Finally, the *Coleman Report* also found that when asked the question, "If something happened and you had to stop school now, how would you feel," 81 percent of the sample said they would "try hard to continue" (36 percent) or would "do anything to stay in school" (45 percent.)[9] Negroes gave these responses just as often as whites and, in fact, reported more often than whites that they wanted to be "one of the best students in the class."[10]

At the same time that most students are exposed to outside pressures to achieve and place a high personal interest on school themselves, not all of them succeed in meeting school standards of performance and progress. For reasons that will be discussed later in the chapter, lower income and non-white students are most often unsuccessful in school, whether the indicator of failure is achievement test performance, academic grades, non-promotion, or dropping out of school. For example, Sexton found in "Big City" that almost one-third larger proportion of high school students in the lowest income schools than from the highest failed one or more subjects.[11] She also reported that in the eighth grade the highest income schools were on the average two full years ahead of the lowest in achievement test scores.[12] Finally, she found drop-out rates six times greater in the lowest than in the highest income schools.[13] A similar pattern was reported for non-promotions.[14]

---

[6]Ralph Turner, *The Social Context of Ambition*. San Francisco: Chandler Publishing Company, 1964, p. 43.

[7]Albert J. Reiss, Jr., and Albert Lewis Rhodes, *A Sociopsychological Study of Adolescent Conformity and Deviation*. United States Office of Education, Cooperative Research Project Number 507 (1959); also see Reiss and Rhodes, "Are Educational Norms and Goals of Conformity, Truant, and Delinquent Adolescents Influenced by Group Position in American Society?" *Journal of Negro Education*, XXXVII (Summer, 1959), pp. 252–67.

[8]*A Sociopsychological Study . . . , ibid.*

[9]*Coleman Report, op. cit.*, p. 278.

[10]*Ibid.*, p. 278.

[11]Patricia C. Sexton, *Education and Income*. New York: The Viking Press, 1966, p. 163.

[12]*Ibid.*, p. 28.

[13]*Ibid.*, p. 201.

[14]*Ibid.*, p. 54.

Schafer found similar differences in two Michigan high schools. For example, he reported that 35 percent of working class students were in the bottom quartile of their graduating class in academic achievement, while the comparable middle class figure was 15 percent.[15] In addition, middle class students dropped out only one-fourth as often as working class students.[16] Differences in reading test scores were just as striking.[17] Finally, Reiss found that in his Nashville sample, over twice as many low status students received a D or E in English, while in an Oregon study of high school students, Polk and Halferty found that over five times as many blue collar as white collar boys received a modal grade of D or F.[18] Hollingshead, Abrahamson, Havighurst and many others have reported similar findings for many different types of schools and communities.[19]

Similar differences have been reported between whites and non-whites. In the New York City schools, for example, Puerto Rican and Negro elementary children were considerably lower than white pupils in reading test scores.[20] The *Coleman Report* describes similar patterns on a national scale with respect to tests of verbal ability, non-verbal ability, reading comprehension, mathematics, and general information.[21]

As we will see later, a very important feature of achievement differences between pupils from varying economic and social backgrounds is that the gaps increase over time, as lower income and non-white pupils fall progressively farther behind.

Educational failure, whether experienced by lower or higher income pupils or by whites or non-whites, often begins early, then builds up and accumulates, setting into motion a series of reactions both among others and within the student himself that sometimes leads to delinquency. Perhaps the most important consequence of failure is the reaction of others.

---

[15]Walter E. Schafer, *Student Careers in Two Public High Schools: A Comparative Cohort Analysis* (unpublished doctoral dissertation), University of Michigan, 1965, p. 88.

[16]*Ibid.*, p. 179.

[17]*Ibid.*, p. 68.

[18]Reiss and Rhodes, *A Sociopsychological Study . . .* , *op. cit.*; Kenneth Polk and David Halferty, "Adolescence, Commitment and Delinquency," *Journal of Research in Crime and Delinquency* (July, 1966) pp. 82–96.

[19]A. B. Hollingshead, *Elmtown's Youth*. New York: John Wiley and Sons, Incorporated, 1949, p. 172; Stephan Abrahamson, "Our Status System and Scholastic Rewards," *Journal of Educational Sociology* 25, No. 8 (April, 1952); Robert J. Havighurst, Paul Hoover Bowman, Gordon P. Liddle, Charles V. Matthews, and James V. Pierce, *Growing Up in River City*. New York: John Wiley and Sons, Incorporated, 1962, p. 38.

[20]Miriam L. Goldberg, "Schools in Depressed Areas," in Passow, *op. cit.*, p. 83; *Youth in the Ghetto*. New York: Harlem Youth Opportunities Unlimited, Incorporated, 1964, pp. 189–95.

[21]*Coleman Report, op. cit.*, p. 219.

In the eyes of the school and the outside world the pupil who receives certain 'low marks' is regarded as a failure and treated accordingly, regardless of whatever other assets he may have or whatever satisfactory growth he may achieve in his other activities.[22]

The effect of these reactions was graphically described to the authors by one of several former delinquents we recently interviewed who had dropped out of school in a major Eastern city, but are now employed as community workers in the Poverty Program.[23]

(What would the school make him feel like before he dropped out? Would it make him feel like something or would it make him feel differently?) That would depend on how his standing is in that school. If he's intelligent, he has his standing, he wants to go along with the school. The school's going to put his name up on the board and say—"honor roll student" and things like that. Teachers come by and look at him—"he made the honor roll." If he's got low standing and every teacher every time they see him say, "Get out of here," and "I don't want you in my class" and things like that, he's going to come on out (drop out).

Students who fail are not only likely to be perceived and defined as "failures," "slow learners," or "goof-offs," but there are likely to be more objective negative consequences as well, both among peers and teachers. Vinter and Sarri recently reported, for instance, that:

Those who performed below a certain standard received adverse grades and might *also* be denied, as a direct consequence, a wide variety of privileges and opportunities within the school. They lost esteem among their classmates, they were seldom chosen for minor but prestigeful classroom or school assignments, and they were excluded from participation in certain extra-curricular activities. This process, in turn, often subjected such students to negative parental responses, representing a third penalty.[24]

In addition, students who fail may be assigned to a special track or classroom for "slow learners," usually resulting in decreased expectations and attention, not increased educational service.

---

[22]William C. Kvaraceus, *Juvenile Delinquency and the School*. New York: World Book Company, 1945, p. 140.

[23]We wish to thank Mr. Karl Gudenberg of the United Planning Organization of Washington, D.C., Mrs. Terry Alt of the United States Office of Education, and Mr. Martin Timin of the National Crime Commission staff for arranging and participating in the group interviews from which the following quotation is taken. Above all, we owe a great debt to the members of Rebels with a Cause from Washington, D.C. who participated in the interviews. Uncited quotations throughout the rest of the paper are from these interviews.

[24]Vinter and Sarri, *op. cit.*, p. 9.

These findings, which have been closely paralleled by those of Polk in the study of Oregon pupils,[25] clearly suggest that as a result of being negatively perceived and evaluated, students who fail tend to be progressively shunned and excluded by other achieving students, by individual teachers, and by the "system as a whole." Partly as a result of the internal frustrations generated by blocked goal attainment and partly as a result of the stigma which others tend to attach to educational failure, failing students' own assessment of themselves, their place in the world, and their future tend to progressively deteriorate and, understandably, the school experience becomes highly unsatisfying, frustrating, and bitter. The frequent result, as reported by Polk, Vinter and Sarri, Gold, and others, is an increase in negative attitudes toward school performance, rules, and activities; devaluation of the importance of education; and turning toward other youths who have also failed.[26] The consequence, in turn, is often the collective substitution or acceptance of alternative standards of conduct that are more easily reached.

Commitment to these new standards or norms often produces behavior that immediately is far more rewarding and satisfying, but that sometimes violates community laws and comes to be defined as delinquent. Such behavior may represent an attack, through some such psychological process as reaction-formation, on the system that labeled them as "failures"; or it may simply be conformity to new standards that are illegitimate or delinquent but that to delinquents themselves do not represent a direct attack against the school or the middle class community.

Miriam Goldberg has clearly summarized these connections between educational failure and delinquency, especially among disadvantaged projects, as follows:

> Early difficulty in mastering the basic intellectual skills which the schools and thus the broader society demands leads to defeat and failure, a developing negative self-image, rebellion against the increasingly defeating school experiences, a search for status outside the school together with an active resentment against the society which the school represents. The child early finds status and protection in the street and the gang which requires none of the skills which are needed in school but makes heavy use of the kinds of survival skills which he learned in his early home and street experiences.[27]

While there are relatively few studies that trace these social and psychological processes through time, there is considerable evidence that

---

[25] Kenneth Polk and Lynn Richmond, "Those Who Fail" (unpublished paper), Lane County Youth Project, Eugene, Oregon, 1966.

[26] Vinter and Sarri, *op. cit*; Martin Gold, *Status Forces in Delinquent Boys.* Ann Arbor: The University of Michigan, 1963; Polk and Richmond, *ibid.*

[27] Goldberg, in Passow, *op. cit.*, p. 87. Reprinted with permission of the publisher. ©1963 by Teachers College, Columbia University.

failure and delinquency are associated. In a study of delinquents and non-delinquents in Flint, for example, Gold found no difference between the two groups in concern about future jobs and belief in the importance of education for future opportunities.[28] Despite this, and the additional fact that delinquents and non-delinquents were matched to within ten points on measured intelligence, delinquents had significantly lower grade point averages than non-delinquents prior to first police contact, as well as more negative attitudes toward school.[29] Short also found an association of poor "educational adaptation" with delinquency in a study of Chicago gangs.[30] Regardless of educational aspirations or occupational level of parents, both Negro and white youth who were unsuccessful in school had higher delinquent rates than those who were successful. Short points out, however, that delinquency did not represent a total rejection of legitimate standards of school and community and a total commitment to the illegitimate alternative, but rather was an on-again, off-again pattern at the same time that a basic commitment to education and the "legitimate system" was retained.[31]

In an earlier investigation, Kvaraceus found that a disproportionate number of delinquents in his New Jersey sample received failing or inferior grades in comparison with non-delinquent youth in the same community.[32] Similarly, Toby and Toby state that:

> . . . the kind of school status that was most strongly related to delinquent outcomes was intellectual status—whether measured by teacher placement in bright or slow classes, by academic grades, or by student votes as the "smartest, most intelligent boy in the grade."[33]

Finally, Polk found that boys from white collar homes had five times a greater chance of becoming delinquent than those who did not fail, while boys from blue collar backgrounds who failed were delinquent almost seven times more often than those who did not fail.[34]

Cooper has clearly summed up the literature on educational attainment and delinquency as follows:

> The educational status of offenders is inferior on the whole to that of the general population, tending to be slightly inferior in respect to illiteracy,

---

[28]Gold, *op. cit.*, pp. 154, 161.

[29]*Ibid.*, p. 163.

[30]James F. Short, Jr., "Gang Delinquency and Anomie," in Marshall B. Clinard, editor, *Anomie and Deviant Behavior.* New York: Free Press, 1964, p. 107.

[31]*Ibid.*, p. 115.

[32]Kvaraceus, *op. cit.*, p. 141.

[33]Jackson Toby and Marcia Toby, *Low School Status as a Predisposing Factor in Subcultural Delinquency.* United States Office of Education, Cooperative Research Project, No. 526, 1961.

[34]Polk and Richmond, *op. cit.*

somewhat inferior in respect to amount of schooling, decidedly inferior in respect to school progress, and clearly inferior in respect to educational achievement.[35]

The evidence suggests, then, that educational failure is one experience, especially when combined with a desire for success, that contributes to delinquency. While such failure has been shown to relate to delinquency regardless of family status there are at least two reasons why lower income youth are especially susceptible to this influence toward illegitimate behavior. First, they fail more often, as noted earlier; and, second, students from higher status backgrounds who fail are likely to be "held into" the legitimate system by greater pressures from parents and achieving peers and by less accessibility to delinquent or criminal subcultures.

These questions immediately arise from these findings and arguments: How might the school itself contribute to this deepening cycle of failure, alienation, and delinquency? What educational changes can be made that will prevent the cycle from starting and, if started, from culminating in delinquency? As we will see in greater detail below, there are at least two major ways in which the school inadvertently contributes to delinquency insofar as it results from this set of experiences. First, certain conditions and practices, especially as they affect lower status and non-white pupils, tend to contribute directly to educational failure. Therefore, identification and change of those conditions and practices are likely to help prevent delinquency. Second, certain current patterns of school responses to failure increase rather than decrease the chances that delinquency will result. As suggested above, there is evidence that the sanctioning system often tends to push away, exclude, and lower involvement and interest of the student in education, rather than to "rescue," or upgrade instruction and involvement. Thus, changes in some of the ways the school reacts to failing students are also likely to prevent and reduce delinquency.

Perceived Irrelevancy of Education

A second school experience that is often associated with delinquency is the sense that education is fundamentally irrelevant to later life. Because school tasks, demands, and rewards are seen as having no payoff in the future, the school career becomes meaningless and empty. As a result, the illegitimate alternative becomes increasingly attractive and delinquency sometimes results.

---

[35]Clara Chassell Cooper, *A Comparative Study of Delinquents and Non-Delinquents*. Portsmouth, Ohio: The Psychological Service Center Press, 1960, p. 207.

Among some youth this experience is closely tied to educational failure. If they are not achieving, it is only reasonable to expect that their perceptions of future occupational payoff will be highly pessimistic, not only because anything but low status, low paying jobs require at the least a good high school record and a diploma, and at the most college training, but also because most students know this. Thus, Gold reported that the higher a boy's academic achievement, the better he saw his chances for getting the job he wanted, except for white collar delinquents, whose aspirations and expectations were probably bolstered by peer and parental pressures.[36] Similarly, Vinter and Sarri and Polk both noted that low achieving students who became delinquents tended to give negative assessment of later job chances.[37]

At the same time there is evidence that the relationship between perceived irrelevancy and educational failure is sometimes reversed. That is, educational failure sometimes results from the belief that there will be no real rewards after high school, regardless of current efforts or attainment. In the words of Arthur Pearl, ". . . growing failure may be also in part due to a growing recognition that there is no payoff in the system for them."[38] In addition, there is evidence that perceived irrelevancy of education exerts an independent influence on delinquency. Main support for this position comes from a study of California high school students by Arthur Stinchcombe.[39] He found that students who were not taking college preparatory work tended to believe that regardless of their present efforts or achievement, the system was not going to come through with anything but low status, low paying jobs after high school.[40] As a result, present tasks and demands of the school had little meaning or payoff. Thus, perceived prospects for future occupational status was found to be a far more important determinant of "rebellion" than social or economic origin.

> . . . rebellion . . . occurs when future status is not closely related to present performance. When a student realizes that he has not achieved status increment from improved current performance, current performance loses meaning. The student becomes hedonistic because he does not visualize achievement of long run goals through current self-constraint. He reacts negatively to a conformity that offers nothing concrete. He claims autonomy from adults because their authority does not promise a satisfactory future.[41]

---

[36] Gold, *op. cit.*, p. 213.

[37] Vinter and Sarri, *op. cit.*; Polk and Richmond, *op. cit.*

[38] Arthur Pearl, "Youth in Lower Class Settings," in Muzafer Sherif and Carolyn W. Sherif, editors, *Problems of Youth.* Chicago: Aldine Publishing Company, 1965, p. 95.

[39] Arthur L. Stinchcombe, *Rebellion in a High School.* Chicago: Quadrangle Books, 1964, p. 70.

[40] *Ibid.*, p. 70.

[41] *Ibid.*, p. 5.

While Stinchcombe's study is probably the most definitive in supporting the linkage between perceived irrelevancy and delinquency, there are others that also suggest the same conclusion. For example, Short found that poor "articulation between school experience and future orientation" was associated with high rates of delinquency.[42] Similarly, Polk found that delinquency was greater among non-college bound than college bound students, even when grades were the same.[43]

More indirect evidence is contained in a number of studies which show that the greater the extent to which youth perceive future opportunities as closed, the greater the delinquency. Short, for example, also reported that delinquents saw educational and occupational opportunities as more limited than non-delinquents, while Polk found that perception of limited opportunity in the local community and in the system in general were associated with high delinquency rates.[44] Finally, Elliott reported that "delinquents (from both lower and middle status) quite uniformly perceive lower opportunities to achieve success goals than non-delinquents."[45] We suggest that these wider patterns of perceived lack of opportunities partly reflect the lack of connection seen between the current school career and later outcomes.

It seems likely, then, that perceived irrelevance of education for the future is one of the factors contributing to delinquency, at times independently of low achievement, especially among the non-college bound and among non-white and lower income students who live in slums, since their chances of going to college or obtaining a good job as a result of striving or succeeding are remote. We suggest that perceived irrelevancy may partly account for the finding of the *Coleman Report* that considerably higher proportions of metropolitan Negroes (most of whom live in ghettos) than metropolitan whites agree with the statement "Every time I try to get ahead, something or somebody stops me."[46] As a Washington, D.C. drop-out put it "all you have to do is look around at your older friends and brothers, your dad, and your neighbors to know it doesn't make any difference."

At the same time, Stinchcombe's evidence shows that some higher status students take non-college preparatory work, perceive a lack of payoff, and turn to delinquency as an alternative. This form of "blocked goal attainment," then, sometimes contributes to middle class delinquency as well.

---

[42]Short, *op. cit.,* p. 114.

[43]Kenneth Polk, unpublished data, Lane County Youth Project, Eugene, Oregon, 1966.

[44]Kenneth Polk, "An Exploration of Rural Delinquency," in Lee Burchinal, editor, *Youth in Crisis: Facts, Myths and Social Change.* Washington, D.C.: United States Government Printing Office, 1965, pp. 221–32; Short, *op. cit.,* p. 114.

[45]Delbert S. Elliott, "Delinquency and Perceived Opportunity," *Sociological Inquiry,* XXXII (Spring, 1962), pp. 216–22.

[46]*Coleman Report, op. cit.,* p. 202.

Here, too, the evidence and arguments generate questions about the role of the school in contributing to and preventing delinquency. In his conclusion, Stinchcombe leaves little doubt that the emptiness that some students feel in relation to the school experience is largely based on an accurate assessment of the way the non-college bound curriculum links up with the job market.[47] He contends that rebellion is an understandable response to the false promises of education, since most of these youth can only look forward to unskilled jobs that are rapidly disappearing, and since they are virtually locked out of better paying, more rewarding occupations. As Arthur Pearl puts it, such students have a "fair fix on reality."[48]

We believe this source of delinquency in part is avoidable through the updating and modification of noncollege preparatory training so that more youth will be fed into the labor market at middle rather than low levels and will be prepared for upward mobility through channels other than the traditional one of college graduation. We recognize that aspirations of some youth will always be frustrated by lack of occupational opportunities or by their own lack of potential and that some delinquency will almost certainly remain even after changes are made. But we hold that the magnitude of the problem can be reduced with a better fit between the secondary school curriculum and labor market demands that will in turn produce a closer fit between student aspirations and occupational outcomes. This, too, is Stinchcombe's position.

> The major practical conclusion of the analysis above is that rebellious behavior is largely a reaction to the school itself and to its promises, not a failure of the family or community. High school students can be motivated to conform by paying them in the realistic coin of future advantage. Except perhaps for pathological cases, any student can be motivated to conform if the school can realistically promise something valuable to him as a reward for working hard. But for a large part of the population, especially the adolescent who will enter the male working class or the female candidates for early marriage, the school has nothing to offer. . . . In order to secure conformity from students, the high school must articulate academic work with careers of students.[49]

Lack of Commitment

It will be recalled that the theories of Karacki and Toby and of Miller take the position that delinquency is sometimes the result of lack of com-

---

[47] Stinchcombe, *op. cit.*, p. 179.
[48] Pearl, in Sherif and Sherif, *op. cit.*, p. 93.
[49] Stinchcombe, *op. cit.*, p. 179.

mitment to adult roles, school standards, and community laws. That is, they contend that some delinquent youth, for different reasons in working and middle classes, tend to develop early and continuing loyalties to standards and activities outside the normal, legitimate stream of things.

Miller contends that uncommitted working class youth sometimes adopt these illegitimate orientations and behavior patterns because they have been acculturated into a lower class pattern of life that includes in the natural course of events engagement in activities that sometimes are defined by the larger system as unacceptable or delinquent.[50] Karacki and Toby, on the other hand, argue that some middle class youth fail to develop a commitment to the legitimate system early in adolescence because of imperfect socialization by the adult world or because of plain choice.[51]

There is some evidence that the uncommitted are in fact "candidates for delinquency." Karacki and Toby, for example, reported that the middle class gang they studied did not get "hooked into" the legitimate system in early adolescence.

> . . . it is our impression that the Dukes failed to develop early in adolescence commitments to adult roles and values which would have mobilized their interest and energies and which would have served to relate them to school and work. In lieu of this, they drew instead upon the youth culture for meaning and purpose and out of this emerged the delinquent gang . . . this involvement in the youth culture was incompatible with diligent performance in school. School was not viewed by the Dukes as an opportunity to prepare for adult occupations or for college. Nor did they select their course or pursue goals with the future in mind. Instead they regarded school within the framework of adolescent interest.[52]

In a different context, Miller reported that the lower class street gangs he studied in Boston tended to be drawn into a culture with a greater emphasis on "trouble, toughness, smartness, excitement, fate, and autonomy" than on conformity to community laws or achievement in school.[53] Finally, Polk and Halferty recently reported an association between lack of commitment and delinquent involvement.

> The uncommitted delinquent youth, it would appear, is characterized by behavioral withdrawal from school. He does not study, he receives poor grades, and he does not participate in activities. This withdrawal tends to

---

[50] Walter B. Miller, "Lower Class Culture as a Generating Milieu of Gang Delinquency," *Journal of Social Issues,* 14:5–19; No. 3, 1958.

[51] Larry Karacki and Jackson Toby, "The Uncommitted Adolescent: Candidate for Gang Socialization," *Sociological Inquiry,* 32 (Spring, 1962), pp. 203–15.

[52] *Ibid.,* p. 207.

[53] Miller, *op. cit.*

be accompanied by concomitant withdrawal from identification with the pathways to adult status as well, since the educational and occupational aspirations of the uncommitted delinquent youth are lower than those of the successful and committed non-delinquent youth. . . . The essential notion of this view is that, as a result of the lowering of an individual's commitment to success and conformity, there is an increased probability of his turning to a characteristically rebellious peer culture or significant social attachments which, in turn, increase the chances of involvement in delinquency.[54]

It should be clear from our earlier argument that lack of commitment is sometimes likely to be a reaction to educational failure and perceived irrelevancy of education. We argued in both of the above sections that those experiences sometimes lead to alienation from school personnel, activities, and demands and a turning toward substitute or rebellious behavior. Part of this process is likely to be withdrawal of a basic legitimate commitment. Yet, Karacki and Toby are quick to point out that among the middle class boys in their samples, lack of commitment seemed to develop prior to low achievement. The problem seemed to be that they "were unable or unwilling to devote themselves to school or work . . . thus, one Duke in explaining his lack of concern for school commented, 'I wanted fun more than I wanted to go to school.' "[55]

This raises an important question about the possible role of the school itself in deterioration or lack of commitment. While both Miller and Karacki and Toby attribute lack of commitment to socialization patterns in the family and neighborhood, we believe that the school itself plays an essential role in the motivational and behavioral disengagement of some youth from the legitimate system. We contend that the character of the authority system, the decision-making process, and the basic teaching-learning structure in most public secondary schools limit the chances for most youth, especially if they are not involved in extra-curricular activities, to become actively engaged in the educational process. That is, there are fewer opportunities than there might be for youth, in both lower and middle class schools, to get "hooked into" the legitimate system of conformity and achievement. In short, we suggest that lack of commitment may result from the fact that, as a result of some of the essential characteristics of the school structure, the educational system is sometimes unable either to "hold" middle class youth within normal channels of development and commitment or to draw the lower class "unacculturated" pupil toward legitimate paths of learning and development. Specific defects contributing to delinquency in this way are discussed below.

---

[54] Polk and Halferty, *op. cit.*, p. 93.
[55] Karacki and Toby, *op. cit.*, p. 210.

Misconduct in School

Finally, there is considerable evidence that students who violate school standards pertaining to such things as smoking, truancy, tardiness, dress, classroom demeanor, relations with peers, and respect for authority are more likely to become delinquent than those who conform to such standards. This finding has been reported by Healy and Bronner, the Gluecks, Havighurst, and others.[56]

It is likely, of course, that violations in both the school and the community represent a single pattern of rebellion, rejection, or lack of commitment. Available data, however, show that misconduct in school frequently but not always precedes delinquency in the community. We take the position, therefore, that there is not a necessary linkage of misconduct in school with delinquency and that one of the determinants of whether or not delinquency follows is the way the school itself reacts to students who get into trouble.

As noted in an earlier part, one of the determinants of whether deviance will be reduced or repeated and widened are the effects on the deviant and his circumstances of the group's labelling process and subsequent sanctions. The relevance of this general principle to the problem at hand is evident. One of the factors affecting the chances that misconduct in the school will be reduced or will be repeated and extended to include misbehavior in the community is the character and effect of the school's sanctioning system. On one hand, the school can prevent behavior problems from re-occurring by imposing firm sanctions, while at the same time involving the student in the legitimate system, rewarding him for conforming behavior, and developing academic and social competencies. On the other hand, the school can inadvertently push the student toward illegitimate commitments by imposing overly-punitive sanctions in a degrading way; by locking the individual out of the legitimate system through such mechanisms as expul-

---

[56]Havighurst, Bowman, Liddle, Matthews, and Pierce, *op. cit.*, p. 75; William Healy and Augusta F. Bronner, *New Light on Delinquency and Its Treatment.* New Haven: Yale University Press, 1963; Sheldon Glueck and Eleanor Glueck, *Unravelling Juvenile Delinquency.* New York: The Commonwealth Fund, 1950; William Wattenburg, *Relationship of School Experience to Repeated Delinquency Among Boys with Intelligence in the Bottom Fifth of the Population,* United States Office of Education, Cooperative Research Project, No. 201 (1960); Kvaraceus, *op. cit.*, p. 148; Polk and Richmond, *op. cit.*; Toby and Toby, *op. cit.*; Alfred E. Simons and Nelson S. Burke, "The Probable Syndrome in Terms of Educational Experience Which Precipitates Dropouts, Delinquency, and Eventual Incarceration," *Journal of Negro Education* 35:1 (Winter, 1966), pp. 27–34; for a review of literature on school experiences and delinquency, see Maynard L. Erickson, Max L. Scott, and LaMar T. Empey, *School Experiences and Delinquency.* Provo, Utah: Brigham Young University, 1964.

sion, suspension, withdrawal of extra-curricular privileges, and placement in a special classroom for the "emotionally disturbed."

It is our position that the balance has traditionally been on the side of debasement, exclusion, and locking out, rather than on the side of respect, re-involvement, and re-commitment of the misbehaving student. This position is illustrated by the following incident involving another former delinquent-turned community worker. The incident began during the first day of ninth grade shop class when the youth unknowingly began to do his assignment on a machine reserved for the teacher.

> "You know what you're doing?" "No." "What you on it for then?" "You told us to work on the machines." Bam—right upside the head. "Now get back over there." He finally called everyone together and said, "Look nobody touch this machine. I run this machine myself." But he didn't tell anyone that at first. And you know, you get *mad*. When you leave, you be mumbling, you know. He say, "what did you say? Come back into this classroom." And then he get this big paddle, you know, and he say, "Okay touch your toes." You know, you look at him like he sick or something and he saying "touch your toes." Then he calls the teacher down the hall and he comes and he grabs you and turns you over and then—whack—he hits you a couple of times on the back and then says, "now what you want to do?" Then you call him a couple of names or something, and he hits you on the chest a couple of times and say, "okay, we'll put you into tardy hall." They have a basic section for girls and boys that they call a "trouble section." All they do is sit in the room all day.

> I haven't done nothing—and I got punched in the chest, got my tail whipped, and got slapped on the side of the head, and you try to explain something to them and they still don't understand. Well, you know, you get fed up with it.

There are several ways in which the teacher in this incident, which may or may not be atypical especially in urban schools, is likely to have heightened rather than lessened subsequent attractions to delinquency. First, the teacher virtually induced misconduct by suddenly making known and enforcing the rule. Second, the "labelling ceremony" was highly degrading and humiliating. Third, the physical punishment was likely to have alienated the student still further from that teacher, teachers in general, school norms, and educational objectives. Fourth, one of the outcomes of the involvement of the second teacher in the incident was that the boy's reputation suffered. Fifth, the fact that the teacher refused to listen to the boy's side of the story was an additional indication to him that the "system" was essentially closed to him and that he was essentially being shut out. Sixth, the unhesitating assignment of the boy to the "trouble section" (which as we will see later served a custodial function, at best) represented an even more definite closing off of involvement in the legitimate system. The boy not only lost all opportunity to make amends, but he lost the chance to keep up with the rest of the class as well.

We contend, then, that experiences such as these—during and after an act has been defined as deviant—play a key part in the rejection by many youth of the educational system and in their subsequent rebellion against the school and all it stands for. If this position is valid, fundamental modifications in the schools' conception of deviant behavior, as well as in their procedures for coping with behavior problems, are required in the prevention of delinquency.

school
conditions
contributing to
delinquency

Conditions Contributing to Educational Failure

Earlier, we pointed out that available evidence suggests that educational failure, which occurs most often among lower income and non-white pupils, is one of the school experiences contributing to delinquency. The question immediately confronting anyone interested in a broad program of delinquency prevention is this: What are the major factors contributing to school failure and hence to delinquency, especially among lower income and non-white pupils?

One explanation for low scholastic performance among lower income children is that home influences are such that they enter school with serious "cultural" deficiencies that are all but impossible for the school to overcome. As a result, educational retardation and failure are almost inevitable. Because of broken homes, crowded and inadequate housing, anti-intellectualism, and lack of effective discipline, it is contended that these children come to school with educational handicaps such as the following: lack of "elaboration" of communication styles; poor auditory and visual discrimination; inability to think conceptually; inability to use "adults as sources of information, correction, and reality testing, and as instruments for satisfying curiosity"; unfamiliarity with books and writing material; inability to sustain attention; lack of development of internal controls over personal behavior; unfamiliarity with school rules of behavior; and inexperience in formal situations like the classroom.[1] In view of evidence that these deficiencies are frequently present, some account must be taken of this argument. But there is an alternative explanation for the low scholastic performance of lower income and non-white children that also must be carefully examined. This explanation holds that, while these handicaps are frequently present, the school itself contributes to failure by not designing its program, curriculum, and techniques of instruction so that such deficiencies are taken account of and effectively offset, and so that the life experiences and cultural assets of such children are used and built on in a positive way. This position has been aptly stated by Roberts as follows:

This chapter was previously published as part of "Delinquency and the Schools" by Walter E. Schafer and Kenneth Polk in Task Force Report: Juvenile Delinquency and Youth Crime, *The President's Commission on Law Enforcement and the Administration of Justice (Washington, D.C.: U.S. Government Printing Offiice, 1967), pp. 234–58.*

---

[1]For an annotated bibliography on this literature, see Susan B. Silverman in Benjamin S. Bloom, Allison Davis, and Robert Hess, *Compensatory Education for Cultural Deprivation.* New York: Holt, Rinehart and Winston, Incorporated, 1965, pp. 65–179.

Potential to learn is affected not only by the culture in which the child is raised, by the ethnic subculture to which he was born, by the socioeconomic position of his family in the social structure, by his earlier experience in learning activities; but also by the school and teachers who may, through inhibiting procedures, decrease the child's capacity to use his learning potential.[2]

Advocates of this position point to research indicating that (1) most lower income children do recognize the importance of education and place a high personal value on educational success and attainment; (2) most of them do have the potential to learn and to develop into capable, responsible, and productive adults; and (3) many of them have shown remarkable development under educational conditions different from those prevailing in most schools, especially in the urban slums. A frequently cited example of such progress is the Higher Horizons Program of the New York City public schools, which has produced substantial improvement in achievement among participants. Another is the Bannecker Group Schools in St. Louis, which have had equally striking success.

The latter explanation clearly places part of the burden of failure at the doorsteps of the school and calls for educational changes that will make it possible for the schools to do whatever is necessary to stretch capabilities and aspirations of all students as far as possible. This position has been clearly summarized by Martin Deutsch as follows:

> The lower class child probably enters school with a nebulous and essentially neutral attitude. His home rarely, if ever, negatively predisposes him toward the school situation, though it might not offer positive motivation and correct interpretation of the school experience. It is in the school situation that the highly charged negative attitude toward learning evolves, and the responsibility for such large groups of children showing great scholastic retardation, the high drop-out rate, and to some extent the delinquency problem, must rest with the failure of the schools to promote the proper acculturation of the children. Though some of the responsibility may be shared by the larger society, the school, as the institution of that society, offers the only mechanism by which the job can be done.[3]

Supporting evidence for the second explanation—that the school as well as the family and community contributes to educational failure—is to be found in a number of studies showing that lower income and non-white chil-

---

[2]Joan I. Roberts, *School Children in the Urban Slum*. New York: Free Press, 1967, p. 31. Reprinted with permission of the Macmillan Company. © 1967, the Macmillan Company.

[3]Martin Deutsch, "The Disadvantaged Child and the Learning Process," in A. Harry Passow, editor, *Education in Depressed Areas*. New York: Teachers College Press, Columbia University, 1963, p. 178.

dren not only begin at low levels of performance, but their achievement shows progressive deterioration the longer that they are in school. Sexton found, for example, that children from the lowest income schools in "Big City" were already one-half year behind average in achievement test scores by the fourth grade, but that this gap had increased to three-quarters of a year by the sixth grade and to one and one-quarter years by the eighth grade.[4] When compared to students from the highest income schools in the city, these children were 1.36 years behind in the fourth grade, 1.82 years behind in the sixth grade, and 1.90 years behind in the eighth grade.

Similar findings have been reported in the predominantly Negro Washington, D.C. schools by a recent task force of the Committee on Education and Labor of the U.S. House of Representatives. For example, the percentages of students reading at grade level declined from the third to the sixth and eighth grades from 67 to 55 to 46, while the percentages reading at one or more years below grade level increased from 33 to 45 to 55.[5]

In the same vein, the *Coleman Report* indicates that:

> For most minority groups . . . and most particularly the Negro, schools provide no opportunity at all for them to overcome this initial deficiency; in fact, they fall farther behind the white majority in the development of several skills which are critical to making a living and participating fully in modern society.[6]

Finally, the same pattern has been reported for Negroes and Puerto Ricans in the New York City schools, and especially in the central Harlem areas. For example, the Haryou Report states that 22 percent of the third grade students in that area were reading above grade level, while 30 percent were reading below grade level.[7] But by the sixth grade, 12 percent of the students were reading above grade level and 81 percent were reading below level. The same finding was reported for tests of arithmetic, word knowledge, and general intelligence.[8] The Haryou Report concludes from these data:

---

[4] Patricia C. Sexton, *Education and Income*. New York: The Viking Press, 1966, p. 38.

[5] *A Task Force Study of the Public School System in the District of Columbia As It Relates to The War On Poverty*, conducted by the Committee on Education and Labor of the United States House of Representatives, Washington, D.C.: United States Government Printing Office, 1966, p. 27.

[6] James S. Coleman and others, *Equality of Educational Opportunity*. Washington, D.C.: United States Government Printing Office, 1966, p. 21. In subsequent references, we will refer to this document as the *Coleman Report*.

[7] *Youth in the Ghetto*. New York: Harlem Youth Opportunities Unlimited, Incorporated, 1964, p. 168.

[8] *Ibid.*, pp. 169, 170, 179.

From this we can infer that the sources of educational problems of Harlem pupils lie in processes which occur during the time they are in school, *rather than in processes prior to their entry into school.*[9]

After reviewing a considerable amount of literature on education of the disadvantaged, Silverman arrived at much the same conclusion:

> The fact that the achievement deficit of these children is cumulative and increases over time seems to reflect some basic weaknesses in both curriculum and school practices for these children.[10]

Our position is identical to those just expressed, namely, that the school not only fails to offset initial handicaps of lower income and minority group children, but actively contributes to educational failure and deterioration. While available data do not allow us to assess the precise amount of the school's negative effect, we take the position that it is probably considerable. If this is true, the school itself becomes an important active force in the generation of delinquency insofar as it is linked to failure.

In the following pages, we seek to substantiate this position by identifying some of the defects in the schools that heighten educational failure and deterioration, and hence delinquency. Most, though not all, attention will be given to school conditions affecting lower income and non-white children and youth, especially in urban areas.

Belief in Limited Potential of Disadvantaged Pupils

The first necessary condition of effective instruction is the belief by school personnel in the intellectual potential and the educability of the students being taught. If one begins with this assumption, it is then possible—and necessary—to develop approaches, techniques, and content that will elicit achievement. On the other hand, if one begins with the opposite assumption, that students have limited capabilities and are essentially ineducable, it becomes fruitless to attempt to accomplish very much in the classroom.

There is increasing agreement that educational failure and deterioration among lower income and non-white pupils, especially in the large city, result in part from the widespread acceptance of the second position; that is, that most of these children have limited capabilities and that not much can be done as a result. The Haryou Report, for example, states that "the data from the questionnaires and depth interviews support the contention that

---

[9]*Ibid.*, p. 227.
[10]Silverman, in Bloom, Davis, and Hess, *op. cit.*, p. 74.

teachers and other school personnel feel that the central Harlem child is intellectually limited."[11]

This view is sometimes, if not often, promulgated and supported by school administrators. For example, the report of principals in a major metropolitan school system recently declared "there isn't too much we can do with our children. Most of them are slow learners."[12] It is small wonder that so many new teachers in lower income schools quickly lose their optimism and zeal when such views emanate from or are at least supported by administrators.

The connections between belief in limited potential and educational failure has been clearly described by Davidson and Lang in their report of a study of the interrelations between childrens' perceptions of teachers' feelings, school achievement, behavior, and socioeconomic status:

> It is therefore likely that a lower class child, especially if he is not doing well in school, will have a negative perception of his teacher's feelings toward him. These negative perceptions will in turn tend to lower his efforts to achieve in school and/or increase the probability that he will aggravate the negative attitude of his teachers toward him, which in turn will affect his self-confidence and so on.[13]

A commonly used term to denote this deepening cycle of negative perception and failure is the "self-fulfilling prophecy," as noted by Ravitz:

> Not infrequently teachers, counsellors, principals assigned to the depressed area schools have been people without any real concern for these children and with the common stereotype of them as children of low ability. As a result of this low estimate of potential, the self-fulfilling prophecy went into effect. The children were not encouraged to learn very much; the teacher expended little energy on anything but maintaining order and bemoaning her lot; as a consequence, the children fulfilled the lowest expectations, which in turn enforced the original assumption to prove that the teacher was right.[14]

This argument receives additional support from several studies showing that the more positive the student's own belief in his ability to achieve,

---

[11] *Youth in the Ghetto, op. cit.,* p. 227.

[12] *A Task Force Study . . . , op. cit.,* p. 64.

[13] Helen H. Davidson and Gerhard Lang, "Children's Perceptions of Their Teachers' Feelings Toward Them Related to Self-Perception, School Achievement and Behavior," *Journal of Experimental Education,* Vol. 29, Number 2 (December, 1960), p. 114.

[14] Mel Ravitz, "The Role of the School in the Urban Setting," in Passow, *op. cit.,* p. 19. Reprinted with permission of the publisher. ©1963 by Teachers College, Columbia University.

the greater his performance; and that the more positive the perception by the teacher, the greater the confidence of the student. Research by Gottlieb further suggests that the greater the social and cultural differences between students and teachers, the more negative the perceptions of students. That is, white teachers had more negative perceptions than Negro teachers of lower income, predominantly Negro pupils.[15]

As noted by Riessman, underestimation of the learning potential of lower income and non-white students often takes the form of "patronization" and condescension.

> The specific forms of patronization are manifold: the tendency to talk down to the deprived child, to speak his language, to imitate slang and speech inflections; the assumption that these children are lacking intellectual curiosity and conceptual abilities; the lowering of academic standards and the failure to set high goals for the deprived; the too-quick taken for granted that they are not interested in learning.

> Much of this is well meant. Academic standards are lowered because it is felt the educational traditions and aspirations of these children make it impossible for the teacher to demand more. The many people who defend these practices feel that they are being considerate and sensitive to the needs of children. Actually, they are being too "understanding" in surrendering to the level at which the child seems to be. Perhaps, it is not the disadvantaged who have capitulated to their environment, but the teachers who have capitulated to theirs.[16]

Belief in the educability of such students, whether it takes this or another form, is seen by the Haryou Report as the major determinant of inferior achievement among Harlem pupils.

> On the evidence available to date, it must be concluded the major reason why an increasing number of central Harlem pupils fall behind in their grade level is that sub-standard performance is expected of them.[17]

While no one who has ever visited an inner-city classroom would deny that the difficulties confronting the teacher are not small ones, there is every reason to believe that the academic and social problems which are so clearly manifested can be overcome, as has been demonstrated in isolated instances throughout the country. This position is also expressed by Kenneth Clark:

---

[15]David Gottlieb, "Teaching and Students: The Views of Negro and White Teachers," *Sociology of Education* (Summer 1964), pp. 345–53.

[16]Frank Riessman, *The Culturally Deprived Child*. New York: Harper & Row, Publishers, 1962, p. 22.

[17]*Youth in the Ghetto, op. cit.*, p. 237.

Given no evidence to the contrary, the assumption can be made that the cultural and economic backgrounds of pupils do not constitute a barrier to the type of learning which can reasonably be expected of normal children in the elementary grades. . . .[18]

There is no question, then, that especially in inner-city schools where by 1970 one in every two students was disadvantaged, "this vicious entanglement must be interrupted at some point."[19] One approach for upgrading the perceptions and expectations of teachers is to focus on the teachers directly, by fostering more positive views during the period of teacher training and by seeking to change the views of those currently serving in schools with low income and non-white pupils. This is the position taken by Davidson and Lang. "The best point of attack may well be the teachers whose capacity to reflect feeling to the child's growth should be a concern to educators."[20]

Our position, which will be elaborated in Section VI, is that direct efforts to develop and sustain high expectations by teachers are essential. However, we believe that these beliefs are in turn developed and supported by other conditions in the schools and, therefore, that the problem will not be solved unless the schools themselves are reorganized.

Irrelevant Instruction

A second essential component of effective education is presentation to students of reading materials and other content that will attract and hold their interest. It is increasingly recognized, however, that:

One specific way the schools have unconsciously augmented feelings of alienation [among lower income and non-white pupils especially in large cities] is by introducing children to the world of reading and books through readers which hold up as an exclusive model a cultural pattern of the white middle class suburban family. The child knows in his heart that the school gives the highest prestige value to books, and yet everything that is familiar to him is excluded from the ways of life presented in the books which the schools provide.[21]

---

[18]Kenneth Clark, *Dark Ghetto: Dilemmas of Social Power.* New York: Harper & Row, 1965, p. 139.

[19]Davidson and Lang, *op. cit.,* p. 144.

[20]*Ibid.,* p. 114.

[21]John Niemeyer, "Some Guidelines to Desirable Elementary School Reorganization," in Staten Webster, *The Disadvantaged Learner: Educating the Disadvantaged Learner.* San Francisco: Chandler, 1966, p. 393.

In short, current textbooks and other curriculum materials are largely irrelevant to the experiences, language, style, skills, and orientation of lower class children, especially in the urban slums. The language, the pictures, the content of lessons—all are from a world many steps removed from the disadvantaged child. As Klineberg has remarked, reading materials are generally oriented to the middle class suburbs where

> ... life in general is fun, filled almost exclusively with friendly, smiling people including gentle and understanding parents, doting grandparents, generous and cooperative neighbors, even warm-hearted strangers.[22]

Thus, the ... "school presents predominantly middle class illustrations, rarely concerning themselves with problems or heroes of the disadvantaged."[23]

As Ralph Tyler has noted:

> The fact that writers of textbooks and teachers have come from a fairly restricted middle class environment may account to a great extent for the limiting of content of elementary school reading materials and of the books used in other subjects to those aspects of life which are largely middle class in character. Elementary school books do not deal with homes as they are known by a large percentage of American children. The books in use treat of business, industry, politics, and the professions usually in the terms of the white collar participants rather than in terms of that which would be most understandable to a large fraction of the children.[24]

A recent survey of 116 basic and supplementary books authorized by the California State Board of Education for use in elementary and secondary schools clearly demonstrated the irrelevancy of reading materials from the lives of minority group children.

> The results are shocking. The illustrations are populated almost exclusively by Anglo-Saxons, and the texts rarely mentioned a minority group except in a traditional, stereo-type situation. The Negro or Mexican-American student seldom sees a member of his own group depicted as an executive, professional, or skilled worker.[25]

---

[22] Otto Klineberg, "Life is Fun in a Smiling, Fair-Skinned World," *The Saturday Review* (February 16, 1963), p. 77.

[23] Riessman, *op. cit.*, p. 30.

[24] Ralph W. Tyler, "Can Intelligence Tests Be Used to Predict Educability?" in Kenneth Eells et al., *Intelligence and Cultural Diversity*, Chicago: University of Chicago Press, 1951, p. 45.

[25] Paul Bullock and Robert Singleton, "The Minority Child and the Schools," *The Progressive*, Vol. 26 (November, 1962), p. 34.

Ethnic and racial irrelevancy is compounded in city schools by the almost total detachment of events, scenes, and people from the lives of the urban child. Nothing we could say could as well describe the linkage between irrelevant textbooks and disengagement from the educational process and the resulting learning void that comes to be filled "in the streets" as do the following recollections of the ex-delinquent mentioned earlier.

(What about the stuff you read in school?) It wasn't interesting to me, I liked the science books but I didn't dig that other stuff. Dick and Jane went up the hill to fetch a pail of water and all that crap. Mary had a little lamb. Spot jumped over the fence. See Spot jump over the fence. I mean I got this stuff in the seventh grade too. I got a little book no bigger than that. I opened it up. Dick and Jane was in the house. Mom and Dad was going to the market. Spot was outside playing with the ball with Sally. I say, ain't this the cutest little story. And I took the book one day and shoved it straight back to the teacher and said I ain't going to read that stuff.

When I took the test I think I was four point something so I was real low in English, but I mostly got all my English listening in the streets, from listening to people. I didn't pick up my English mostly from school. (Can you read now?) I can read something that I am really interested in.

Irrelevancy of school to present surroundings and problems does not only apply to elementary instruction but extends to secondary school materials and content as well. Textbooks—and the teachers who use them —generally devote very little if any time attempting to develop an understanding of experiences and surroundings of disadvantaged pupils and attempting to use their experiences and settings as a baseline from which to extend their horizons. There is almost no attempt to develop an understanding of the social, economic, and political conditions that produce slums, depressed areas, poverty, and unemployment; of alternative social solutions; or ways of individually coping with, improving, and moving out of these conditions.

The yearning for this understanding yet extension of the world of the ghetto was expressed to us as follows:

(Going back to junior high, what kind of stuff would you have liked to have read, that would have made you interested?) Well, I could see Dick and Jane when I was in elementary school, but in junior high school I was ready to know about life, about how it really is out there. In elementary school it's painted like it is beautiful, everything is beautiful. (In a sing-song.) Get your education and you can go somewhere. I didn't want to hear that no more, because I had seen my brother go through the same thing. He quit school, he ain't making it. So I wanted to know, okay how can I get somewhere if I go to school. How is life in general? How is the government ran? What's in the government right now that makes it hard for young people that graduate from high school to get somewhere? Why is it that people are fighting each other in the United States? Why is it that people can't communicate with each other? Society in general—what is it that society has said that we have to follow? How is the police structure set up? Why is the police hard on youth?

These are all the things I would have loved to learn in school. (Is that the way you think now or the way you thought then?) I used to want to know about the government. How it was structured. I wanted to learn how it was run—really. Back then I didn't know people were marching for their rights. I didn't know about that. (When did you find out?) In the streets.

Finally, the following observations of Kvaraceus point up not only the irrelevancy of high school instruction, but its latent dishonesty and perversion of reality.

Since the high school is careful to skirt and detour around real-life problems and controversial issues regarding race relations, alcoholism, materialism, religion, politics, collectivism, consumer competency, it involves the learner in a type of artificially contrived busy work and shadow boxing that either dulls the adolescent into a stupor or drives him in his resentment out of school to overt agression and resentment. In protecting youths from real-life problems, the school enters into a tragic conspiracy of irresponsible retreat from reality. The perversion of the high school curriculum to neutral and petty purposes emasculates the school program and disintegrates the ego.[26]

Clearly, then, one of the ways the school itself contributes to progressive disengagement of youth from education—and sometimes from the illegitimate system as a whole—is its detached and consequently empty instruction. There should be little question of the immediate need to develop new materials and approaches that will generate and hold the attention, interest, and commitment of youth.

Inappropriate Teaching Methods

A third component of effective instruction is the use of teaching approaches and techniques that are geared to the backgrounds, skills, and deficiencies of particular groups of pupils. As we noted earlier in the paper, maximum development of potential talent requires the use of divergent,

---

[26]William Kvaraceus, "Negro Youth and Social Adaptation: The Role of the School as an Agent of Change." Medford, Massachusetts: Lincoln Filene Center of Tufts University, 1963 (unpublished paper), cited by Harry Passow in John Curtis Gowan and George D. Demos, editors, *The Disadvantaged and Potential Dropouts, Comprehensive Educational Programs: A Book of Readings.* Springfield, Ill.: Charles C. Thomas, 1966, p. 287.

not uniform, teaching styles for different populations. There is increasing—though belated—recognition among educators that the approaches required for effective teaching of the disadvantaged are different from those used in the middle class schools. Goldberg has clearly articulated this position in the form of three interrelated assumptions.

> First . . . a pupil's learning is in large measure a function of the kind of teaching to which he is exposed. Thus, the extent to which a pupil masters a given set of academic tasks reflects not only his aptitudes and attitudes but also the appropriateness of the particular approach by which he is taught. The second assumption . . . rejects the notion of the universally "good" teacher, equally able to adapt his style to varying pupil populations, and substitutes a conception of a variety of "good" teachers, differentially suited (by temperament and training) to teaching different groups of students. The third assumption proposes that children from culturally disadvantaged backgrounds, though highly variable, nevertheless represent a describable pupil population in need of teachers who are uniquely "good" for them.[27]

The claim that lower income and minority group pupils are lacking in cognitive or behavioral preparation fails to distinguish between cultural differences and cultural deficiences. Riessman has called attention to the differences between the "deprived child's style" and the style of the typical middle class pupil:

> 1. physical and visual rather than oral, 2. content-centered rather than form-centered, 3. externally-oriented rather than introspective, 4. problem-centered rather than abstract-centered, 5. inductive rather than deductive, 6. spatial rather than temporal, 7. slow, careful, persevering (in areas of importance) rather than quick, facile, flexible.[28]

Judgments about skills, experiences and attributes must be made in relation to the school, not according to some objective standard. Usually, however,

> The judgment of "verbal deficiency" is attached to the *child,* not to the child in relation to the demands of the formal learning situation designed for the needs of *certain* children and destined to succeed with only those children.[29]

---

[27]Miriam Goldberg, "Adapting Teacher Style to Pupil Differences: Teachers for Disadvantaged Children," *Merrill-Palmer Quarterly,* Vol. 10, No. 2 (1964), pp. 161–62.

[28]Riessman, *op. cit.,* p. 73.

[29]Sema Brainin, "Language Skills, Formal Education and the Lower-Class Child," New York: Mobilization for Youth, Incorporated (mimeographed), 1964.

It is our position, with Pearl, that:

> Schools must be prepared to meet and treat with the poor child on his own level as he enters. If his skills and coping ability lead him toward physical activity rather than verbal manipulation in his adaptation to environment, then why must they be judged inferior or worthless?[30]

Inappropriate teaching approaches clearly inhibit the learning and development of lower income and minority group children. Thus, Deutsch has reported that, partly as a result of inadequate understanding and inappropriate control and instruction techniques, some teachers in lower income areas spend as much as 80 per cent of their time in the classroom attempting to exert control and trying to deal with non-academic tasks. This compares with 30 per cent of teaching time devoted to control of students in middle class schools.[31] The amount of instructional time in slum schools is considerably less than in middle class schools, then, despite the fact that children in slum schools generally require more, not less, teaching to reach the same level of development.

A major reason for the inappropriateness of teaching methods in lower income schools is that teacher training institutions persist in training all teachers as though they were going to be fed into the suburban middle class school. They fail to devote sufficient time and attention to developing an understanding of and techniques for dealing with the environmental circumstances, motivational patterns, problems—and potentialities—of lower income children. Ornstein recently reported that, although more than 200 teacher training institutes now have such programs in operation or in the planning stage,

> ... they are unrealistic, because the courses are mainly on the graduate level and do most prospective teachers no good, and the few colleges that offer undergraduate programs make them voluntary; therefore, they are vastly undersubscribed.[32]

We contend that use of inappropriate teaching methods, largely resulting from inadequate and unimaginative preparation of teachers, is one of the factors contributing to educational failure, progressive loss of

---

[30] Arthur Pearl, "Youth in Lower Class Settings," in Muzafer Sherif and Carolyn W. Sherif, editors, *Problems of Youth.* Chicago: Aldine Publishing Company, 1965, p. 96.

[31] Martin Deutsch, *Minority Group and Class Status as Related to Social and Personality Factors in Scholastic Achievement.* Monograph No. 2. Ithaca, New York: Society for Applied Anthropology, 1960.

[32] Allan C. Ornstein, "Learning to Teach the Disadvantaged," *Journal of Secondary Education,* Vol. 41 (May, 1966), p. 207.

interest, alienation, and subsequent delinquency among many lower income and non-white pupils, especially in the cities. The urgent need for training for slum schools in particular has been vividly portrayed by a young teacher in the ghetto in a letter, which was later published, to one of her former professors.

> I would like to emphasize now the even greater need to train teachers to be able to deal with and attempt to overcome their own "culture shock" and "culture bias." Most middle class teachers, for example, have little experience, training, or understanding to be able to deal with parole officers, truant officers, social workers, and welfare investigators. Teachers who work in slum schools need to be prepared to work also with these people. They need to be told beforehand that they might have children in their classes who have police records. They need to be *prepared* so that they can understand and deal with these problems, rather than go in unprepared and be shocked, frightened, and/or resentful of them. They need to be prepared to deal with parents who may be illiterate or partly illiterate, concerned but helpless, or hostile or abusive. More than anything else, I think that teachers who work in slum schools must be helped to become more community minded. They must be made aware of the social and economic backgrounds of the community. They must know the community values, interests, and problems.[33]

As Ornstein correctly points out, the need for such training is not just limited to future slum teachers.

> . . . the fact remains, not only will new teachers who work in urban areas most probably be assigned to slum schools; not only will they probably teach disadvantaged children even in the "good" schools, but if our schools are totally integrated, which seems to be the trend, just about every teacher will have to teach these children, and in large numbers at that.[34]

Testing, Grouping, and "Tracking"

It is increasingly recognized that accumulation of academic failure is heightened, especially among lower income pupils, by heavy reliance on ability and achievement tests and on grouping and "tracking" procedures.

There is no longer any question that intelligence tests do not in any sense measure innate potential alone, but rather strongly reflect past learning opportunities and experiences.

---

[33]Betty Levy, "An Urban Teacher Speaks Out," *Harvard Graduate School of Education Association Bulletin*, Vol. X, No. 2 (Summer, 1965).

[34]Ornstein, *op. cit.*, p. 207.

Few thoughtful people today believe that the intelligence quotient reflects a purely innate hereditary ability of humans. Half a century of intelligence testing and research has made it clear that the person's environmental experiences help determine the I.Q. score he achieves.[35]

Intelligence is a plastic product of hereditary structure developed by environmental stimulation and opportunity, an alloy of endowment and experience.[36]

Evidence is also clear that intelligence scores are heavily influenced by situational factors during the test and by familiarity with this kind of task and situation. Thus, Riessman refers to "the big three: practice, motivation, rapport" as critical ingredients in test performance.[37]

There are two implications of these environmental and situational influences on test scores. One is that scores are highly unstable through time. For example, "P. E. Vernon found an average increase of 11 points on I.Q. scores as a result of a few hours coaching on material similar to that found in I.Q. tests."[38] Similarly, Haggard found with three hours of practice and encouragement, he was able to sharply increase the I.Q.'s of a sample of disadvantaged children.[39] In sum,

Numerous studies of identical twins and children in institutions, nursery schools and foster homes have shown that I.Q. scores can be raised by changing the environment, improving needed skills, and teaching children how to take tests.[40]

A second implication is that tests of intelligence underestimate the talent of lower income and non-white children, because of middle class-oriented test content, lack of environmental stimulation (or more properly, a different kind of environmental stimulation) among lower income pupils, and their unfamiliarity with the testing situation itself.

Most presently used intelligence tests . . . are so constructed and so administered that scores on them are influenced by the cultural backgrounds of

---

[35] W. W. Charters, Jr., "Social Class and Intelligence Tests," in W. W. Charters, Jr., and N. L. Gage, editors, *Readings in the Social Psychology of Education*. Boston: Allyn and Bacon, Incorporated, 1964, p. 12.

[36] Thomas F. Pettigrew, *A Profile of the Negro American*. New York: Van Nostrand Reinhold Company, 1964. © 1964 by Litton Educational Publishing Inc. Reprinted by permission of publisher.

[37] Riessman, *op. cit.*, p. 53.

[38] P. E. Vernon, "Coaching For All Advised," *The London Times Education Supplement* (February 1, 1952 and December 12, 1952), p. 290.

[39] Ernest A. Haggard, "Social Status and Intelligence," *Genetic Psychology Monographs,* Vol. 49 (1954), pp. 141–86.

[40] Sexton, *op. cit.*, p. 48. ©1961 by Patricia Cayo Sexton. All rights reserved. Reprinted with permission of the Viking Press, Inc.

the children they test in such a way that children from certain kinds of cultural backgrounds receive scores that are not accurate reflections of their basic intelligence.[41]

Yet, Clarke and Clarke report from their investigation:

> The results show clearly that intellectual retardation among such deprived people as have been studied here is not necessarily a permanent and irreversible condition.[42]

The problem here is not so much the tests themselves but rather the uses to which they are put. Despite these well-known facts of instability and class bias, most school systems and teachers still use intelligence tests as though they were stable measures of innate potential, independent of environment. One consequence is that individual teachers frequently underestimate the ability of particular youngsters and scale down their expectations and level of instruction accordingly. Another more formal result is that scores are used, often very early, as the basis for grouping students according to so-called "ability" or "readiness." For example, in Washington, D.C. elementary schools, . . . "metropolitan (form R) reading readiness tests are given in kindergarten or first grade, and on the basis of these scores, pupils are sorted into 'ready to read' first grade groups or 'not ready' junior primary groups."[43]

Such practices are usually carried on, not to increase educational input for those who need it most and therefore to equalize educational opportunity and to maximize the development of "submerged talent," but to decrease performance standards and levels of instruction, thus ensuring eventual failure and heightening the chances of delinquency.

> In segregating students the I.Q. test is used as the principal grounds for determining which students are "slow" (and should be made even slower) and which are "fast" (and should therefore be given special advantages and removed from contamination from other students.)[44]

This problem has been noted in the particular case of the Washington, D.C. schools (which have recently taken steps to eliminate the "tracking" system):

---

[41]Kenneth Eells, "Some Implications for School Practice of the Chicago Studies of Cultural Bias in Intelligence Tests," *Harvard Educational Review*, XXIII (1953), pp. 284–97.

[42]A. D. B. Clarke and A. M. Clarke, "How Constant is the IQ?" *Lancet,* ii, pp. 877–80.

[43]*A Task Force Study . . . , op. cit.,* p. 37.

[44]Sexton, *op. cit.,* p. 43.

Critics have attacked the "junior primary" as the beginning of basic track grouping; they claim that school officials or principals set ceilings on how much can be taught them, and that as a result needy pupils never reach their "ready" point, but are doomed to basic classes for the rest of their school life.[45]

In short, the "self-fulfilling prophecy" is again set in motion whereby pupils who, according to test performances, have low innate potential are grouped and instructed as though that were in fact the case, resulting in a further falling behind in their progress in development. Thus,

> As time goes on the children of the slower group get further and further behind the children of the fast. The rationale for this phenomenon is two-fold: (1) The children in the slow groups are incapable of doing what children of the fast groups can do, so why burden them with what they cannot achieve? (2) The less that is offered the poorer becomes their reading in comparison with the other children, until the time comes when their reading levels are so far behind the levels of the fast that they truly can no longer expect to compete with them.[46]

As Kenneth Clark has noted, "It is conceivable that the detrimental effects of segregation based upon intellect are similar to the known detrimental effects of schools segregated on the basis of class, nationality, or race."[47]

Adverse consequences are not just limited to delinquency but are more general: because intelligence tests underestimate available talent, substantial talent is lost—at a time in our national life when there is already an oversupply of undeveloped talent but a shortage of fully developed talent.

These remarks have referred to testing and grouping practices at all stages of the educational career. While they are particularly damaging during the elementary years, as the "gap" quickly widens between the "slow" and "fast," the negative effects of "tracking" in the secondary schools are just as serious in producing delinquency. The traditional procedure in American secondary schools has been to place students at the onset of junior or senior high school in two, three, or four tracks of curricula, according to past performance, parental preference, teacher or counselor judgment, test scores, or student aspirations.

These practices may have several adverse consequences for those assigned to the lower tracks. First, studies by Warner, Kitsuse and Cicourel,

---

[45] *A Task Force Study . . . , op. cit.*, p. 37.

[46] Nathaniel Hickerson, *Education for Alienation*. Englewood Cliffs, New Jersey: Prentice-Hall, Inc., p. 34. ©1966. Reprinted with permission.

[47] Kenneth B. Clark, "Educational Stimulation of Racially Disadvantaged Children," in Passow, *op. cit.*, p. 152. Reprinted with permission of the publisher. ©1963 by Teachers College, Columbia University.

and Schafer and Armer suggest that lower status pupils are at a disadvantage in competing for upper track positions.[48] This is illustrated by the following observations of a junior high school teacher upon being asked if there was "much class feeling in the school."

> Oh, yes, there is a lot of that. We try not to have it but of course we can't help it. Now, for instance, even in the sections we have, it is evident. Sections are supposed to be made up just on the basis of records in school but it isn't and everybody knows it isn't. I know right in my own A section I have children who ought to be in B section, but they are little socialites and so they stay in A. I don't say there are children in B who should be in A but in the A section there are some who shouldn't be there. We have discussed it in faculty meetings but nothing is ever done. . . .[49]

Although parents theoretically have the right to overrule the judgments of teachers or counselors, Kitsuse and Cicourel, Schafer, and the House Task Force on the Washington, D.C. schools, found that few lower income parents felt at liberty to do so.[50]

> Parents, according to printed policy, have always had the right to protest the placement of their children in basic or regular track. Relatively few did, or do, however. Most parents of poverty area pupils would feel themselves incapable of arguing the point, even if they were aware of it.[51]

Second, assignment of a student to a lower track usually means that the quality of instruction and the expectations held of him are scaled down. Effects on lower income pupils are especially devastating, as noted by Pearl: " 'special ability classes,' 'basic track,' or 'slow learner classes' are various names for another means of systematically denying the poor adequate access to education."[52]

Third, a student who ends up on a non-college preparatory track finds his chances for going to college almost totally closed and his occupational career chances severely hampered. Tracking may, then, directly contribute

---

[48]John I. Kitsuse and Aaron V. Cicourel, *The Educational Decision-Makers.* New York: The Bobbs-Merrill Company, 1963; Walter E. Schafer and J. Michael Armer, "High School Curriculum Placement: A Study of Educational Selection," paper presented at the Annual Meetings of the Pacific Sociological Association, Vancouver, B.C. (April, 1966); W. Lloyd Warner, Robert J. Havighurst, and M. B. Loeb, *Who Shall Be Educated?* New York: Harper, 1944.

[49]*Ibid.*, p. 74.

[50]Kitsuse and Cicourel, *op. cit.*; Walter E. Schafer, *Student Careers in Two Public High Schools: A Comparative Cohort Analysis.* (unpublished doctoral dissertation), University of Michigan, 1965, Chapter 3; *A Task Force Study . . . , op. cit.*, p. 39.

[51]*Ibid.*, p. 39.

[52]Pearl, in Sherif and Sherif, *op. cit.*, p. 92.

to the perceived lack of payoff mentioned earlier, as well as to deterioration of interest and commitment.

Fourth, assignment to a lower track almost inevitably leads to low status among teachers and pupils. A girl in a midwestern high school recently remarked to one of the authors, for instance, that she was always ashamed to carry her "basic" books face up for fear other students would see them and look down on her. Quite clearly, however, status differences cannot be so easily concealed.

> It really don't have to be the tests, but after the tests, there shouldn't be no separation in the classes. Because, as I say again, I felt good when I was with my class, but when they went and separated us—that changed us. That changed our ideas, our thinking, the way we thought about each other and turned us to enemies toward each other—because they said I was dumb and they were smart.

The frequent result is that students' estimates of their own worth and potential deteriorates.

> When you first go to junior high school you do feel something inside—its like a ego. You have been from elementary to junior high, you feel great inside. You say, well daggone, I'm going to deal with the *people* here now, I am in junior high school. You get this shirt that says Brown Junior High or whatever the name is and you are proud of that shirt. But then you go up there and the teacher say—"well, so and so, you're in the basic section, you can't go with the other kids." The devil with the whole thing—you lose —something in you—like it just goes out of you.

> (Did you think the other guys were smarter than you?) Not at first—I used to think I was just as smart as anybody in the school—I felt it inside of me. When the first year into junior high school—I knew I was smart. I knew some people were smarter, but I knew I could be just as good as they were— and I *wanted* to go to school, I wanted to get a diploma and go to college and help people and everything. I stepped into there in junior high—I felt like a fool going to school—I really felt like a fool. (Why?) Because I felt like I wasn't a part of the school. I couldn't get on special patrols, because I wasn't qualified. (What happened between the seventh and ninth grades?) I started losing faith in myself—after the teachers kept downing me, you know. You hear "a guy's in basic section, he's dumb" and all this. Each year—"you're ignorant—you're stupid."

Fifth, "basic" or other lower track students are not only denied status but they are frequently denied objective opportunities to become engaged in certain prestigeful and rewarding activities.

> (What happened after you were separated?) (You said you didn't have any opportunities any more. What kind?) I mean—they'd get special things. When you're ready to graduate from junior high, you get to take pictures

and go on picnics and stuff. Basic classes don't do this. You don't get to take any pictures in basic classes. You don't get a chance to be in the recital, you don't get the chance to do certain things. You know, 9–7, 9–8, and 9–9, they used to give plays—they gave a big play. But none of the basic section was included, although we was classified as the ninth grade.

The direct connection between tracking and delinquency could hardly be made more clear than this:

> You can't get on this, you can't get on that and the girls that were in my class back in the sixth grade—they look at you—"you're in the basic section aren't you." You know, all of a sudden the guys you used to hang out with won't hang out with you nomore. They hang out with a new class of people. Like they're classifying themselves as middle class and you're low brow and, you know, you start feeling bad and I said I can prove that I'm middle class and I don't have to go to school to prove it. And so I did. I got out of school. All those kids' mothers buying them nice things in ninth and tenth grades. I said, baby, you ain't talking about nothing—and what your mother has to buy you I can get everyday. I used to sport around. Yeah—I used to show them $125—*every* day. I used to say—you have to go on to school for 12 years and I only went for 9. (How did you get this money?) I'd take it. (How did you take it?) I broke into things. I used to have a little racket set up. I used to have a protection fee—anybody who wants to cross the street, anybody who wants to come into my territory, they has to pay me 25 cents. I gave boys certain areas where they couldn't cross. A cat used to live up there. I say, "okay that's your deadline right there. If you want to go through this way, you give me 25 cents. If I ever catch you coming down through this way, you got a fight on your hands." And they gave me 25 cents.

It is clear that the denial of status and opportunity to this youth as a result of having been assigned to the "basic" track had a direct effect on his rejection of the legitimate system and on his subsequent turn toward delinquency.

In view of these inadvertent defects and outcomes of testing, grouping, and tracking procedures, we believe the public schools should re-examine these procedures very carefully. Where the effects are more negative than positive, they should be modified or eliminated.

Inadequate Compensatory and Remedial Education

Another way in which the schools contribute to educational failure is through inadequate compensatory and remedial programs for offsetting initial and continuing physical, psychological, intellectual, and social difficulties of some children. As noted above, part of these problems result from the failure of the system to meet the individual, but, at the same time, recognition must be given to the fact that some part of these difficulties inhere in the child as well.

Inaction by the schools, especially in urban areas, has traditionally been justified on two grounds. First, cognitive and social deficits are irreversible, and, second, even if they were reversible, it is not the schools' responsibility to compensate for learning handicaps produced by the family or community. One or both of these assumptions are still implicitly held in many if not most school systems, despite evidence that these difficulties can be reversed and despite increasing agreement that it is both appropriate and necessary for the public schools to do everything to maximize education for all children. In the words of the Educational Policies Commission, "compensatory education is fundamental. . . ."[53]

Compensatory and remedial education programs in the past have been inadequate in at least two ways. First, the amount of expenditures and number of programs has simply not met the need as we will see in more detail later. Second, they have almost exclusively tended to emphasize pre-school and early elementary services at least until very recently. No one, of course, denies the massive need for programs at this level, and that they have been effective in increasing the chances of later success. At the same time, there has been a neglect of older students who have fallen behind.

As we will discuss in more detail later in the chapter, the compensatory and remedial provisions of the Economic Opportunity Act of 1964 and the Elementary and Secondary Education Act of 1965 are likely to make considerable impact on the educational chances of the disadvantaged, but they are currently inadequate because of their relatively small appropriations relative to the size of the problem and the almost exclusive use of such funds by local schools for pre-school and early elementary programs.

Inferior Teachers and Facilities in Low Income Schools

The effects of educational defects discussed up to now are compounded for lower income and non-white children by the fact that quality of teachers and facilities is generally inferior in the schools that they attend. On a nationwide basis, the *Coleman Report* used a number of rough indicators of teacher quality, including the type of college attended, years of teaching experience, salary, educational level of mother, and performance on a 30 word vocabulary test. Results showed, first, that "the average Negro pupil

[53]Educational Policies Commission of the National Education Association, *American Education and the Search for Equal Opportunity*. Washington, D.C., 1965, p. 7.

attends a school where a greater percentage of the teachers appears to be somewhat less able . . ."; second, the better the quality of teachers, the higher the achievement; and, third, "teacher differences show accumulative effects over the years in school."[54]

Variations in teacher quality are especially marked in metropolitan areas, as younger, less experienced teachers, as well as unqualified substitutes tend to concentrate in lower income, non-white, inner-city areas, while more experienced and stable teachers tend to concentrate in white, middle class, outer city or suburban areas. Sexton found, for example, that the lower the average income of city areas, the greater the percentage of the teaching staff consisting of poorly qualified substitutes and the less the experience of full time teachers."[55]

Similarly, Havighurst found in Chicago that while . . . "younger teachers and those with least experience tend to be assigned to schools in the lower socio-economic areas . . . the teachers over 50 years of age and with 16 or more years of experience are heavily clustered in the higher status and in the mixed, middle and working class areas."[56] Viewed another way, "the median years of teaching experience of regularly assigned teachers in these (low income) schools is only four compared with 19 for teachers in the most favored."[57] Likewise, he found that 36 percent of all teachers in the "Inner-city" schools were substitutes compared to 14, 9, and 6 percent in the "Common Man," "Main Line," and "High Status" schools.[58]

This situation has become worse in Washington, D.C. over the past decade as the proportion of Negroes in the public schools has increased.

> In 1955, 16.4 percent of the teachers employed had temporary status—without tenure because of failure to meet the prescribed qualifications. In 1965, 40 percent of all teachers had temporary status.[59]

These patterns result from a desire of experienced teachers to move as soon as possible to more "desirable" schools in outlying, middle or higher income areas—and from the support given this tendency by school administrators who hire, assign, and promote teachers.

Since . . . "it seems likely that, other things equal, an experienced teacher is much to be preferred to an inexperienced teacher . . . ," it also

---

[54]*Coleman Report, op. cit.*, pp. 12, 318.

[55]Sexton, *op. cit.*, pp. 118, 211.

[56]Robert J. Havighurst, *The Public Schools of Chicago*. Chicago: The Board of Education of the City of Chicago, 1963, p. 341.

[57]*Ibid.*, p. 346.

[58]*Ibid.*, p. 170.

[59]*A Task Force Study . . .*, *op. cit.*, p. 12.

seems likely that lower income and non-white pupils, especially in inner-city schools, receive an inferior quality of instruction.[60]

Such students attend schools that are not only manned by inferior teachers, but are also older, more crowded, and less well equipped. In the nation as a whole, non-white children go to larger classes; have less access to physics, chemistry, and language laboratories; have less access to library books; and more often are faced with an insufficient supply of text books.[61] Each of these factors is in turn associated with low achievement.[62]

Again, facilities and equipment are especially deficient in lower income schools in the large cities. Sexton, for instance, also reported that—

> The school buildings, and the facilities that they contain are *much less adequate* in lower income than in upper income areas—in the lower income half (below $7,000) 30.5 percent of all children—about one of every three— go to schools that are fifty years old or older. By contrast no students in the upper income half attend schools of this age . . . school buildings in the lower income half are about twice as old as the buildings in the upper half.[63]

She also found facilities in and around the schools to be vastly inferior in low income areas.[64] Finally, she found marked differences in over-crowding and class size. Despite beliefs that—

> . . . class size is smaller in lower income areas where students tend to be harder to handle and in need of extra attention by the teacher . . . , class size is not smaller in lower income areas; in fact, it is somewhat higher.[65]

Similar patterns were reported in Washington, D.C.

> Despite the fact that 70 percent of all elementary schools constructed since 1958 have been placed in areas where the median yearly family income is below $6,000, the oldest, most overcrowded schools continue to be in the poorest parts of the city.[66]

As a result, 5,652 elementary school children in Washington remained in classrooms intended for other purposes in 1965.[67]

---

[60] Sexton, *op. cit.*, p. 122.
[61] *Coleman Report, op. cit.*, p. 9.
[62] *Ibid.*, pp. 312–16.
[63] Sexton, *op. cit.*, pp. 123–24.
[64] *Ibid.*, pp. 122–34, 212–13.
[65] *Ibid.*, pp. 113–14, 215–22.
[66] *A Task Force Study* . . . , *op. cit.*, p. 9.
[67] *Ibid.*, p. 10.

Finally, vast discrepancies were reported in the Washington schools in the number of library books available to higher and lower income children.

> A junior high school in an upper-income neighborhood of families with relatively high educational backgrounds and with "books in the house" had a library of 5,600 books in the fall of 1965. A junior high school in a neighborhood with a high incidence of welfare clients and other low income families with limited schooling and with "no books in the house," had 3,500 books for 1,400 children. The former had 5 complete sets of encyclopedias, with additional sets in the various classrooms; the latter had one. Similarly, at one elementary school "feeding" into the affluent junior high school, the home and school association had provided 12 sets of encyclopedias, while in the less favored neighborhoods there are schools with not a single set.[68]

The evidence clearly suggests, then, that low quality teachers, facilities, and equipment prevail in schools serving low income and non-white pupils, heightening failure and subsequent delinquency in those areas.

School-Community Distance

> That the public schools in America cannot shut themselves off from the communities served has been a long-accepted tenet of our educational philosophy.[69]

Even though this may be true "philosophically" it is less than completely applied in practice. Schools serving middle class populations tend to be relatively "close" to the community, neighborhood, and families served. This results from the fact, that, on the one hand, middle class parents are not only highly supportive of educational aims, but are comfortable in taking an interest if not an active part in school affairs and in their children's educational careers. Sometimes, in fact, the school's problem may be to fend off undue pressures and intervention by over-zealous or over-protective middle class parents. On the other hand, school personnel understand the motivations, styles, and aspirations of middle class parents and are able to communicate openly and with no resentment or hostility.

The story is different with respect to lower income or minority group parents, however, especially in urban ghettos. At the same time that school expectations in relation to frequency and type of parental involvement are

---

[68]*Ibid.*, p. 30.

[69]Henry Saltzman, "The Community School in the Urban Setting," in Passow, *op. cit.*, p. 322. Reprinted with permission of the publisher. ©1963 by Teachers College, Columbia University.

likely to be the same as for middle class parents, lower income parents frequently perceive the school as hostile, cold, and alien, and, as a result, they are often too fearful, uncomfortable, or hostile in return to offer much active support.

The following hypothetical statements of an educator and a disadvantaged parent aptly portray the standoff that frequently exists:

Educator: What right have these people to charge down to the school and accuse us of keeping their children out of the college prep courses? They don't give a hoot about education. They never have supported us. They are only raising hell now, because protesting has become fashionable. Do you think they usually care enough about their kids to join the PTA? I am tired of hearing everybody yell that all of the problems of communities such as this are the school's. We do the best we can and with too little help from parents or their kids. We hold meetings to explain what we do here, but they don't care enough to take advantage of them. If a kid cuts up and you have to send for them, they come in all pushed out of shape and looking for trouble. You try to explain the problem and whose side do they take? They side with their children, of course.

Parent: Those school people don't give a damn about us or our kids. Hell, they don't even live around here, so how can they tell me what I want, or what I want for my kids? The only time they want to see you is when your kid has got them all shook up. Rest of the time they don't care if you are dead. I don't like to even talk to those people. Their big $10 psychology words bug me. They really don't want you to know what they are talking about. My kid is just as good as those other kids. They use all of those big science words to try and con me that he is dumb. I work too damn hard for too damn little money, and pay too much taxes to take that crap off those people.[70]

It is increasingly recognized that education of lower status students will be effective only to the extent that such conflict is eliminated. As the Educational Policies Commission has stated:

One of the most serious obstacles to successful education in disadvantaged areas is the lack of communication between school and community. In a pathetic sense, the schools are not schools *of* the disadvantaged community but schools *in* the disadvantaged community. A new mutual confidence and mutual understanding between school personnel and parents is desperately needed.[71]

Educational attainment will be heightened insofar as the school and the family cooperate in the true sense of the word—with the parents sup-

---

[70]Staten Webster, "When Schools and Parents in a Disadvantaged Community Clash: A Proposal," in Webster, *op. cit.*, p. 408.

[71]Educational Policies Commission, *American Education . . . , op. cit.*, p. 22.

porting the aims of education, and creating conditions that will facilitate their children's progress; and with the school understanding and appreciating the circumstances and views of families, and doing what is necessary to develop family support of educational tasks and aims. As we will see later, this requires new educational measures for bringing the family closer to the school and for extending the school into the community.

Economic and Racial Segregation

The school condition which has perhaps the greatest effect of all on educational failure and hence delinquency is economic and racial segregation. There are a number of points that must be made in support of this position.

First, a major finding of the *Coleman Report* was that pupils' achievement and aspirations are strongly related to the educational backgrounds and performance of other students in the same school.[72] This single factor accounted for much more variation in student achievement than any other school conditions. Pupils who attend schools mostly filled with other students who achieve at low levels are lower in their own achievement than pupils who attend schools which have a better cross section or which have large numbers of students who achieve at high levels.

Second, we noted earlier that despite equivalent or even higher levels of educational aspirations, non-white and lower income pupils attain lower levels of educational achievement than white and higher income pupils. Partly as a result, Coleman found that at least in certain parts of the country, "Negro pupils are more likely to be exposed to fellow students who have feelings of powerlessness over their environment."[73]

Third, most students attend schools mainly comprised of other pupils of their own racial and economic background. With respect to race, for example, the *Coleman Report* states that nearly 80 percent of all white pupils attend schools that are from 90 to 100 percent white while more than 65 percent of all Negro pupils attend schools that are between 90 and 100 percent Negro.[74] In the South, most pupils attend schools that are 100 percent white or Negro. While less adequate data are available on economic homogeneity within schools, there is some evidence that segregation by income is also very high. Havighurst in fact contends that:

There has probably been a growing amount of economic segregation in American public schools since 1940. That is, there has been a growing

---

[72]*Coleman Report, op. cit.*, pp. 22, 302.
[73]*Ibid.*, p. 202.
[74]*Ibid.*, p. 3.

percentage of middle and lower class schools and a decreasing percentage of mixed class schools.[75]

Because of a series of forces that need not be elaborated here, economic and racial segregation is especially high and is actually increasing in central cities of major metropolitan areas. These patterns reflect a growing bifurcation of metropolitan population: central cities are becoming increasingly non-white and lower class, while suburbs are becoming or remaining white and middle class.

Fourth, it follows from what has been said that more students from lower income and non-white backgrounds than from higher income and white families are exposed to other students with inferior educational backgrounds and levels of achievement. Although we know of no direct evidence in support of this conclusion in terms of economic level, the *Coleman Report* clearly affirms it in terms of race.

> The average Negro has fewer classmates whose mothers graduated from high school; his classmates more frequently are members of large rather than smaller families, they are less often enrolled in a college preparatory curriculum, and they have taken a smaller number of courses in English, Mathematics, Foreign Language, and Science.[76]

Fifth, it further follows that lower income and non-white pupils attain lower levels of educational performance than they would if they attended mixed or predominantly middle class or white schools.[77] This is not only the conclusion of the *Coleman Report* with respect to race, but it has also been reported by a number of other investigators with respect to economic level (which partly overlaps with race, of course). Wilson found, for example, that at both the elementary and secondary levels in the San Francisco Bay–Oakland area, working class boys received higher grades if they were in predominantly middle class or mixed class schools.[78] In addition, he found that boys from a given income background and with a given I.Q. were more likely to go to college if they were in a middle class or a mixed class school. Numerous other investigators have reported similar findings.[79]

Sixth, by inference, economic and racial segregation exert an indirect effect on delinquency, insofar as it arises from educational failure. For-

---

[75]Robert J. Havighurst, "Urban Development and the Educational System," in Passow, *op. cit.*, pp. 217–35.

[76]*Coleman Report, op. cit.*, p. 20.

[77]*Ibid.*, p. 29; Havighurst, in Passow, *op. cit.*, p. 30.

[78]Alan B. Wilson, "Social Stratification and Academic Achievement," in Passow, *ibid.*, pp. 217–35.

[79]For a summary of these studies, see William H. Sewall and J. Michael Armer, "Neighborhood Context and College Plans," *American Sociological Review*, Vol. 31 (April, 1966), pp. 159–68.

tunately, Albert Reiss' Nashville study allows us to go beyond mere inference to establish this relationship empirically, at least with respect to economic composition of schools.[80] He, as others, found that lower status students obtain higher levels of performance in mixed or predominantly middle class schools than in predominantly lower class schools. Of great importance here, however, is the additional finding that predominantly lower status schools also appeared to produce higher rates of delinquency.

> On the average, the schools which cross cut the status structure and avoid concentration at lower status levels were closest to optimizing the kind of conforming conduct we want from adolescents both in the school and in the community.[81]

If we accept the above evidence and arguments, then the schools themselves help contribute to delinquency, insofar as they duplicate homogeneous housing patterns, or impose school boundaries or other attendance criteria (like race) that create uniformity within particular schools with respect to educational backgrounds and performance of students. Clearly, one educational change—perhaps the most important one, on the basis of the *Coleman Report* conclusion—that will help prevent delinquency in the long run is economic as well as racial desegregation of schools.

The objection will surely be raised that to mix school populations racially or economically in the interest of delinquency prevention—or for any other reason—would produce mediocrity and would inevitably bring more fortunate students down to a lower level. The *Coleman Report* very clearly shows, however, that racial or economic mixing has no such "depressing" effect; even the less advantaged student stands to benefit.

> Thus, if a white pupil from a home that is strongly and effectively supportive of education is put in a school where most pupils do not come from some such homes, his achievement will be little different than if he were in a school composed of others like himself. But if a minority pupil from a home without much educational strength is put with schoolmates with strong educational backgrounds, his achievement is likely to increase.[82]

There are, of course, conditions that need not be discussed here that affect the educational outcomes of racial economic integration. In general,

---

[80] Albert J. Reiss, Jr. and Albert Lewis Rhodes, *A Sociopsychological Study of Adolescent Conformity and Deviation.* United States Office of Education, Cooperative Research Project, No. 507 (1959).

[81] *Ibid.;* also see Albert J. Reiss and Albert Lewis Rhodes, "The Distribution of Juvenile Delinquency in the Social Class Structure," *American Sociological Review*, Vol. 26 (October, 1961), pp. 720–32.

[82] *Coleman Report, op. cit.*, p. 22.

however, the *Coleman Report* concludes that . . . "in the long run, integration should be expected to have a positive effect on Negro achievement . . ."[83] In fact, . . . "there is evidence even in the short run of a positive effect of school integration on the reading and mathematics achievement of Negro pupils."[84] The arguments and evidence presented here strongly suggest that similar effects should follow from economic integration.

Conditions Contributing to Perceived Lack of Payoff of Education

A facade of affluence and abundance hides the spreading blight of social crisis in America—a crisis compounded by insufficient economic growth, a rising number of unemployed, increasing racial tensions, juvenile delinquency, swelling public welfare rolls, chronically depressed areas, and an expanding ratio of youth to total population, as well as a growing disparity of educational opportunities. At the center of the crisis is a system of education that is failing to prepare individuals for a new world of work in an advanced technological society.[85]

As implied in this statement by Grant Venn, there are far broader consequences of the failure of the educational system to produce an adequately prepared work force than just unemployment or a less than fully efficient economy, important as these problems are. As he suggests, one of these additional consequences is a heightened incidence of juvenile delinquency.

Earlier we pointed out that the major way in which this occurs is that many youth see secondary education as fundamentally irrelevant to later rewards. The school is seen as offering only false promises. The signs say, "Education is for the birds. (The birds who need to get ahead.) To get a good job, get a good education." However, if one is taking a non-college preparatory course—and especially if one is non-white—such promises are in large part false ones. For one is almost certain to be fed into the labor market along channels that lead nowhere.

(What kind of school program were you doing? Vocational education?) Yeah, vocational training. (Did that prepare you for a job?) It was supposed to prepare me for a job but it didn't. (Did you try to get a job?) Yeah, I tried to get a job. The men said I wasn't qualified. (Did you think

---

[83] *Ibid.*, p. 29.

[84] *Ibid.*, p. 29.

[85] Grant Venn, *Man, Education and Work*. Washington, D.C.: American Council on Education, 1964, p. 157.

while you were in school that you would get a job?) That's right—that's why I stayed in school so I could get a job upon completion of high school because they put so much emphasis on getting a high school diploma. "If you get a high school diploma, you can do this and you can do this, without it you can't do this." And I got one and I still can't do nothing. I can't get a job or nothing, after I got one.

The deep disillusionment felt by this youth not only produces shattered hopes, but increases the potential attraction of delinquency for him. Further, his experiences—and thousands of others like them—understandably are communicated back to younger brothers, neighbors, and friends, contributing to a deterioration of commitment among them as well.

As James Conant has noted, poor articulation between the high school career and later job possibilities is also at the root of the drop-out problem: "Why bother to stay in school when graduation for half of the boys opens onto a dead-end street?"[86]

We pointed out that this perception is sometimes tied to academic failure, but is partly independent as well. It is our contention, therefore, that educational changes designed to decrease academic failure will not suffice by themselves to substantially reduce delinquency rates. For failure will continue or reappear; perceived irrelevancy of education will remain; and therefore delinquency will persist or appear unless the high school career is made more meaningful for all youth—so it is seen as having a purpose, a connection with the future, a clear payoff.

Although education for those students who are college bound and especially for those who are regarded as "gifted" has received a great deal of attention since Sputnik, much less attention has been given to the education of those who are not college bound. As a result there continue to be a number of defects in the way non-college preparatory programs in the secondary school link the school career to the later occupational career.

First, too few students who are not college bound are given sound occupational preparation. There are usually two, three, or four alternatives to the college preparatory track in American high schools: "basic," "general," "vocational," or "business" courses. There is increasing recognition that "basic" or "general" tracks are usually little more than a watered down "general education" for working class living, providing no real preparation for the world of work. According to Pearl, "Students assigned to the 'basic track' in most metropolitan schools are simply counted and kept in order; they have been relegated to the academic boneyard and eventual economic oblivion."[87]

---

[86] James B. Conant, *Slums and Suburbs.* New York: McGraw-Hill, 1961, p. 33.
[87] Pearl, in Sherif and Sherif, *op. cit.,* p. 92.

Yet, data reported by the U.S. Office of Education indicate that one in every four students is enrolled in the "general" curriculum (the equivalent to the "basic" track in their categories).[88] Research by Hollingshead, Sexton, Polk, Schafer, and others shows that this figure rises to over half among lower income pupils.[89] At the same time, the Office of Education study shows that less than one in five are enrolled in a track that is work-oriented.[90] More than half of these, most of whom are probably girls, are taking "commercial" courses. This leaves only about two or three percent of all boys taking "vocational" or "industrial arts" training. Clearly, then, a large number of youth are neither headed for college nor are they adequately prepared for anything but the most unskilled work.

Second, a basic problem with vocational or industrial arts programs in which boys do enroll is that they are too often job-specific. According to Venn—

> First job preoccupation has resulted in the narrowing of vocational education to a point where an unduly high proportion of classroom time is taken up with instruction in skills presumably needed for jobs in the local community.[91]

There are two specific consequences of this overspecialization that are relevant here. One is a constant lag between what is taught in the school and what is actually required in the work place.

> The schools that invest heavily in shop and laboratory equipment in an attempt to duplicate industrial conditions soon learn that they cannot afford the constant replacement that industry finds necessary.[92]

Venn later refers to this problem as "institutionalization of obsolescence" in the face of increasing need for highly technical and skilled personnel.[93] The result is that many youth find themselves unable to get work even after successful completion of an education built on the promise of work after high school. It is only reasonable to expect that this message will be communicated back to students still in school and will lessen their commitment to school and its promises.

---

[88]Edith S. Greer and Richard M. Harbeck, *What High School Pupils Study.* Washington, D.C.: United States Government Printing Office, 1962, p. 40.

[89]A. B. Hollingshead, *Elmtown's Youth.* New York: Wiley, 1949, p. 168; Sexton, *op. cit.*, p. 177; Schafer (dissertation), *op. cit.*, p. 66; Kenneth Polk, "An Exploration of Rural Delinquency," in Lee Burchinal, editor, *Youth in Crisis: Facts, Myths and Social Change.* Washington, D.C.: United States Government Printing Office, 1965.

[90]Greer and Harbeck, *op. cit.*, p. 40.

[91]Venn, *op. cit.*, p. 32.

[92]*Ibid.*, p. 33.

[93]*Ibid.*, p. 34.

Another consequence of over-specialization is that subsequent opportunities for upward mobility or for shifts into different jobs are often precluded.

> With unpredictable changes in the job market, the workers need versatility and adaptability to qualify for a number of alternative jobs. The worker trained in only one type of work is at an overwhelming disadvantage.[94]

Yet many students get "locked into" the particular level and type of work for which they are trained, with the only possibility for change being downward to less skilled and less demanding lines of work. Vocational education usually has no steps built into it for progressive movement into higher level jobs nor does it provide enough education in basic skills to facilitate later job changes and retraining. Pearl has summarized these negative consequences of over-concentration with first job as follows:

> In many cases the trades for which such training is intended are rapidly being made obsolete by automation. In other instances modern tooling, equipment, and techniques are lacking and an already existing technical schooling is compounded by failure to provide even the minimum basic skills—reading and mathematics—necessary to face the current scene. . . . [In addition,] the vocational student is securely "locked" into a job for life, which means, conversely, that he is *locked out* of opportunities to gain entrance into other fields. The products of an occupation-specific vocational curriculum who lack adequate basic learning skills must become casualties when there is technological change and dislocation.[95]

Third, there is little opportunity in school for work experience. While work-study programs are growing in number, most non-college bound students have little opportunity to engage in productive, rewarding work in conjunction with their formal academic training. In Washington, D.C., only five to ten percent of vocational students participate in work-study programs.[96] The result is a heightened sense of detachment between immediate school tasks and the world of work. We contend that this deficiency is one of the conditions contributing to the failure of the educational system to retain a "hold" over many pupils.

This position is also taken by Havighurst, who notes that most work-study programs are usually limited to junior and senior high school pupils and thus—

> . . . come too late to be of much use to the delinquency prone youth. Furthermore, these popular work experience programs are often limited

---

[94] Bullock and Singleton, *op. cit.*, p. 35.
[95] Pearl, in Sherif and Sherif, *op. cit.*, p. 91.
[96] *The Task Force Study . . . , op. cit.*, p. 25.

to pupils with a reasonably good work record and therefore are not available to the failing student.[97]

Fourth, the strong emphasis in American high schools on college attendance is a situation in which second class status is accorded vocational, general, and technical programs.[98] Thus, neither top-quality teachers nor students are attracted and students who do enroll become even more pessimistic about themselves and their future because of the way they are evaluated.

Fifth, it is increasingly recognized that many sub-professional jobs in the human services need to be created that do not require a college education and that there is a shortage of personnel to fill those that do exist.[99] Yet the public schools have shown little recognition of this and as a result offer virtually no training or work experience that would enable youth to move into such positions immediately after high school.

Sixth, occupational guidance and placement services are usually non-existent or are grossly inadequate.[100] As Conant has remarked, "Although half or more of the graduates of many high schools seek employment immediately on graduation, only in a few cities does one find an effective placement service."[101] In the Washington schools, "Arrangements for job placement are often solely dependent upon the teachers, already over-burdened with teaching loads."[102] Thus, entry into the labor market is frequently random and nonplanned, and when a student is taking courses he has little knowledge of later occupational requirements and little assurance of later rewards.

Seventh, a related defect is that the responsibility of the educational system terminates immediately after the student has either graduated or dropped out, rather than when he enters productive and stable adulthood. For students who go on to college, the educational system's responsibility for guiding or directing the work-bound youth into full adult status continues. Conant, as well as others, has called for an extension of the schools' responsibility to fill this gap in the career from pre-adulthood to adulthood. As we will see later, this has important implications for the school's approach to the drop-out problem.

---

[97] Robert J. Havighurst, "Research on the School Work-Study Program in the Prevention of Juvenile Delinquency," in William R. Carriker, editor, *Role of the School in Prevention of Juvenile Delinquency*. Washington, D.C.: United States Government Printing Office.

[98] Venn, *op. cit.*, p. 34.

[99] Arthur Pearl and Frank Riessman, *New Careers for the Poor*. New York: Free Press, 1965, Chapter 1.

[100] Venn, *op. cit.*, p. 147.

[101] Conant, *op. cit.*, p. 39.

[102] *The Task Force Study . . . , op. cit.*, p. 26.

The obligations of the school should not end when the student either drops out of school or graduates. At that point the cumulative folder concerning a student's educational career is usually brought to an end. It should not be. To my mind, *guidance officers, especially in the large cities, ought to be given the responsibility for following the post-high school careers of youth from the time they leave school until they are twenty-one years of age.* Since compulsory attendance usually ends at age sixteen, this means responsibility for the guidance of youth ages sixteen to twenty-one who are out of school and either employed or unemployed.[103]

These defects have all referred to non-college preparatory education. We contend that perceived irrelevancy of education and hence delinquency are also heightened by the failure of the educational system as a whole to encourage, prepare, and open up ample avenues of access to institutions of higher education. As Ramsoy has shown, more youth actually attend college than enroll in college preparatory courses in high school.[104]

Conditions Contributing to Low Commitment

Earlier we noted that one of the conditions that sometimes contribute to delinquency is lack of commitment to the school, to conventional adult rules and values, and to community standards of behavior. We also pointed out that this may partly result from "imperfect socialization," assimilation of "lower-class culture" or simple choice. At the same time, we noted that low commitment is often tied to educational failure and pessimism toward the future and that the school may even more directly contribute to the problem in the way it meets and deals with students.

The plausibility of this position is strengthened by a considerable amount of sociological evidence from other settings showing that the attitudes of subordinates in an organization are partly shaped by their experiences within the organization, as well as by earlier or outside experiences.[105] Specifically, inmates, patients, soldiers, or factory workers develop positive or negative attitudes toward the respective type of organization partly as a result of the way they are viewed and treated by those who are in control. When those in positions of superiority (e.g., guards, supervisors, foremen)

---

[103]Conant, *op. cit.*, p. 39.

[104]Natalie Rogoff Ramsoy, "College Recruitment and High School Curricula," *Sociology of Education*, Vol. 38 (Summer, 1965), pp. 297–311.

[105]For summaries of this literature, see Peter M. Blau and W. Richard Scott, *Formal Organizations: A Comparative Approach.* San Francisco: Chandler Publishing Company, 1962, Chapter 4; and Amatai Etzioni, *A Comparative Analysis of Complex Organizations.* New York: Free Press, 1961.

impose their demands and authority on those in positions of inferiority without involvement of the latter in the formulation of the organization's policy, policies, objectives, or norms or in their implementation, negative orientations are likely to develop. But when involvement of those in subordinate positions is high, attitudes toward the organization and its objectives, demands, and norms are likely to be more positive.

This general principle has been found to operate in schools as well as in these other kinds of organizations. That is, the greater the involvement of students in the planning and operation of the school, the more active and intense their interests in learning, achieving, and conforming.[106]

We hold that low commitment and sometimes delinquency is heightened by the failure of most schools to apply this principle in a wholehearted and serious way. Rather, students tend to be kept in a "colonial" status, and are excluded from serious or intense involvement in the educational process.

We believe that there are several respects in which this is so. First, students are usually excluded from any serious participation in educational planning and decision-making. The result is not only a lower stake among students in later implementation than would otherwise be the case but also the neglect of a potentially useful source of insight, creativity, and innovation.

Second, students are generally excluded from the exercise of authority in the school and instead are subjected to outside control by teachers and administrators. Under these conditions, it is small wonder that the school fails to develop the active identification and support of so many students.

Some research has shown that many teachers favor greater involvement of pupils in the formulation and enforcement of school rules. A recent study by Vinter and Sarri of five midwestern secondary schools indicates that on the average about two out of ten teachers say students are involved "quite a bit" or "a great deal" in the establishment of school regulations regarding student conduct, while about half the teachers think students *should* have that much influence.[107] Similarly, less than one of ten teachers

---

[106]This is the conclusion of a recent review of literature on social conditions for effective learning. See Sarane S. Boocock, "Toward A Sociology of Learning: A Selective Review of Existing Research," *Sociology of Education*, Vol. 39 (Winter, 1966), pp. 1–45.

[107]We wish to thank Robert D. Vinter and Rosemary C. Sarri of the University of Michigan School of Social Work for permission to cite these and subsequent unpublished data from the project, Deviancy in the Public Schools. The project was supported by a curriculum development grant from the Office of Juvenile Delinquency and Youth Development, Welfare Administration, United States Department of Health, Education, and Welfare in cooperation with the President's Committee on Juvenile Delinquency and Youth Crime.

says students are involved to that degree in the enforcement of school regulations pertaining to student conduct, but about four of ten think they should have "quite a bit" or "a great deal" of involvement.

Third, the very teaching-learning structure itself is such that active involvement of students is minimal. They usually have little or no choice of subjects, must endure endless hours of passive rather than active participation in classroom activities, and are given little chance to help or be helped by classmates, or to apply what they learn.

In all these respects we suggest that youth are essentially excluded and locked out of the educational enterprise, one result of which is a deterioration of commitment to educational norms and goals. Under these conditions the delinquent alternative becomes increasingly attractive to some youth.

Although there is no systematic evidence that we know of to support us, we believe this set of school conditions contributes both to lower class and middle class delinquency. Such exclusion and subordination is probably greatest in lower income schools, since students served there are especially likely to be seen as too incompetent and irresponsible to be given a share in the operation of the school. At the same time, the suburban school fails to keep hold of some students because of this same problem. As one of Karacki and Toby's Dukes explained:

> I guess I tried until the eighth grade. I started slumping then. Other things were more important to me, I guess, I started hanging around [the park] at night. . . . I guess I was kinda wild when I was a freshman and sophomore. Things seemed so far away I didn't care.[108]

This problem of exclusion is best seen as part of the larger problem of prolonged dependence and subordination felt by most adolescents in our society.

> Given the adolescent stage of life when youth are unsure of themselves and their significance in the social order, and given a society that belittles the ideas of youth, rejects their innovations, and is intolerant of their participation, conditions are ripe for non-commitment to the goals of the existing society, identity confusion, and in general, the alienation of youth from the larger social system which does not accept them and sometimes rejects its adolescence. Hostile withdrawal and violent aggression are two kinds of delinquent responses typically exhibited by alienated youth uncommitted to a society, and therefore, uncontrolled by its values.[109]

---

[108] Larry Karacki and Jackson Toby, "The Uncommitted Adolescent: Candidate for Gang Socialization," *Sociological Inquiry,* Vol. 32 (Spring, 1962), p. 110.

[109] Charles V. Willie, "Antisocial Behavior Among Disadvantaged Youth: Some Observations on Prevention for Teachers," *Journal of Negro Education,* XXXIII (Spring, 1964), p. 178.

As Yablonsky has observed, the "beat" subculture with its parallel emphasis on rejection of traditional commitments partly arises out of the same roots as delinquency.[110] We believe that the pervasiveness of adolescent exclusion in American life is all the more reason to give increasing attention to the creation of means that will foster progressive development of responsibility, independence, and commitment through allowing greater involvement in the adult world.

Two additional implications for change, one long-term and one short-term, follow from what has been said about lack of commitment and the social conditions producing it. First, we contend that the traditional emphasis on individualism in this country, while responsible for much of our growth and vitality, has at the same time been responsible for a pervasive middle class emphasis on exclusion of certain groups from full participation and opportunity: Negroes; the poverty stricken; people in trouble, including adult criminals and ex-criminals, delinquents, and deviants in school; and adolescents in general. We further contend that the middle class school is the primary agent for perpetuating this "exclusion orientation." Therefore, we believe a major re-orientation of the values taught in those schools is essential. Not only must exclusion of adolescents in general and deviants in particular be greatly lessened, but the middle class school must cease producing students who grow into "exclusion oriented" adults. We further believe the schools should take the lead in re-educating parents themselves in this respect. Thus, the school would become an active agent in change and alleviation of social problems, rather than a passive and at times irrelevant institution.

Second, it is frequently argued that delinquency is fundamentally rooted in lack of respect among today's youth for law and order and that one way to develop such respect is to instruct them about what the laws of the community are and why they should be obeyed. Our position on the matter of lack of respect for law and order is a less simplistic one than this. We grant that almost by definition delinquents do exhibit disrespect and disdain for laws and police. However, the thrust of our argument should have made clear that this lack of respect is not an attitude that appears in the minds of youth out of nowhere. Rather there are certain forces—some of them in the school, including unending subordination—surrounding youth that combine to produce opposition, resistance, and disrespect. Too often attribution of delinquency to lack of respect for law and order is simply another way of deflecting attention away from conditions in the schools and the larger society that generate that attitude in the first place.

At the same time, we recognize that one small way of developing a commitment to law-abiding behavior, especially among high delinquency-

---

[110] Lewis Yablonsky, *The Violent Gang*. New York: Macmillan, 1962.

risk populations of youth, may be effective instruction in school about the nature of and rationale behind the legal system, about the character of law enforcement machinery, and about ways in which the legal system can be used as a means for realizing one's own interest. Theoretically, these issues are covered in junior and senior high school civics courses. In practice, however, such classes most often deal in the most formal and superficial way with "blueprints," paper definitions, and ideal objectives and operation of the legal and law enforcement systems. Later in the chapter we will propose modifications in the secondary school curriculum that will include forthright and relevant instruction about the legal and law enforcement systems that may help to foster respect for law and order, as well as to develop a more enlightened citizenry generally. Such instruction must have immediate relevance and meaning and must actively engage students in exploration of pertinent issues. Otherwise, it is likely to degenerate into tasteless and ineffectual moralizing.

Misbehavior in School, School Sanctions, and Delinquency

Earlier we contended that the chances that students who get into trouble in school will, on one hand, continue such behavior and even widen it to include delinquency in the community, or, on the other hand, that they will conform to school standards in the future and not become delinquent depend upon the character and effects of the schools' responses to the initial behavior. Just as responses of the school to academic failure may or may not effectively break into the deepening cycle of frustration, alienation, and rebellion, so responses to misconduct may have similar effects.

We contend that school responses to misbehavior often tend to intensify rather than weaken forces toward delinquency. In order to identify some of the ways in which this occurs, we will briefly examine the structure that exists in most schools for dealing with students in trouble, then discuss some of its weaknesses and adverse effects. For want of a better name we will refer to this structure as the "Behavior Control System."

Behavior Control Systems in the Schools

Any discussion of ways the school handles behavior problems must begin with the classroom teacher, since she is the one on "the firing line," so to speak, who first encounters various forms of rule violations to which she must respond. If a student is aggressive, disruptive, or disrespectful, there are several ways in which the teacher may react, depending on such things as her own style of teaching, the school, the incident, the grade level, and the pupil. She may, for example, (1) ignore the problem; (2) use verbal sanctions of one kind or another, including public reprimand, a lecture, public humiliation, persuasion, or a threat of more serious sanctions in the future; (3) withdraw informal and minor privileges in the classroom; (4) use physical punishment; (5) mobilize collective influence of other students in generating support for conforming behavior; (6) move the student's seat or temporarily send him to a corner; (7) send him to the hall for a short time; (8) lower his grade for the day or the marking period; (9) call his parents in for a conference about his behavior; (10) permanently expel him from her class; (11) refer him to a counselor, to a "special service" person such as a social worker or a school psychologist, to a vice-principal, or to the principal.

The role of counselor tends to vary considerably from one school system to the next and, as a result, particular counselors may play varying parts in the school's reaction to misbehaving students. In some systems, they are restricted to academic counseling and occupational guidance. In others, they carry on these activities, but are also available to counsel students with "personality," "adjustment" or other individual problems, who have been referred by teachers or who have sought the counselor's assistance on his or her own. Some school systems have explicit policies of not involving counselors in disciplining or sanctioning, the rationale being that these activities inhibit effective guidance and counseling. Others, however, rely heavily on counselors to mete out sanctions to students who have violated school rules pertaining to attendance, punctuality, dress, smoking, cars, classroom conduct, or hall behavior.

Particular counselors may become involved in the school's reaction to behavior problems in a number of alternative ways, depending on some of the same factors influencing teacher responses, as well as on the school definition of the counselor role. He may, for instance, (1) use counseling techniques to try to influence the student's future attitudes and conduct; (2) call in parents for a conference; (3) work with the teacher involved in hopes of modifying her discipline techniques or increasing her understanding of the child's behavior; (4) remove the student from a class temporarily or permanently and reassign him to another; (5) assign the student to a special track or classroom for "problem students" or students who are "emotionally disturbed"; (6) suspend the student; (7) refer him to a special service person for help, or to a vice-principal or principal for further discipline.

In many systems, each school has a vice-principal whose total or partial responsibility includes disciplining students who misbehave. The alternatives open to him are generally the same ones open to counselors as outlined above. Principals generally have final authority in relation to the treatment of behavior problems, though they may be involved in such matters in varying degrees, depending on the level and size of the school, the school system's policy for principals, the principal's individual definition of his job, and the nature of the rest of the "coping system" in the school. In many high schools, the principal only becomes involved in extreme or difficult cases, although at the elementary level they are likely to be more frequently involved.

In addition, most school systems have "pupil personnel" or "special service" staff who are charged with the special responsibility of handling students who are "emotionally disturbed," "upset," or "maladjusted." Such a staff may include a wide variety of specialists, but social workers and school psychologists are likely to be those most directly concerned with students in trouble. They are likely to serve several schools out of a centralized office, though they sometimes are assigned to a particular school. In some instances, they may be entirely responsible to their superior in the central office, while in others they may be mainly responsible to a particular principal or number of principals.

Special service personnel generally receive referrals of students from teachers, counselors, vice-principals, or principals and employ a variety of techniques or approaches for attempting to alleviate deviant behavior in the future, depending mainly on the professional training and commitment of the particular staff person. Such techniques may range from individual therapy or counseling, to group therapy or counseling, to home visits, to conferences with teachers. The objective generally is to change the student's personality or attitudes through direct influence of one kind or another, though attempts may also be made to alter conditions in the home or classroom that affect his attitudes or behavior.

In some schools, special teachers and classes exist for students who are persistent violators of school regulations and whose continued presence in normal classrooms is thought to disrupt the learning process for other children. Such teachers are generally forced to spend most of their time keeping control, though attempts may be made to alleviate personal or academic problems of individual students. Since such students are generally doing inferior or failing academic work and since resources are usually limited, the pace of instruction is usually slow.

Mention must also be made of the truant officer who is charged with tracing down and returning truant students and increasingly with doing some amount of individual counseling or consulting with parents.

The internal "coping system," which we have seen may vary considerably, links up with various external organizations which also deal with children and youth who are in trouble or are otherwise defined as in need of special attention. These organizations include the police, the juvenile court, and various social and psychological agencies and clinics.

We believe this outline is in general an accurate description of the structure of behavior control systems and of the types of responses invoked when students violate school rules, although details vary from one community to another. While we do not question the dedication or zeal of those in the schools who must seek to control and reduce deviant behavior within this structure, we believe there are fundamental defects and shortcomings in the structure itself that substantially restrict the effectiveness of the school in alleviating behavior problems. We hold, in fact, that certain features of these systems may inadvertently contribute to delinquency among students who are behavior problems in the school. In the following paragraphs we seek to identify some of these defects.

Weaknesses in Behavior Control Systems

Assumptions About Student Misbehavior. First, responses invoked by teachers or others are by and large based on the assumption that misbehavior results almost entirely from the motivation or deeper personality system of the child, or from defective family values and relationships. As a result, it is either assumed that the way to change such behavior is to direct sanctions, counseling, or therapy at the individual pupil himself; or that there is little the school can do as long as family conditions remain unaltered.

Illustrative evidence showing the pervasiveness of these beliefs comes from Vinter and Sarri's study of five Midwestern secondary schools.[111] Among their findings was that when teachers were asked "what factor contributes most to the problem of misbehavior in this school," over one-half responded "nature of the misbehaving students," slightly less than half responded "family values and relationships," while less than ten percent said "conditions and practices of the school." At the same time, they found that in four out of the five schools about two-thirds of the teachers expressed the belief that "most" or "all" students with academic or behavior difficulties "don't have enough incentive or don't care enough." In the fifth school this proportion went down to about one-half.

In view of these beliefs, it is not surprising that large numbers of teachers advocate student responses that are directed at the individual deviant, rather than at the school itself: from one-third to one-half of the

---

[111] Vinter and Sarri, unpublished data, *op. cit.*

teachers thought that one of the reasons for student misbehavior was that the deviants were not suspended often enough. This belief was strongest in a predominantly middle class school where misbehavior of students presumably interfered most with preparation of other students for college. At the same time, from 15 percent to 41 percent of teachers in the various schools indicated that "most" or "all" of students with academic behavior difficulties had "psychological or emotional problems." Acceptance of this belief helps account for the persistent call for more counseling and "clinical" staff—at the same time that conditions in the school or the classroom that help produce so-called "emotional problems" are almost entirely ignored.

Labelling of Deviant Behavior. We have taken the position that deviancy is a complex process through time involving behavior by individuals (pupils in this case), reactions by others (teachers, counselors, principals, and other pupils), effects of those reactions of the individual, and so forth. Further, we have contended that the likelihood that deviant behavior will be repeated and broadened or inhibited in the future is partly determined by the sequence of events during the labelling and sanctioning process. In this section, we suggest ways that the school itself inadvertently contributes to alienation, rejection, misbehavior, and delinquency—in its very attempt to do the opposite.

As we saw in the shop incident described earlier by the ex-delinquent, an alienating cycle is sometimes set in motion by school personnel themselves who arbitrarily or unpredictably enforce a rule which a student had no intention of violating. Moreover, other instances sometimes arise in which a teacher sometimes directly produces rule violations.

> . . . and it was the teacher's fault for not giving me a pass. You be walking down the hall, this man grabs you. You say, "what did you grab me for?" "Where is your pass?" "I ain't got no pass—I'm sick, I'm going to see the doctor." "Come with me." He takes you down to see the principal. The principal gives you a card this long, that wide and says "you are in tardy hall for three months."
>
> It was the teacher's fault for not giving you a pass. I said, "look teacher, I got a stomach ache. The grub I ate down stairs wasn't too good, you know, and can I go to the doctor." And she said, "Go ahead," to get you out of her class sometimes because she say, "you ain't interested anyway." She ships you on down there and she might forget to give you this little pass that you had to carry in the hall with you. And here you got to stay in the tardy hall for three months for something the teacher did. So, you know, I got sick of this and I said the devil with the whole school system.

Teachers and other school personnel may also "create" deviant behavior by basing their definitions of the acceptability of behavior on criteria other than the character of the act and its place in immediate events. For example, the clothes that a student wears, the way he combs his hair, who his friends are, what his reputation is among other teachers, whether he is Negro or white—all these factors are quite irrelevant to the relation of an act to a school or classroom rule, but they are likely to be highly crucial in determining whether or not that act is labelled as unacceptable and the individual sanctioned in one way or another. Responses to questionnaires and interviews by boys in the schools studied by Vinter and Sarri indicate that most of them are aware of these contingencies in teacher reactions and are highly sensitive to what they feel are unfair perceptions and judgments.[112] We suggest that this may often be a first step in progressive "separation" of school from pupil.

This problem is often aggravated further by the fact that many schools unknowingly support formal and informal "mechanisms" whereby negative reputations of students are diffused among other staff. All too often the teachers' lounge or coffee room is the burying ground for students' success chances, as teachers openly inform each other about students "to watch out for," or conform each other's negative assessments of so and so's attitude or conduct. Vinter and Sarri found that from one-fourth to two-thirds of teachers in the various schools indicated that they hear "quite a bit" or "a great deal" informally from teachers or other members of the staff about the conduct or reputation of their students.[113] The smaller the school, the greater the exchange of such information. The damage may be severe.

> When I got in trouble one day in shop, the shop teacher went down to the English teacher—"pass the word around, this boy is not coming to school for anything." When I come into class, the teachers ask me, "what did you come here for." I said, "I'm here for the same reason all the other students come here." "No you don't, you don't belong here. You go out. You go on downstairs to the office. You go down there and sit." Next period I go to another class—they say the same thing. Day after day. I stayed though. I didn't drop out. I had stayed in school too long to drop out.

More formal mechanisms for broadcasting reputations sometimes exist as well. For example, some schools regularly circulate lists to teachers of students who have been officially sanctioned in one way or another. Moreover, most schools keep official files on students which follow—or precede—

---

[112] *Ibid.*
[113] *Ibid.*

them from year to year and school to school. They are usually accessible
to all staff members, and are often read early in the year—sometimes before
the student has ever appeared on the scene. If a student has a past record
of "trouble" it is highly likely that new teachers will use such information
to anticipate trouble in the future, or to confirm suspicions. As Vinter and
Sarri have reported, students themselves often see the process operate.

> When you get in trouble, they never let up on you. They keep calling you
> in. Like you get caught for smoking and they suspend you. Then they
> watch out for you so they can catch you again.
>
> I have a bad reputation here. Last year in junior high I gave teachers a lot
> of trouble and I guess the record follows everywhere I go. Teachers here
> [in high school] have the record. They have to find out about all the kids.[114]

In some San Francisco schools, steps have been taken to eliminate
this formal mechanism of "reputation diffusion" by destroying all student
records of conduct every two or three years and by making certain that no
records are passed from one school to the next as the student's career
progresses.

Once a teacher or another staff member decides that an act is unacceptable, he enters into a "labelling ceremony" in which the student is
defined as deviant. Such ceremonies are not infrequent, of course, but go on
continually in classrooms, halls, and offices. The labelling act may vary in
at least two ways. It may be more or less degrading, demeaning, and
humiliating; and it may be more or less public or private. We suggest that
schools frequently increase rather than decrease students' disengagement
and rejection by making the labelling ceremony both degrading and public.
The following incident in a New York school, which may be all too typical
and which also illustrates labelling of an "innocent" act as deviant, suggests
that degradation and public humiliation tend to go together.

> Turning to the assembled class the teacher interrogates them as follows:
> "Class, here is a boy who was running in the shop this morning and hit a
> piece of machinery and cut the palm of his hand so deeply that they had to
> take him to the hospital and have stitches put in it. Now whose fault is it
> if a boy cuts his hand when he is running in the shop—where he shouldn't
> run?" In chorus, the class responds "His" as the boy leaves with his forms
> in hand.[115]

---

[114]Robert D. Vinter and Rosemary C. Sarri, "Malperformance in the Public
School: A Group Work Approach," *Social Work*, Vol. 10 (January, 1965), p. 10.

[115]Elizabeth Eddy, *Walk the White Line*. Garden City: Doubleday Anchor,
1967. ©1967 by Elizabeth M. Eddy. Reprinted with permission of the publisher.

One of the outcomes of incidents such as this one is that the student's reputation suffers in the eyes of other pupils. Another result is more private: the personal sense that one is different, or "an outsider." The damage from public and degrading labelling ceremonies for the individual's self-definition is vividly conveyed in the following remarks to us by another ex-delinquent.

(Did you feel like a hoodlum?) Then I did. And there were a couple of times I got in a little trouble and the police came and got me. (In the school?) Yeah, they came in the school and got me. Teachers say, "take that hoodlum out of here. He ain't nothing but trouble—he so and so this and he so and so that." I got fed up with the crap. (Did you feel like a hoodlum?) Well, then I did after the day I got branded a hoodlum. I said I'm going to live up to the name so I became a hoodlum.

I used to feel like I was a hoodlum when they put the label on me. You try to back it up.

I could see them trying to help you along instead of branding you with a name. It's no good. It makes a guy feel bad. Everything that happens, she brings it up to the whole class. You know, the class will be looking at you and everything. You feel funny inside. You feel embarrassed. Let's say they are forty or forty-five students in there. Well, the guys you don't feel too bad about. When the girls are there you crouch down a little. And the girls look at you like you are dirt—it makes you feel bad inside. No guy—no girl either—likes to be embarrassed.

Along with adverse effects mentioned earlier of being placed in a basic section or track, such students may also find themselves "marked" as well. The following not only illustrates how this sometimes happens, but also highlights again that reputations easily become public knowledge—to affect later perceptions and judgments by others.

Do you know what you get mostly in basic sections—you get lectures. You get lectured on your hoodlum life. (Doesn't that do you any good?) What you mean? That'll do you some good if you want to be a hoodlum all your life. You know, the teacher used to ask us "I'm curious. I want to know what each of you all know—just out of the street—what do you know. I don't want to know nothing about classes—nothing about math, English, nothing like that, but what you know in the streets. What you know as a hoodlum." Right there, you know—she says "what you know as a hoodlum?" So you're going to tell her what you know. "Well, I know how to take a twelve volt battery and hook it up to burglar alarm systems and burn it out—then break the window and go inside; and how to get away from the police. I know how to yoke somebody and put 'em to sleep and get their money, or take their clothes. I know how to beat somebody beside the head." This is what you get, this is what I used to listen to when I was in school. Now why should I stay in school? Give me one good reason?

(You mean the guys were saying those things in front of the class?)

Yeah, they used to tell the teachers and the rest of the class what they used to do. The girls used to tell what they used to do. And then the next time you go into the next class, this teacher done told that teacher about each student. If the teacher is a female, she's nervous, she's worried. "I don't want him in my class." Or she'd go to the principal "look, can you transfer him to section F–2, cause he looks like he's going to give me trouble."

Up to now, we have emphasized that incidents such as these tend to adversely affect pupils' status and reputation in the eyes of others. The other side of the coin, however, is that as the individual finds himself seen more and more negatively by teachers and other students, he is likely to experience a growing recognition that he has much in common with other students who have encountered similar or more serious problems and who feel the same way about themselves and the school. The frequent result is the gradual emergence of a deviant peer group that comes to establish new standards of conduct that call for open opposition to and flouting of school demands and rules. Such growing resentment and rejection sometimes widens into broader patterns of rebellion against community standards as well, resulting in delinquency.

School Responses to Misconduct. In our description of behavior control systems, we identified a wide range of alternative responses available to teachers and others in the school once an act has been defined as unacceptable. In this section we seek to identify ways in which some of these responses serve to intensify rather than weaken deviant tendencies.

Carl Werthman has noted that:

> . . . the school difficulties of these [delinquent] boys occur only in some classes and not in others. Good and bad students alike are consistently able to get through half or more of their classes without friction. It is only in particular classes with particular teachers that incidents leading to suspension flare up . . .[116]

This suggests that there may be something about the teacher and the classroom situation he creates that has as much to do with misbehavior as the student's own motivation. If this is true, the problem arises of identifying some of the effects of different teacher responses to earlier trouble.

Students behave in a variety of ways in the classroom. Some time is spent in concentrated reading, writing, or listening; other time is spent in

---

[116]Carl Werthman, "The Function of Social Definitions in the Development of Delinquent Careers," paper prepared for the President's Commission on Law Enforcement and Administration of Justice (August, 1966), p. 28.

passive idleness and mind wandering. Still other parts of class time are taken up with behavior that is not directly related to the teaching-learning process. "If they are tired, they sleep; if they are bored, they read comic books; if they are energetic, they may feel like 'having fun'."[117] At other times they may talk to their neighbors, write notes, eat, or carve on the desk. For example:

> If I'm bored, then I have to do something to make it exciting. First, second and third ain't too bad because I get me two comic books and they last three periods. (You read comic books for the first three periods?) Yeah. See, in my first three periods I got typing, English, and some kind of thing—social studies I think. In them three periods I read comic books, and the next three periods I got shop and I got gym and then I got that math. Them last three periods I don't read comic books because I only bring two, and they only last three periods.
> Friday we had a substitute in class named Mr. Fox, and I had a headache so I went to sleep. (Why were you sleeping? Were you out late the night before?) No, I wasn't. I just had a headache. They wasn't doing nothing but talking about this and that. Sally and John, and I just went to sleep. The class wasn't doing nothing but fussing, fooling around talking, so I went to sleep.[118]

Once a teacher is aware that students are engaged in activities unrelated to "teaching and learning," he may respond in one of several ways. One way is "to overlook whatever other activities besides 'learning' are taking place and decide to 'teach' those people who show signs of wanting to learn. In these classes, there is rarely 'trouble.' "[119]

> (Have you ever had any good teachers, Ray?) Yeah, Mr. F, and Mr. T. in junior high school. (What made them good?) They just help you, you know. They didn't want you always working all the time. As long as you keep your voices down, you know, and don't be talking out loud and hollering, you could go on and talk in groups and have a good time. (They let you have a good time. Did they flunk you?) Yeah, they flunked me. But I mean it was my fault too because they gave me all the breaks, you know. Anything I asked for, they gonna give me a break. But, you know, I just never do right anyway.[120]

---

[117] *Ibid.*, p. 32.
[118] *Ibid.*, pp. 28–29.
[119] *Ibid.*, p. 29.
[120] *Ibid.*, p. 29.

This kind of response, which essentially represents a surrender, is often reported by observers in ghetto schools, though it is likely to be found in "slow" sections in middle class schools as well. The consequence for the individual may not be as apparent in the short-run as in the long-run, when his growing academic deficiencies accumulate.

As Werthman notes, a short-run danger in ignoring misbehaving pupils is that they sometimes want to re-enter the teacher-learning process but find the door closed.

> Like this one stud, man, he don't try to help us at all. He just goes on rapping (talking) to the poopbutts (squares), and when we ask a question he don't even pay no attention. I don't think that is fair. We were trying to learn just like anybody else. (All the time?) Well, sometimes.[121]

Another form of surrender, which is also likely to provide an immediate solution to the control problem but to have detrimental effects in the long-run, is teacher agreement to participate in activities that are usually considered unacceptable. "Activities such as talking to friends, having 'fun' or 'horsing around' then become 'normal' events that go on at different times in the same room. In these classrooms also there is rarely 'trouble.' "[122]

> Like my Civics teacher, he understands all the students. He knows we like to play. Like, you know, he jokes with us for about the first 15 minutes and then, you know, everybody gets settled down and then they want to do some work. He got a good sense of humor and he understands.[123]

In giving in, the teacher is not only condoning behavior that may be antithetical to socialization aims of the school, but he is surrendering time from academic instruction as well. "Lack of trouble" may be more pleasant in the sense that teacher-student confrontations are avoided, but in the long-run probably does the student more harm than good.

When confronted with activities other than learning, other teachers often feel not only that the educational process is being disrupted, but that their personal authority is being challenged. This in turn often leads to the belief by the teachers that "trust" is no longer warranted. In such instances, the teacher is likely to convey his alarm at being challenged by beginning to issue "commands" which in turn is clear indication to misbehaving students that they are no longer being trusted. At the same time, they are likely to view these commands as infringements on their rights to autonomy. Thus, a "character contest" arises:

---

[121]*Ibid.*, p. 30.
[122]*Ibid.*, p. 30.
[123]*Ibid.*, p. 30.

The teachers that get into trouble, they just keep pounding. You *do* this! You know, they ain't gonna ask you nice. You just do this or else, you know I'm going to kick you out of school. All that old foul action. Like in math class, this teacher always hollers. He always raises his voice and hollers, "Do this work!" All that old crap. Everybody just looks at him. Don't say crap and just sit down, talk, wait around, you know.[124]

This breakdown of trust by teachers may begin the very first day of class. That is, there are some teachers whose previous experiences or beliefs lead them to define their students in general as "untrustworthy" from the beginning and who initiate their exchanges with the class by communicating this lack of trust. Thus, a situation of deepening teacher-student estrangement may be set in motion from the beginning. This too may feed into a progressive withdrawal of commitment by the student to the school and what it stands for.

It is important to point out that there are variations among teachers in the way they enter into these exchanges and in their effects on students. For example, students who have been in trouble before will frequently begin a new class by "feeling a teacher out." After a rule has been purposely violated, the student may carefully size up the teacher's reaction.

If the teacher responds to this move by becoming either angry or afraid, the boys know that they are dealing with someone who is either "tough," "smart," or "lame." On the other hand, if the teacher responds by acknowledging the right while insisting that rules still be obeyed, he is considered "straight."[125]

Subsequent exchanges also vary.

If the request to stop is made politely, their own sense of honor is not offended and they are likely to cease whatever they are doing. If the teacher's retort is derogatory, however, the boys are likely to view the teacher's defense of his rights to authority as a violation of their own rights to autonomy and thus the character contest is on.[126]

These illustrations underscore the importance of individual teachers' attitudes and styles in coping with difficult students in class. Past research indicates that such students do not seem to respond as well, in terms of attitudes, subsequent behavior, and academic performance, to a great deal of freedom as they do to firm controls that are administered with respect, honesty, and consistency.[127] One of the great needs in the training of new teachers is more complete development of insights and skills in classroom control.

---

[124] *Ibid.*, p. 31.

[125] *Ibid.*, p. 31.

[126] *Ibid.*, p. 33.

[127] *Ibid.*,; also Boocock, *op. cit.*

In an earlier part of the paper, we suggested that the behavior control system tends to be organized around the principle that students who get into trouble should be excluded from and denied access to conventional activities and opportunities. The assumption presumably underlying this principle is two-fold: one, the instructional process can proceed better if troublesome students are removed; and two, denial of opportunities, rewards, and activities that are highly valued serve as a negative sanction for inducing the deviant to change his ways.

Implementation of this principle usually begins in the classroom itself. That is, another alternative response open to the teacher is to remove the student from his class either temporarily or permanently. As we saw in several of the quotes, a student may be sent to the office for a short time or removed for the rest of the year. The Vinter and Sarri research shows that from one-third to nearly two-thirds of teachers in the schools in their sample said that they "frequently" or "very frequently" make the "student aware that he will be sent out of class" if misbehavior is repeated.[128] In terms of responses to particular kinds of infractions, they found that in one high school 74 percent of the teachers said they would send a student to the office if he "had a cigarette behind his ear during class," while in another high school 79 percent reported that they would do the same thing if a student were "five minutes late for class without a pass or a good excuse."

Another example of a response which closes off opportunities is the incorporation of deviant behavior into academic grades. In this instance, the student is essentially denied access to scholastic rewards for non-scholastic behavior. Vinter and Sarri found that on the average about two-thirds of the teachers in their sample reported that they take the "student's conduct in class" into account in giving grades.[129] In addition to being graded down, the student is likely to be denied minor but meaningful privileges by the teacher.

There is also a wide range of sanctions outside the classroom that tend to push away, exclude, and deny opportunity for further involvement in the main stream of the educational process. One of these is assignment of troublesome students to special classrooms. As we have pointed out several times, this generally represents a final stage in the school's surrender, since basic sections tend to be custodial at best and degrading and impossible at worst. The teacher's efforts are generally limited to maintaining control and the instruction that does take place is at a very restricted level and pace.

Recent experience in a Virginia school clearly shows that permanent separation of misbehaving students has more adverse than positive outcomes even when services are increased. Despite the fact that for a two-year period

---

[128] Vinter and Sarri, unpublished data, *op. cit.*
[129] *Ibid.*

93 students with academic and behavior problems were taught by specially selected teachers who gave the children individualized instruction, the outcomes were overwhelmingly negative. According to the report, the pupils tended to:

> ... multiply their unhealthy attitudes when the less motivated were placed together in one class. ... Potential dropouts did not improve their self-images as a result of being in a group homogeneous in terms of social and mental abilities. Profane and vulgar language became the accepted language and antisocial behavior a thing to boast about.[130]

Another example of an exclusion-oriented sanction is denial of opportunity to participate in student activities or special programs. For example, athletic eligibility is sometimes contingent on proper behavior in and around school as well as on maintenance of a certain scholastic average. In one of the schools studied by Vinter and Sarri, students could no longer remain on a cheerleading squad when their grades fell below C or when they misbehaved in school.[131] In another school, several high school students met with a junior high school principal in an attempt to offer suggestions for modifications in the school's program for students in trouble. The principal later remarked to one of the researchers that after the meeting he learned that two of the students had been in trouble before in school and in the community—and that he was going to be absolutely certain they were not included in any future meetings. In a Philadelphia high school, potential dropouts were automatically dropped from a "model" work study program if the school learned of any law violations in the community.[132] In each of these cases, the very students who needed most to be engaged were the ones who were excluded and pushed out.

Suspension and expulsion practices represent perhaps the most serious instances of exclusion.

> And in the last years of high school, the boy either graduates or departs, usually at the school's request. For most of these years, the school regards him as hopeless, and they suspend him regularly for his activities in the presence of other boys as well as for his attitude toward the authority of the school itself.[133]

In at least one of the high schools studied by Vinter and Sarri, each suspension was automatically accompanied by a one-third drop in the student's

---

[130] *Washington Post* (August 24, 1966), p. 8.
[131] Vinter and Sarri, unpublished data, *op. cit.*
[132] Personal communication from Marvin Wolfgang.
[133] Werthman, *op. cit.*, p. 38.

grade for that term and by failing marks for any assignments on the days that were missed.

It should be clear from this analysis, then, that existing machinery in public education for responding to students in trouble serves mainly to push away, to alienate, to cut off opportunity for future achievement and engagement in legitimate activities in and out of school. While counseling, social work, and psychological treatment are not to be discounted, they are far less significant in the school's response to deviants—including delinquents—than the routine practices of isolation from the classroom, assignment to a special classroom or track, suspension, intentional or unintentional withdrawal of privileges, expulsion, and so forth—all of which serve to block future opportunities for pupils to become enmeshed in the legitimate system.

Clearly, "the dropout problem" more accurately should be called "the forceout problem." Practices such as these represent an attitude of defeat by school personnel, though such defeat is hidden behind figures of college attendance. As students are pushed out rather than pulled back into the educational process, the legitimate commitment of which we have spoken becomes less and less attractive—or acceptable—and therefore delinquency becomes more and more attractive and likely.

This process of exclusion rather than reintegration partly results from inadequate preparation of teachers for dealing with problem children, especially in slum schools. But it also results from the creation and reliance upon a negative, punitive, and exclusion-oriented machinery for reacting to students in trouble.

There should be no question, then, of the need to completely reassess conceptions and practices in the school for dealing with pre-delinquent and delinquent youth and to devise new means for responding in ways that will produce reinvolvement and recommitment of students who have begun to head down the wrong path toward adulthood. If the educational system is to equip a maximum number of individuals for responsible adulthood, it must organize itself and do everything in its power to "bring back" students in trouble, to reintegrate and re-engage them in the process of education. To the extent that it fails to do this, the educational system fails to fulfill its mandate to produce a new generation of developed, trained, and responsible adults.

Efforts must be made to devise new responses that serve to bind the individual into the system and to reward him for achievement and conformity. We contend that such responses must be primarily geared to channeling deviant youth into stepped-up academic and work-study programs, as well as into opportunities for teaching younger students or helping formulate and enforce school rules of conduct. This approach is likely to be more effective than setting students off in separate programs or classes, as shown by the Virginia experience.

School Responsibility for Dropouts and Other Out-of-School Youth. As we noted earlier, public school responsibility for youth generally terminates in this country when a student leaves school either through graduation or early exit. We also noted that for the minority who go to college, this presents few problems, since the college takes over the "protective" or "guidance" function during the ensuing years of attendance. For the majority of out-of-school youth, however, this has serious consequences, since there are no agencies to take over the task of further preparing or guiding them into relatively permanent, responsible adult positions, especially in terms of work. Yet according to a recent Census report, 604,000 persons between 16 and 24 had dropped out of school during the 12 months prior to October, 1964.[134] While the overall dropout rate is steadily declining, the 1960 Census showed that 18 percent of all white youth and 27 percent of all non-white youth ages 16–17 were not enrolled in school.[135] We contend that this lack of attention to occupational placement partly accounts for the following unemployment rates in 1964 for out-of-school youth ages 16–17: white females, 17 percent; non-white females, 37 percent; white males, 16 percent; non-white males, 26 percent.[136] High school dropouts are especially affected, as reflected in the fact that in 1963, 32 percent of all high school dropouts between 16 and 24 were unemployed, compared with 18 percent of all high school graduates in that age group.[137]

Both immediate unemployment and the lack of a better prospect in the future almost certainly help to some extent account for the higher delinquency rates of dropouts. In one study, dropouts were reported to have ten times higher delinquency rates than high school graduates.

Especially in view of accelerating changes in the world of work that lead to the necessity for greater and greater training, we contend that the schools must modify traditional conceptions of their responsibility for youth to include responsibility for out-of-school youth until, say, age 21. Of particular relevance in delinquency prevention is the need to develop special means for "reaching out" to draw dropouts back into some part of the educational system. We believe this extension of responsibility should also cover community behavior of out-of-school youth. If a dropout gets into trouble with the law, the school ought to be partly accountable and should seek to do what it can to reduce the chances of recidivism by re-integrating him into the educational system and providing experiences and rewards that will "hold" him to the legitimate system.

---

[134] *School Enrollment: October, 1964, Current Population Reports, Population Reports, Population Characteristics.* Series P–20, No. 148, February 8, 1966, p. 1.

[135] Bureau of the Census, 1960.

[136] A Report on Manpower Requirements, Resources, Utilization and Training, United States Department of Labor (March, 1966), p. 168.

[137] *Ibid.*, p. 188.

Conflict of Professional Perspectives. A recurrent problem facing the school is to coordinate and articulate the perspectives and actions of various professionals who deal with pupils in trouble.[138] The psychologist, the speech therapist, the social worker, the attendance officer, the counselor, the principal and the classroom teacher all tend to view the problems of students, education, and misbehavior from different perspectives. Hence, they seek out different types of information and follow varying courses of action. The result is frequent "atomization" of the school's response to students in trouble.

Segregation or separation of the activities of ancillary personnel from the activities of classroom teachers and other personnel directly concerned with educating students is especially problematic. Either overt conflict occurs between "clinical" and "educational" perspectives, or activities are simply not relevant to each other.

Conditions must be established, therefore, which ensure a closer connection of special service and counseling programs with primary educational activities in the school. New mechanisms must be developed for making various activities mutually supportive and complementary rather than conflicting or detached from each other.

Coordination of School and Community Responses to Youth in Trouble. In our description of the structure of the school's behavior control system, we noted that it links up in various ways with external agencies that deal with children and youth in trouble. It is increasingly recognized that the effectiveness of both school and community practices is hampered by lack of coordination and articulation of the various activities, approaches, and perspectives. As Harry Passow has noted:

> The duplication of effort, overlapping of services, lack of coordination, and failure to share information continue to plague various social and welfare agencies [serving youth] in many a community . . .[139]

One part of this problem is mutual lack of awareness of what other agencies are doing in handling particular pupils. The result is not only lack of a coherent approach for alleviating problems but frequent overlap, dupli-

---

[138] Ideas in this section, and in others cited below, were first developed in a paper by Eugene Litwak, Frank M. Maple, Henry J. Meyer, Jack Rothman, Rosemary C. Sarri, Walter E. Schafer, and Robert D. Vinter, in "A Design for Utilization of Special Services in the Detroit Public Schools." Ann Arbor, Michigan: University of Michigan School of Social Work (mimeographed), 1965.

[139] Passow, in Passow, *op. cit.*, p. 350. © 1963 by Teachers College, Columbia University. Reprinted with permission of the publisher.

cation, and actual conflict between school responses and responses of other agencies. At best, various responses may be irrelevant to each other, and at worst, they may offset potential positive effects of each other or even combine to aggravate tendencies toward delinquency. One example of inadequate linkage is the absence of mechanisms within the school for re-integrating delinquents into the educational process after they have returned from correction institutions or detention homes.

Another defect—which is another instance of the school's "exclusion principle"—is that responsibilities for pupils in trouble often tend to get shunted off from the school to other youth serving agencies. This takes a number of forms: truants are made wards of the juvenile court; the school abdicates responsibility for youth in correction institutions or detention homes; students who are defined as "emotionally disturbed" are turned over to psychological clinics; and city police are relied on to keep order not only on school grounds but sometimes inside the school itself—a practice that we believe is most antithetical to a climate of dignity, liberty, and trust.

We contend that these are all ways in which the school deflects attention from its own approaches and practices and represents an abdication of educationally relevant responsibilities. If the school is to become a truly effective and responsible agency for bringing youth into adulthood, we contend that its responsibility should be extended not only over a greater number of years, but over a greater range of activities as well, especially in relation to students in trouble. While we recognize the dangers in the creation of a single "monolithic" institution affecting youth, we believe that many educationally relevant activities are now pushed off to other agencies, with the consequence that responses to students in trouble tend to be segmented and uncoordinated.

Rigidity, Educational Lag, and Delinquency

At the beginning of the chapter, we noted that major economic and social changes have occurred in this country, to which the schools have not adequately adapted. As a result, there are serious lags of public education behind changes in other parts of society, one by-product of which is heightened delinquency. We contend that these lags result largely from rigidity, inflexibility, inadaptability within the educational establishment itself. It is not just that this is the way the public wants it, but that the schools are incapable of adapting or innovating. There are at least three reasons for this that lay within the educational system itself.

Educational Lag and Local Quality Control

First is the inability of schools and school systems to monitor themselves.[140] In contrast to business and industrial organizations, where evaluation of outcomes is partly constrained by the press of competition, the schools are almost completely lacking in quality control, assessment of current operating patterns, and assessment of outcomes. Schools simply do not confront themselves with the questions of how they are currently operating and how effective they are in meeting their objectives. As a result, the objectives themselves are usually not well formulated or understood. Moreover, the publics who support and "own" the schools are deprived of judging their achievements.

Even though schools already possess large amounts of information—about students' backgrounds, deficiences, skills, performance; about families; about teachers' evaluations of students; about staff performance and behavior; about who gives and who receives specialized services—this information is seldom used for "feedback" or evaluation purposes, simply because means have not been created for systematically collecting, analyzing, and using information.

Insofar as (1) lack of information about itself and its outcomes affects the ability of schools to adapt; (2) lack of adaptability contributes to failure, meaninglessness, and exclusion among students; and (3) these school experiences lead to delinquency; then a pressing need in long-run delinquency prevention is the establishment of a structure and machinery for gathering, processing, and evaluating information and for feeding that information into the decision-making process. As we will see, it is absolutely essential that such a structure be established in such a way as to avoid becoming simply another instrument for delay and for justification of the status quo, and to ensure its use as a positive means for educational innovation and change.

Educational Lag and Lack of Local Support
for Change

Second, inflexibility in education partly results from the failure of local school systems to encourage and support innovation and change.[141] Far more emphasis in the training, hiring, and rewarding of teachers and other personnel is placed on fitting well into the existing framework than on being inventive, imaginative, and change-oriented. We contend that this deficiency

---

[140] We are especially indebted to Robert Vinter for emphasizing this defect to the authors; Litwak, *et al., op. cit.*
[141] *Ibid.*

partly accounts for the inability of schools to adapt to external change, especially in the economy; to new increments in knowledge; and to new approaches and material.

A very critical need, then, is to anchor adaptability and innovation into the on-going pattern of operation of schools. Means and conditions must be developed for fostering individual and collective concern about change, for rewarding efforts to change, and for incorporating creative and innovative changes into the educational process. This is highly important with respect both to the school's machinery for responding to students in trouble and to the broader underlying conditions of teaching and learning that produce such youngsters.

Problems in Implementing Innovations

A closely related problem is that innovations emanating from universities, professional groups, and the federal government tend to be rapidly subverted by traditional conceptions and patterns of operation. Countless instances could be cited in which potentially fruitful programs and ideas get channeled into existing frameworks of operation. The greater the departure of innovations from current ways of doing things the greater the chances they will never be implemented successfully.

In our view, the fundamental difficulty is in the administrative ranks in education—ranging from middle to low levels in the U.S. Office of Education, to state departments of instruction, to local superintendents, curriculum coordinators, and principals. We believe that experience has shown that creative, imaginative, and forward ideas are not entirely absent from the top levels of the Office of Education, from the universities, and occasionally even from professional educational groups. At the same time, we believe it is valid to assume that local teachers are fundamentally interested in good education and are not entirely resistant to changes that will improve instruction. The difficulty, however, is that existing channels of authority, patterns of organization, and conceptions in the middle administrative ranks serve to insulate these latent sources for change at the top, outside the formal system, and at the "operational" level. While we can reasonably assume that middle level administrators are also fundamentally interested in good education, the constraints and pressures from inside and outside the educational system under which they must operate usually make it exceedingly difficult to depart from existing patterns of behavior.

We contend, therefore, that serious consideration must be given to the creation of a new framework for freeing innovative energies at the top and the bottom levels. We believe that when new ideas or programs are designed above or outside local school systems, new channels should be created for introducing these programs at the local level. Similarly, those at the top should be empowered—not with dictating local educational policies—but with creating the framework and making available resources that will permit local personnel to innovate and experiment. Finally, many attempts at change fail, not for want of imaginative thinking about how new programs would work, but because of insufficient attention to careful planning about how they can best be introduced into on-going patterns of operation.

We contend that these problems of resistance, inflexibility, and poor implementation represent perhaps the greatest difficulties of all in making the schools effective instruments for deterring delinquency—as well as for producing productive and responsible adults.

Summary and Recommendations

The foregoing analysis should have made three things clear. First, juvenile delinquency in this country is partly heightened by conditions in American public education. Second, these conditions are deeply anchored into prevailing conceptions and organization of the educational system. Third, proposals for preventing, reducing and controlling delinquency cannot refer only to programs that relate directly to control problems in the schools, but must reach deeply to the underlying and core conditions that help produce educational failure, perceived irrelevancy, lack of commitment, and exclusion—and, therefore, delinquency. To stop short at proposing such stop-gap and surface proposals as more counselors, more social workers, more truant officers, special classes for troublemakers, and tighter enforcement of attendance laws would simply be a failure to recognize the broader dimensions of the problem. Their implementation would have only the slightest effect on prevention of delinquency. Unless basic, radical, and immediate educational changes are made, delinquency will continue to increase—and will be accompanied by the spread of other social ills that stem from the same roots.

4

recommendations

The foregoing analysis should have made three things clear. First, juvenile delinquency in this country is partly heightened by conditions in American public education. Second, these conditions are deeply anchored into prevailing conceptions and organization of the educational system. Third, proposals for preventing, reducing, and controlling delinquency cannot refer only to programs that relate directly to control problems in the schools, but must reach deeply to the underlying and core conditions that help produce educational failure, perceived irrelevancy, lack of commitment, and exclusion—and, therefore, delinquency. To stop short at proposing such stopgap and surface proposals as more counselors, more social workers, more truant officers, special classes for troublemakers, and tighter enforcement of attendance laws would simply be a failure to recognize the broader dimensions of the problem. Their implementation would have only the slightest effect on prevention of delinquency. Unless basic, radical, and immediate educational changes are made, delinquency will continue to increase—and will be accompanied by the spread of other social ills that stem from the same roots.

Recommendations

It should be clear that comprehensive educational changes are required to make the schools an effective institutional force in the prevention of delinquency. Preventive measures must range from the pre-schooler to the late adolescent; from high risk categories of pupils to identified delinquents; from the basic teaching-learning structure to procedures for dealing with students in trouble; from the urban slum to the middle class suburb to the rural slum; from the local school classroom to the federal government. For these reasons, the recommendations that follow include a wide variety of programs, all of which we believe to be essential.

Because of the scope and deep roots of delinquency, our recommendations call for large-scale, institutional changes in the American educational system. Past experience in education, as well as in other institutions—a good deal of which has been negative experience—has clearly shown that two equally essential ingredients must enter into the planning of effective institutional change. One is careful conception and formulation of programs them-

This article was originally published as part of "Delinquency and the Schools" by Walter E. Schafer and Kenneth Polk in Task Force Report: Juvenile Delinquency and Youth Crime, *The President's Commission on Law Enforcement and the Administration of Justice (Washington, D.C.: U.S. Government Printing Office, 1967), pp. 258–304.*

selves, in terms of objectives, rationale, and operational blueprints. But just as important is the careful development of implementing strategies for introducing innovations into the ongoing system. Countless instances could be cited in which best laid plans for change have gone awry because of inadequate concern with and planning for implementation at the administrative and operational levels. Organizations and the people who man them seem to have an infinite capacity for advertently or inadvertently subverting attempts at change by retaining traditional conceptions and patterns of operation and by translating or diverting new funds or ideas into existing frameworks.

While we do not have the space here to proceed very far in making recommendations for either type of planning, we will give some attention to both problems. At the same time, we strongly urge that planners and decision makers who take up where we leave off give as much attention in their planning to problems of implementation as they do to problems of program formulation.

The recommendations that follow are ordered according to the foregoing analysis, not according to priority.

Local school districts must make effective use of available funds and additional federal funds must be appropriated for the following changes, in order to increase the educational success chances of high delinquency-risk populations.

FOSTERING BELIEF IN EDUCABILITY OF ALL PUPILS. As we saw, an essential ingredient in effective instruction is belief in the learning potential of all youngsters. At the same time, we saw that many teachers, often supported by administrators, harbor the belief that large numbers of lower-income and nonwhite pupils are incapable of being educated beyond the most minimum level. As a result, expectations and levels of instruction are scaled down and the belief is eventually borne out.

While these conditions in part emanate from other educational conditions that make effective instruction difficult, an urgent need is for the development of specific mechanisms that will foster and support the belief that all students can learn and can develop into productive adults. Examples of such mechanisms are these:

1. Professional education groups must make concentrated efforts to develop positive and optimistic attitudes and beliefs about low achieving and disadvantaged students among existing teachers, administrators, and school boards.

2. Programs of reeducation of teachers, administrators, and other school personnel must be vastly increased and must have as a major focus the development of more positive attitudes and beliefs about the potential

of all students. (Programs of reeducation are discussed in greater detail later in the chapter.)

3. Teacher training institutions must not only develop skills for teaching low achieving and disadvantaged pupils, but must continually support the belief that such pupils can be educated. (Modification of teacher training programs are discussed in greater detail later in the chapter).

4. Teachers, administrators, school boards, universities, and professional groups must make concerted efforts to reeducate the public so it will support and even encourage intensified efforts to teach "slow learners." Such efforts must be directed both at lower income and other disadvantaged parents, whose children stand to benefit the most, and at middle class parents, who now tend to be apathetic or resistant to efforts to improve education for underachieving children.

EXPANSION OF PRE-SCHOOL EDUCATION. As we pointed out, educational failure results in part—though we hasten to add, not entirely, from the fact that many children are ill equipped to fit into the educational system. At the same time that the educational system itself must be modified in important ways, the schools must develop means to better equip lower income children for subsequent educational development. Federal funds are now available for pre-school education through local Community Action Programs of the Economic Opportunity Act and Title I of the Elementary and Secondary Education Act of 1965. In addition, personnel from the National Teacher Corps can be used for this purpose.

A publication jointly published by OEO and the U.S. Office of Education, which administers ESEA funds, has this to say about particular pre-school programs and outcomes:

> Experimental classes for deprived pre-kindergartners have been in existence for more than four years. Experience has shown that classes seem to work best when there is a teacher and aide for each fifteen pupils. Teachers bombard children with chatter. They name colors, foods, and animals; they play with puzzles and geometric blocks to help them learn sizes and shapes. They take children on trips to museums, stores, and construction projects. In class children play with telephones to stimulate talk. They speak in tape recorders and enjoy the surprise of hearing their words played back. In one class, children, unaccustomed to conversation, have been found to speak readily if both teacher and pupil have a public through which conversation is made. In another class a tape recorder is built into a mechanical clown. When a child speaks, the clown's nose lights up. This reward is augmented by the thrill [of] a child . . . hearing a play back of his own voice.[1]

---

[1]United States Office of Education and United States Office of Economic Opportunity, *Education: An Answer to Poverty* (Washington, D.C.: United States Government Printing Office, 1966), p. 20.

Experience in many Head Start programs indicates that progress is especially marked when one or both parents are involved as either teacher aides or in supplementary classes for teachers. Such involvement can serve a number of desirable ends: increasing the parents' understanding of and concern about their children's problems of development; increasing their ability to provide more stimulating experiences at home; building a more general bridge between the community and the school; where they are used as aides, making the instructional process itself more effective; and providing more employment and even a new career-line for mothers. As we will see, older students too can be used as aides, as part of programs of instruction and job training, or as means for re-involving troublesome or underachieving students in the educational process.

According to current OEO estimates, less than half of eligible pupils are included in Head Start programs. In addition to expansion of Head Start funds and the use of ESEA—Title I funds for pre-school education, then, local Headstart programs must make special efforts to actively recruit deprived children.

Another problem has been lack of buildings, facilities, and room space. It is highly important that those who run pre-school programs vigorously seek cooperation from various community agencies and organizations in order to maximize use of available space. At the same time, if pre-school education is to become a permanent fixture in American education, new funds must be appropriated for needed buildings and facilities.

As the OEO—OE booklet notes, pre-school programs have produced remarkable gains in the educational readiness of disadvantaged children.[2] The Coleman Report arrives at the same conclusion, especially with respect to educational motivation.[3]

Experience has shown, however, that these gains tend to disappear as the students enter the traditional elementary instructional process.

> These early experimental classes produced highly significant increases in the average IQs and school readiness of children. It should be pointed out, however, that the longest running of these experiments indicated some decline of IQ scores after the children had entered primary grades. Such findings suggest the need for continued emphasis on intensive effort in the early grades.[4]

We would go a step further to call for changes in the elementary instructional program itself, as well as in the pupils.

---

[2]Ibid., p. 20.
[3]James S. Coleman, *The Adolescent Society* (New York: The Free Press of Glencoe, Inc. 1961), p. 516.
[4]*Education: An Answer to Poverty.*

DEVELOPMENT OF RELEVANT INSTRUCTION. Earlier we pointed out that the content of lessons tends to be largely irrelevant to the current experiences and circumstances of disadvantaged youth, who quickly lose interest in education as a result. Further, we pointed out that secondary school materials are often typified by an underlying lack of honesty, avoidance of controversial issues, and detachment from the current and future concerns of many youth, especially those from lower income or nonwhite backgrounds.

As a result, there is a great need to develop new, relevant textbooks and other materials and to present content that will be immediately meaningful, useful, and interesting, as well as beneficial in the long run. This is a special problem for disadvantaged children. As one writer has remarked, "how to educate the child out of his subculture into society's main stream while preserving and developing personal elements of his culture—is the problem we face."[5]

Past efforts to develop relevant curriculum materials have largely failed, as noted by the Panel on Educational Research and Development of the President's Science Advisory Commission.

> Much time is already spent on this area, but irrelevance, hypocrisy, and misplaced emphasis destroy the value of many of these efforts. What the child needs is a growing knowledge of who he is, what kind of world he is living in, how his future role in the world may be shaped, and how he may help shape it. This is a matter for self-scrutiny, honesty, and careful observation. It is not a matter for didactic oversimplification.[6]

Development of new curriculum materials must proceed very carefully, as shown by the following experience.

> The artist doing illustrations for the series depicted some typical housekeeping situations, (brooms leaning in the corner, a kitchen sink with exposed pipes beneath it) and this—at least relative to other preprimers, which do not treat the realities of housekeeping quite as fully—was taken simply as poor housekeeping, and thereby derogatory of the Negro since this was the home of a Negro family. The first preprimer was only one-third the length of the normal preprimer, because we wanted each child to have the satisfaction of completing a book in a short time. Thus, we inadvertently left the father out of the first preprimer; indeed we did not even refer to him. This was also interpreted as a derogation, not only of the Negro family depicted, but of Negro families in general. Finally, we called the little boy hero of the series "Sammie." It was an unfortunate

---

[5]A. Harry Passow, "Instructional Content for Depressed Urban Centers: Problems and Approaches," from a paper at the Postdoctoral Seminar of the College of Education, The Ohio State University, October 23, 1964.

[6]The Panel on Educational Research and Development, *Innovation and Experiment in Education.* Washington, D.C. (March, 1964), p. 33.

choice, since it was seen by middle-class Negro families as "stereotype by insinuation."[7]

An example of an attempt to develop meaningful content at the secondary level is in the Wilmington, Delaware, public schools.

> A three-year Wilmington project focused directly on the aspect of human relations in an effort to help children and their families to comprehend and deal more effectively with changing neighborhoods: transiency, desegregation, flight to the suburbs, and changing economic forces. The focus of curriculum building was on developing human relations sensitivity, skills, insights, and information. Units relating school instruction to life needs and experience was built for specific classes. Such education is viewed as being at the center of the school's program.[8]

An urgent need, then, is for all educators, beginning at the local level, to develop an awareness of the need for new content of instruction; to carefully develop guidelines for new, relevant materials; and to actually develop some of these materials themselves. Later we propose the creation of new units for continuing innovation at the local level. These might take the lead organizing and administering such efforts. Moreover, teachers might be freed for a term or a year to do this. Another means is for schools to hire teams of local staff for the summer. One New York school screened new applicants for teaching positions by observing their reactions to textbooks and other materials. This idea might be broadened so that all teachers are given a major voice in selection of materials.

As a means of obtaining fresh ideas, as well as of developing parental and community interest and involvement in school, we urge that parents and representatives of various community groups be involved in the development of new materials. In addition, pupils themselves should be included; this represents a great opportunity to tap neglected innovative resources, as well as to involve students in the educational process to a greater extent.

If local educators become genuinely concerned about the real need for new materials and are given the chance to develop guidelines and ideas, and if the school boards will listen to such educators, then school boards in turn can begin to put pressure on publishers to produce relevant materials. Later we also proposed new federal grants to local, state, and professional groups for curriculum development.

----

[7]Carl L. Marburger, "Considerations for Educational Planning," in Passow, "Instructional Content for Depressed Urban Centers," p. 305. © 1963 by Teachers College, Columbia University.

[8]Passow, "Instructional Content for Depressed Urban Centers: Problems and Approaches."

In addition, we urge that federal curriculum development grants be made available to local districts for two purposes. First, they should enable local and regional groups to hold regular institutes or seminars for assessing current curriculum materials and for recommending new materials. Such institutes should include parents, community representatives and students, as well as school personnel. Second, they should enable individuals, groups, or school districts to take time off to actively develop and write new materials or to work closely with publishers and authors as they develop them.

DEVELOPMENT OF APPROPRIATE TEACHING METHODS. As we noted before, different teaching methods are required for different student populations. Despite this, traditional middle-class approaches are usually applied in all schools, with the result that many disadvantaged pupils are not reached, and the school soon loses its "hold" over them.

Miriam Goldberg, among others, has drawn on research and experience to construct her image of the ideal teacher for disadvantaged pupils.[9]

A first step in developing adequately trained teachers is to develop special training in teachers' colleges for teaching disadvantaged pupils. New federal funds should be made available for this purpose. The first components of such training should be extended practice teaching in schools with large numbers of such children. At present,

> The curriculum of college or university may or may not inform and influence prospective teachers about the problems and relevant issues of the depressed urban areas . . . (despite the fact that) . . . these children and their neighborhoods have unique problems that one does not usually encounter in Psychological Foundations I or in student teaching which is done in a "good neighborhood."[10]

The Panel on Educational Research and Development has offered the following proposal for teacher training.

> The schools should serve as educational institutions not only for the pupils but also for the teachers. In a preservice program, schools could provide aide internships for student teachers, working under the supervision of master teachers, and the use of block methods could permit the student teacher to work six months and then study six months. In an in-service program for working teachers, instruction can be tied to the introduction

---

[9]Miriam Goldberg, "Adapting Teacher Style to Pupil Differences: Teachers for Disadvantaged Children," *Merrill-Palmer Quarterly* 10, no. 2 (1964): 161–78.

[10]Vernon F. Haubrich, "Teachers for Big City Schools," in Passow, "Instructional Content. . . ." p. 247. © 1963 by Teachers College, Columbia University.

in the school of a new project. One barrier to change is the insecurity teachers feel during the presence of something new, of uncertainty about what to do tomorrow.[11]

Below is an example of a similar effort in the New York City Schools.

Hunter College, in an effort to improve the preparation of teachers for depressed area schools, selected a group of students who expressed a willingness to remain as regularly appointed teachers in the same "most difficult" junior high schools in which they had accepted appointments as student teachers. As part of their training they were seen more often than was customary by a member of the college faculty and worked closely with carefully selected cooperating teachers. They spent the last 10 weeks of their student teaching in full command of the class, under constant supervision. A number of these young men and women, in due course, took and passed the required examination and were appointed as regularly licensed teachers to the same school in which they had taught as students. But the supervision and assistance continued, reinforcing their earlier learning and providing the needed support and encouragement.[12]

As in pre-school programs, use of adult and student aides in the teaching process can result in multiple gains. Use of older students to help teach younger ones is a particularly novel concept in education since students have traditionally been locked out of the instructional role. However, experience in a number of school systems indicate highly promising results of such a practice.

In Michigan and California pilot experiments were conducted in which sixth grade pupils were assigned to tutor lower graders who showed signs of school difficulty. The lower graders, in almost all cases, showed a noticeable rise in involvement and achievement. Equally significant, however, was a definite beneficial change in the achievement and attitude of the tutors. Some of these tutors had been not only backward learners themselves, but rebellious "problem children." Many tutored effectively and showed remarkable improvement in their own learning, their attitude toward school, and their behavior and dress. In the Michigan experiment, conducted by a university in a school of the disadvantaged, sixth graders spent 45 minutes a day as "academic assistants" in the first, second, third, and fourth grades, helping younger pupils with reading, writing, spelling and arithmetic. Two afternoons a week—also for 45 minutes—the older children met in a seminar to discuss how "olders" can best help "youngers." They discussed what can be realistically expected of children of each age. They exchanged ideas on how to correct errors in a manner that was encouraging instead of discouraging. Through "role playing," older chil-

---

[11]*Innovation and Experiment in Education*, p. 35.
[12]Goldberg, "Adapting Teacher Style to Pupil Differences: Teachers for Disadvantaged Children," p. 172.

dren pretended they were "youngers," by way of testing how they would react to certain kinds of praise or scolding, friendliness or threat. Their habitual disdain for the ways of younger children turned to sympathetic constructiveness.[13]

To be discussed in greater detail later is experience in New York City and elsewhere which confirms the fact that the involvement of underachievers, behavior problems, delinquents, and even dropouts is one effective means by which those students who have traditionally been shut out, not only from the instructional process but by any legitimate student involvement, can be attracted back.

Again, OEO and ESEA funds are available for hiring teacher's aides as well as for other modifications suggested in this section.

Educators are increasingly seeing the potential in teaching machines and other mechanical materials and devices for effective instruction, especially of disadvantaged learners. We encourage intensified efforts to develop and incorporate such devices in the instructional process, at the same time we caution schools about using them in a haphazard fashion. A great deal of additional research is needed on the use of teaching devices before their potential is fully known or applied. It is rather dismaying that very large proportions of ESEA funds went to equipment during the first year, at the expense of creative development and use of human resources in teaching.

USE OF FLEXIBLE GROUPING. An urgent need in all schools is the development of alternative methods of curriculum organization that avoid rigid "segregation" of students on the basis of unquestioning acceptance of questionable test scores. One such alternative that is gaining wide acceptance is the "nongraded" system. This system has the advantage of retaining groups of relatively homogeneous ability in particular subjects, but avoids impermeable boundaries between tracks and takes account of differences in aptitudes and pace of development among and within children.

In one California school organized for individual progress, the labels of grades one through eight have been abolished, and 14 "levels" of curriculum have been substituted. A child moves from level to level as soon as he is ready, without regard to age or to the length of time spent in the previous level. After summer vacation, he resumes where he left off in June. A fast-learning child may be promoted to high school in seven years, but not sooner, lest his social and physical development lead to other problems. In saving the one year, however, he has not skipped a year of lesson material.

As a child demonstrates by testing that he has accomplished the work of one level in a major subject, he is shifted to another group within a class

---

[13]*Education: An Answer to Poverty*, p. 66.

or from one class to another, where he will meet the new challenges for which he is now ready. Readiness for a new level is chiefly determined by reading ability since most other learning is based on it. However, other subjects as well as social and emotion development are considered.[14]

The chief merit of such an arrangement is that all students are given the chance to extend themselves or to catch up in a particular subject, depending on the need.

Remedial education in each area can fit into such a program, without the visible stigma that typically goes along with such classes. It is important that efforts be made to channel all pupils in need of remediation into such classes, regardless of socioeconomic background or race—and that remediation involve stepped up rather than restricted instruction.

Again, experience indicates that the best kind of remediation program may be the use of underachieving students to teach younger students. For example, Mobilization for Youth in New York City paid high school age tutors $1 to $2 an hour for spending time after school with elementary school pupils. The major result was that tutors demonstrated even more remarkable progress than those being helped. We will discuss this program in more detail later, but at this point urge all schools to consider developing such an approach in their own remediation programs.

Another important point to be made about remediation programs is that they are generally limited to the early primary grades. This in essence represents a position of hopelessness and surrender in relation to older students who are behind. In the first year, one-half to two-thirds of ESEA funds went for elementary school projects. While no one would deny the importance of making up for deficiencies as early as possible, the schools must not give up on them at later stages in the educational career.

Along with Conant, we urge flexible, individualized curriculum organization at the high school level as well, an arrangement which requires considerable time, knowledge, and skill in counseling.

In my first report I also recommended individualized programs. I was specifically referring to the elective programs. There would be no classification of students according to clearly defined and labeled tracks such as "college preparatory," "vocational," "commercial," or "general." In advising a student as to his elective program, the counselor is guided by the minimum program recommended as a matter of school policy for the academically talented or by recommending sequences leading to the development of marketable skills. With such a system, many students of similar abilities and interests have almost identical programs, but there is no sharp line between different kinds of programs. Each year it is expected that the counselor will work with the students in appraising his record and plan-

---

[14]Ibid., p. 32.

ning his future elective courses. There is no fixed pattern of courses that, once enrolled in, a student must continue until graduation. Such individualized programs are perfectly compatible with ability grouping in required courses.[15]

A crucial component of such an arrangement is maximum participation of students in the decision-making process. This can be an important means for developing a greater involvement of students in the educational process.

CONTINUING REEDUCATION OF TEACHERS. In view of the natural tendency for teachers, as others, to fall into accustomed conceptions and approaches, there is an urgent need for local schools to develop programs for continually reeducating teachers. "In-service training," as it is traditionally called, must be vastly increased to accomplish at least four objectives in relation to improved education of high-risk populations. First, teacher attitudes and beliefs in regard to the educability (and the nature of deviant behavior, as we will see later) of disadvantaged and other "slow learners," must be modified. Second, methods of teaching and dealing with disadvantaged learners (and troublesome students) must be continually reassessed and new ones developed and adopted. Third, teaching styles must be continuously adapted to new increments in knowledge and to new student populations. This is especially crucial in rapidly changing urban schools. Fourth, teachers must be reequipped to effectively use or fit into new, innovative programs, such as the use of aides, programmed instruction, team teaching, and nongraded classes.

Numerous creative attempts are being made to update techniques and approaches of teachers. One example is described below.

> One large Midwestern city developed an experimental summer school for grades one to six. This program stressed language arts, social studies, and arithmetic in a setting of work projects and play. A formal hour of in-service training—demonstrations and discussions based on occasional lectures by a psychologist from a nearby university—was held every afternoon. Teachers stayed for two or three hours after the one o'clock closing of school for informal discussion, exchange of ideas, and invention of experimental tasks.
>
> Teachers, supervised by a school social worker assigned as a parent coordinator, spent some afterschool time in visiting homes. They also exchanged ideas on how to get the most out of these home visits.[16]

While this example referred to continuing reeducation among elementary school teachers, there may be an even greater need for such efforts

---

[15]James B. Conant, *Slums and Suburbs* (New York: McGraw-Hill Book Company, 1961), p. 58.

[16]*Education: An Answer to Poverty*, p. 61.

among high school teachers, because of rapid changes in the world of work about which many of them teach. As indicated below, there are countless resources available in every community which can help improve the skills of teachers, as well as develop community support of education.

> A nearby college or university might provide lecturers or consultant specialists. These experts may be professors of education who can advise on innovations in teaching techniques; perhaps one is especially equipped on the problems of the educationally deprived child. But there are less obvious resources of expertise in any community—professional and working people in chemical, baking, banking, electronics, paint, cement, steel, transportation, newspaper, and other industries, as well as police and fire stations, hospitals, and jails. People in these places can enhance a teacher's ability to explain the world of work, thus aiding him in development of special lesson units, study materials, and field trips.[17]

While it is not our place to prescribe particular techniques for in-service training of teachers, we do feel called upon to direct attention to a general principle that has been invoked throughout our analysis and recommendation: maximum involvement of those being treated or taught in the learning process.

> A good teacher-training program practices what it preaches. If it tries to train teachers not to lecture to pupils but to demonstrate, the program itself should be based not on lecture, but on demonstration.

> When a discussion technique operates well in the teacher-training class, the group should inspect the technique closely and determine why it went well. What works for the teachers will probably work equally well in their regular class with pupils.[18]

Continuing reeducation for special programs or for general improvement of teaching may be supported by the local Community Action Programs funded by OEO, by Title I ESEA, or Title VI of the National Defense Education Act. Later we will propose expansion of federal funds for this purpose.

INCREASING REWARDS FOR TEACHING IN LOW INCOME SCHOOLS. Since there is evidence that quality education is inhibited by the presence of large numbers of inexperienced teachers or unqualified substitutes; since such teachers abound in low income areas, especially in large cities; and since the schools' responsibility is to do everything possible to maximize the quality of education for low income students; then a needed change is for local schools to provide inducements that will attract and retain high-quality teachers in lower income schools.

---

[17]Ibid., p. 61.
[18]Ibid., p. 63.

There are a number of inducements or rewards that can be created. For example, teachers in "difficult" schools might be given fewer classes per day, with time off for additional preparation and planning. Reduced class size, which should occur for purely instructional purposes as well, is another inducement. Not to be dismissed is the proposal for making teachers' schedules as flexible as those of college teachers, with changes from term to term and ample time for professional development—including released time for advanced training. This proposal has the merit that it not only would attract teachers but would benefit the school system in the long run as well. Additional classroom aides—which we have proposed on the other grounds as well—is another such inducement. Finally, the most obvious—and perhaps potent—inducement is higher pay for teaching in low income schools.

While attraction and retention of quality teachers is especially problematic in low income schools, it is a general problem facing education. Research has clearly shown the unfortuate fact that ability and performance of college students who enter teaching is considerably lower than those who enter most other professions.[19] The most obvious solution to the problem is to increase the monetary rewards for teaching. Teachers' salaries have always been the responsibility of state and local government in the community. We take the position that public education should remain as decentralized as possible. But unless the states and cities take steps to improve teachers' salaries and working conditions, quality education will surely suffer and arguments will become compelling for a greater federal role. The financial plight of large cities—growth of lower income populations which are reluctant to support additional taxes, decentralization of industry —many leave little choice but a greater federal involvement in education, including higher teachers' salaries.

UTILIZING AND EXPANDING BUILDINGS, FACILITIES, AND EQUIPMENT. A closely related need is to better utilize and vastly expand buildings, facilities, and equipment, especially in low income areas. Reduction in class size, an important ingredient in improved education, is dependent on available space, of course, as well as on increased teaching staff. In addition, the quality of instruction is partly dependent on the quality of buildings and the facilities and equipment in them.

We contend that more flexible scheduling, which we will recommend later on other grounds as well, can permit better utilization of available facilities. As the Panel on Education Research and Development has noted, consideration should go to use of rooms and buildings not traditionally used for instruction.

---

[19]James A. Davis, *Great Aspirations,* vol. 1 (Chicago: National Opinion Research Center, 1963), pp. 170–71.

More classroom space is needed, but this does not mean that new buildings must take the same form as familiar buildings, or that new space cannot be found in buildings already in existence but not designed originally as schools. Experimental programs can be housed anywhere and still be part of the school system—in a housing project, a separate small building, a store front, and so forth.[20]

Nevertheless, vast building programs are required to accommodate rapidly growing youth populations, and especially to replace and improve deteriorated schools in low income areas. Again, because of the financial squeeze of big city schools and the apparent reluctance of the states to take up the challenge, federal funds for buildings seem to be required.

In calling for improved equipment, we hasten to add that expenditures in this area should go for basic educational material such as books and learning devices. Below is an extreme example of improving instruction with educationally relevant equipment.

One eastern school superintendent recently obtained a grant of about $10,000 to enable an experiment in one of his elementary schools. Teachers were to develop specific educational goals, be given the sum of money and have complete freedom to buy whatever they wanted to achieve their goals.

The teachers decided to emphasize "real-life" learning tasks in place of conventional class tasks that children often regard as the artificial work of school.

Then preparation of the shopping list began. The teachers quickly learned that, sizable as their grant was, they could not go out on an indiscriminate shopping spree. Thus, it was necessary for them to examine closely the learning value of each item of equipment. By the time they scaled down the list and were ready to buy, their picture of a new learning program was sharply focused in their minds. Also, because they had to reject so many useful items, the teachers were more determined than ever to extract the most value out of those they could acquire.

Discussion had led them to believe that pupils lacked concepts in social studies and that the subject had to be presented more vividly. The teachers decided that carefully selected audiovisual equipment would help turn abstractions into concrete observations. They bought a photocopy machine so that each child might have his personal copy of study materials; an overhead projector and overlay-making machine; an 8mm movie camera and projector for filming aspects of life in their town for class production and discussion; a filmstrip projector and filmstrips, and a previewer to aid in lesson planning; a 35mm camera for slides and a slide projector; equipment and supplies for a photographic darkroom; and tape recorders, record players, and records, as well as headphones so that a portion of the group might listen while the rest were engaged in other tasks.[21]

---

[20]*Innovation and Experiment in Education*, p. 34.
[21]*Education: An Answer to Poverty*, p. 43.

The most basic need is to provide more textbooks in low income areas and to expand library facilities. In the absence of adequate local and state expenditures, federal funds should be made available for this purpose. In addition, the Panel on Educational Research and Development has called for book allowances to supplement those basic materials.

> Students might receive a yearly book allowance, perhaps of ten dollars in the form of stamps. The stamps could be used to buy paperbacks broadly related to the studies in which the student was, or might be, engaged. Teachers in the school system could draw up long lists of acceptable books. Provision of a similar allowance for tools, art supplies, music and musical instruments might also be possible.[22]

We regard large expenditures for vocational education equipment as perhaps doing more harm than good, since the result is an enlarged tendency toward obsolescence. We believe these funds can be more profitably spent for basic instructional materials that will help provide a solid educational foundation for work-bound youth.

Both Titles I and II of ESEA include funds for expansion of equipment and facilities, as does Title III of NDEA.

CREATING DIVERSITY WITHIN STUDENT BODIES. We saw that an important factor determining student achievement—and hence the likelihood of delinquency—is the nature of the student body in the school attended by a particular pupil. The greater the proportion of the pupils with high levels of achievement and aspiration, the greater the chances that a particular student will attain a high level of achievement himself. Since achievement levels tend to be associated with income background and race, this means that the higher the proportion of higher income and white pupils, the more positive the effect on pupils, especially if they come from low income and Negro families. White and higher income pupils tend not to be adversely affected by the presence of Negro and lower income students, although the latter stand to gain.

The implication is clear: educational attainment will be heightened and delinquency lessened to the extent that schools contain cross sections of student populations. In terms of delinquency prevention, this means that efforts must be made to preserve, create, or recreate mixed-class and racially integrated schools. As Havighurst has noted, there are reasons beyond delinquency prevention for such effort:

> It is desirable that working-class and middle-class children should attend the same schools so as to: (1) give each group more understanding and

---

[22]*Innovation and Experiment in Education,* p. 36.

liking for each other; (2) give working-class children the stimulation, competition, and cooperation of the middle-class children. It is desirable for Negro and ethnic and old-American white children to attend the same schools so as to: (1) help all groups develop feelings of equality and mutual trust; (2) avoid deepseated suspicion and hostility by the minority groups, which suffer from discrimination in the past and often in the present.[23]

At present, however, big city schools are becoming more segregated racially and economically, as middle-class families move to suburbs or middle-class areas in the city and as lower-class in-migrants take over deserted inner city housing. To the extent that this trend continues, diversified student bodies will be increasingly difficult to maintain or create. One of the reasons for the middle class exit is concern about quality schools. The schools themselves can help arrest this trend, then, by improving the quality of inner city instruction—and by imposing boundaries in such a way that either the income and racial mix remains above the "tipping point" at which advantaged families move out or that the ratio returns to that point.

While we recognize that de facto segregation, both racial and economic, is closely linked to housing patterns, we urge that local districts do whatever they can within these patterns to eliminate racial and economic imbalance. There are numerous specific means available for effecting these changes, including the following: rezoning (changing boundaries), bussing, strategic location of new buildings, open enrollment, regrouping of grades, closing schools and redistributing pupils, "educational parks," and pairing of schools (Princeton Plan). Whatever the particular means used, we urge local districts to take maximum advantage of available financial and technical assistance available through Title I of the Civil Rights Act of 1964 in planning for and implementing desegregation.

We also urge school systems to give greater attention to the more general educational problem of economic segregation than they have in the past. Although we recognize that there are no constitutional justifications for economic desegregation of schools, we believe, along with Havighurst and others, that maintenance or creation of mixed class schools in the cities, along with increased educational expenditures and input, will not only serve to maintain or upgrade educational achievement among high-risk populations of youngsters, but will help stem the outward movement of middle-class families resulting from fear or distaste for lower class schools. Therefore, we believe that city schools should participate in or initiate community planning in relation to housing problems and population movements, at the same time that they adopt educational measures for maintaining or recreating internally diverse schools. The schools should also take the lead in creating a community climate among middle-class whites which will support economically and racially mixed schools.

---

[23]Havighurst, in Passow, "Instructional Content . . . ," p. 41.

We also urge that Federal funds be made available to local districts for technical assistance for maintaining, creating, or recreating economically mixed schools in the interest of diversity within student bodies.

Each of the changes referred to above has called for local decisions, innovations, and programs. At the same time that we make these recommendations, we recognize that one of the greatest problems of all in bringing about needed changes at the local level is breaking through traditional educational conceptions, arrangements, and approaches. This is especially true in schools serving those who are without influence, power, or sanctions to speed along such change, namely the poor. Therefore, we see a serious need for new local mechanisms for promoting innovation and change. Proposals in this regard are offered later in the chapter.

Local school districts must take advantage of available funds and new federal funds must be appropriated for creating a better linkage between the secondary school curriculum and the changing world of work, especially for the noncollege bound.

We pointed out before that a pervasive belief among those who fail or get assigned to a dead-end academic program of one kind or another is that they ". . . rarely perceive any possibility for ever succeeding in doing work which carries society's respect and in which they themselves can take pride."[24] It is increasingly recognized that attempts to shore up courses and curricula within the existing framework of noncollege preparatory education will continue to be inadequate and to make only the smallest impact on educational failure and delinquency. This position is being taken because current "basic," "general," and even many vocational educational curricula tend to feed youth into job areas that are least demanding and rewarding, and most rapidly disappearing. Current content and methods of instruction, and linkages with the labor market produce youth who are inadequately prepared in basic educational foundations for work, let alone in specific job training, to do much of anything except the most undemanding work, which leads them nowhere in the future. It is questionable whether, within prevailing curricula, an adequate number of youth can either be "held into" legitimate paths toward adulthood or fitted into expanding jobs in the human services and in highly technical areas.

ALTERNATIVE CAREER ROUTES. We begin by accepting Conant's position that "in a highly urbanized and industrialized free society the educational experiences of youth should fit their subsequent employment."[25] As

---

[24]Jacob R. Fishman et al., *Training for New Careers* (Washington, D.C.: Howard University, 1965), p. 5.

[25]Conant, *Slums and Suburbs,* p. 38.

a means to that end, we propose that local school districts, state departments of education, universities, professional groups in education as well as in other fields, labor groups, business and industry, and the federal government jointly initiate immediate and large-scale planning efforts to build into the secondary school training for subprofessional, career-oriented jobs. As proposed by Pearl and Riessman in *New Careers for the Poor,* such training would focus most strongly on preparing the poor for subprofessional jobs in the human service field.[26] In view of the lack of occupational future for the poor and of the great need for expansion of human services in coming years, this focus is a valid one. At the same time, we suggest that this conception be broadened to include all youth who are failing or headed down one or another dead-end street and that it be oriented toward technical, business, and other occupations as well as toward human service areas.

Before discussing the particular features of such a program and citing some examples, we call attention to the fact that while several experiences with the new career concept have been highly promising, very careful consideration and planning must go into the design and implementation of new programs so their potential can be fully realized, rather than subverted by traditionalism, rigidity, and resistance by state departments, professional groups, and local schools. In short, we see the problem of "institutionalizing" subprofessional, career-oriented programs, or building them into the existing educational system, as just as great as the problem of designing them in an operational sense. We suggest that effective implementation requires creation of a new decision-making, planning, and coordinating framework which will be unencumbered by habitual operating patterns and vested interests and which will bring new channels of information, influence, and authority into existence.

In stating the objectives of a program for "alternative career routes," it is useful to draw on one of a series of publications written by the staff of Howard University's Institute for Youth Studies where this concept is being developed and implemented.

The overall goals, then, of an aide training program may be summarized as follows:

1. Developing in socially deprived youth the necessary motivation, identity, values, and capabilities for maximally utilizing the offered training for both holding down a job and beginning a potential career line in human and community services.

2. Enabling these youth to learn the basic interpersonal skills, attitudes, and knowledge common to all human service occupations, so that they might work effectively in these areas.

---

[26]Arthur Pearl and Frank Riessman, *New Careers for the Poor* (New York: The Free Press of Glencoe, Inc., 1965), Ch. 1.

3. Developing flexibility of attitude, role, and the viewpoint in these youth so that they will not be artificially confined to a specific job, but, with additional specialized training, can transfer easily from one type of human service position to another.

4. Teaching specialized skills essential to at least one kind of human service.

5. Developing meaningful jobs and career lines that are a permanent part of community institutions.

6. Training and orienting professionals to work effectively with these aides.[27]

As suggested in this statement, there are several key features of this model, which must be paralleled in nonhuman service lines of work as well.

1. The noncollege preparatory curricula, beginning as early as high school, must be modified to include three basic elements. First, it must include instruction in a core of basic educational courses—reading, mathematics, history, sciences, etc. Second, it must include instruction in a core of knowledge and skills that are essential for the general area of training which an individual student has chosen—the human services, technical work, business work, etc. Third, it must include some training in specific skills in at least one particular kind of job.

2. Academic study in the classroom must be supplemented with part-time employment in a community agency, organization, or firm. Such employment would, of course, be remunerative, but in addition, academic credit would be given for job performance. Technical aspects of job training would occur in the work place, rather than in the classroom. This is especially crucial in what has traditionally been known as vocational education, since the schools cannot hope to keep up with rapid technological changes in industry. Work would usually be carried on in new positions, created by the employing unit in conjunction with schools. Occupants of those positions would be known as aides of one kind or another. The Howard publication refers to the following aides in the human services: Help Care Aide, Community Organization Aide (Neighborhood Workers), Child Care Aide, Family Counseling Aide, Foster Care Aide, Legal Aide, Probation Aide, Recreation Aide, Research Aide, Remedial Aide, School Classroom Aide, and School Library Aide.[28] Comparable positions would be created in conjunction with professional, business, and industrial leaders for nonhuman service work as well.

We believe that the program being proposed should begin as early as junior high school. If so, and if it involves nonschool aide work, modifica-

---

[27]Fishman, *Training for New Careers*, p. 7.
[28]Ibid., pp. 92–105.

tions of child labor laws might be required to allow those involved to become gainfully employed.

Special mention should be made of the school aide positions, since they overlap with earlier references to use of pupils for teaching other pupils. We contend that these positions can be highly important mechanisms for "hooking in" students whom the schools might not otherwise be able to hold. The Howard description of a school classroom aide is illustrative of the use to which such persons might be put and the requirements needed.

> *General Description.* Classroom aides work with teachers, assisting them in the following activities:
>
> 1. Preparation of materials required by the class.
> 2. Care of audiovisual machines.
> 3. Operation of tape recorders, typewriters, teaching machines, projectors.
> 4. Making contact with and tutoring individual children assigned to them or the teacher.
> 5. Supervision of small groups of children while the teacher gives special attention to another part of the class.
> 6. Supervision of activities outside the school building.
> 7. Supervision of homework, lunchroom, and recess rooms.
> 8. Maintenance of attendance and other records.
>
> *Qualifications.* School aides must be able to read, write, and count, like children, and be dextrous.[29]

3. During part of the classroom day (perhaps one period) students involved in such a program would be organized into small groups of, say, from five to fifteen. Several groups would be supervised by a master teacher, and each group would have assigned to it as a resource person, a regular teacher, adult aide, or both. These sessions would be devoted to work-related topics: to problems in applying material from other classes to the work situation, problems in getting along with employers and other employees, technical aspects of the job, career possibilities, etc. The strength of this feature is that it mobilizes collective resources and influences among youth around common problems. As we will see, this has special merits in "binding in" students who are in trouble or are having difficulty in school or work.

4. The school day, week, and year would be extended and made more flexible than at present so that pupils could arrange flexible schedules of work and study. For instance, a group might work days and go to schools in evenings, or work full-time for several weeks during the winter but go to

---

[29]Ibid., p. 104.

school during the summer. At the same time, this would ease the pressure of numbers on existing buildings and facilities, although scheduling and professional manpower problems would necessarily become more complex.

5. An essential feature of such a program is that aides would not be locked into the level at which they begin, but would have the opportunity to move progressively upward into more demanding subprofessional jobs after having shown sufficient progress of development in initial jobs. Two or three advances would open up for students during high school as tangible signs of payoff, and the career line would culminate in full professional status in a particular field after a number of years of experience and progress. Each aide position would be tied in this way to a career line, but flexibility and fluidity would be maintained so students could easily move from one field of work and training to another without being markedly set back. To be avoided is another form of locking students into a particular channel without ample opportunity to change direction at various points along the line.

This plan, then, represents an alternative route out of low status for youth who are not likely to use the traditional one, college education. Not all of them would in fact move up, but progress and advancement would be limited only by capabilities, performance, and aspirations, not by lack of objective opportunities as is now the case for so many youngsters. At the same time, we would be falling into "naive opportunity theory" if we recommended the creation of opportunities without accompanying efforts to equip students to fit into these new positions and to perform satisfactorily. Thus, we go back to the importance of small group training and problem-solving as an essential ingredient. To the extent that these and other features of this "model" are combined together in a package, the "model" is an extremely promising approach in delinquency prevention.

6. Effective coordination of curriculum and in-school training with the world of work requires continuing contact between the school and various employing agencies and organizations. First, the schools must seek continuing guidance from employers in the design and development of the curriculum, insofar as it is work-oriented. This is especially critical in areas in which the schools have traditionally not participated in the training of personnel and in which rapid changes are occurring in the work setting. Although we are likely to encounter resistance from educators here, we recommended liberal inclusion of employers—competent, perceptive ones— in curriculum development. This, we suggest, is one way of breaking down the professional rigidity and parochialism so often displayed by local and state educators. Second, the schools must seek continuing guidance from employers in the training of particular students or groups of students. Third, the schools must take an active lead in helping professional, business, and

industrial employers in creating subprofessional jobs and career lines and in infusing them effectively into their on-going operations. Fourth, the schools must also take an active part in training employers in the effective use of aides, so aides will not be sent down a dead-end trail and so talents and performance can be maximized.

7. Since the demands, requirements, and techniques in training aides are likely to be substantially different from those traditionally involved in classroom teaching, in-service teacher training is likely to be required.

This description of the model "alternative career route," which is similar in many ways to one proposed by Havighurst, has only touched on the barest outlines, since it is not our task to spell out all operational features, but rather to propose the general design for a program of delinquency prevention.[30] There is growing evidence that employment in general can be a highly useful approach for preventing and reducing delinquency. Shore and Massimo, for example, have recently reported significant gains from work experience among delinquents.[31] Mobilization For Youth and others have reported similar results.[32] We suggest, however, that employment by itself will be less effective than the linking of work with future opportunities for advancement. As shown by the Howard experience, expansion of such opportunities can be a major step in restoring hope, optimism, and a sense of control of one's own destiny which is now so absent among youth who are relegated to academic boneyards early in their educational careers and never have the chance to escape. This renewed sense of payoff can be an effective means by which the school can retain or gain the commitment of students who are otherwise likely to give up or rebel.

We propose that this model be opened to all students, but that special efforts be made to channel into it those categories of pupils which are of special relevance in delinquency prevention: underachievers, behavior problems, identified delinquents, and even dropouts. Later we will discuss the need for special mechanisms for introducing and involving such youngsters in the program.

Funds are now available for implementing this model through Title I of ESEA, as well as through the Vocational Educational Act of 1963. In

---

[30]Robert J. Havighurst, "Research on the School Work-Study Program in the Prevention of Juvenile Delinquency," in William R. Carriker (ed.), *Role of the School in Prevention of Juvenile Delinquency* (Washington, D.C.: U.S. Government Printing Office), pp. 27–45.

[31]J. L. Massimo and M. F. Shore, "The Effectiveness of a Vocationally Oriented Psychotherapeutic Program for Adolescent Delinquent Boys," *American Journal of Orthopsychiatry* 4 (1963): 634–42.

[32]Robert D. Cloward, "Studies in Tutoring," (New York: Columbia University School of Social Work [mimeographed], 1966).

addition, however, we urge the appropriation of additional funds explicitly for this purpose—accompanied with guidelines for effective implementation, so monies will not get channeled into existing structures, with little effect.

OCCUPATIONAL PLACEMENT AND FOLLOW-UP OFFICES. As another measure for creating a more effective linkage between the school career and the subsequent occupational career, we recommend new federal funds for the creation of "Occupational Placement and Follow-Up Offices" in every high school.[33] In the past, the schools have not seen it as part of their mission to take a serious and active role in guiding youth into the world of work, in providing continuing counseling and guidance services in connection with work-related problems, or in aiding unemployed youth in developing new skills and finding work. And although schools are usually eager to produce figures on college attendance, they do not see it as part of their responsibility to assess occupational placement and performance of those youth who do not enter college. As a result, they are not forced to confront themselves with the payoff or lack of payoff of the noncollege preparatory phase of their efforts, programs, and expenditures.

These situations have emerged from what we believe to be a narrow definition by the schools of their responsibilities for youth. Traditionally, they have interpreted their charge to include responsibility for youth up to the time when they leave school—through either the graduation or the drop-out route. Once out, youth are presumably on their own or become the responsibility of other institutions.

We hold that while this may have been an appropriate interpretation of the schools' mandate in the past, it is presently outdated. In the past, there was little reason for the schools to be concerned with the work-bound student after exit, since there was an abundance of jobs into which they could move. Now, however, these jobs have become much more scarce, and as a result, many youth drift into the ranks of the unemployed and into subsequent delinquency. . . .

INCREASED ACCESSIBILITY TO HIGHER EDUCATION. A final measure for creating a better articulation between the high school curriculum and the occupational career is to increase the accessibility of youth to institutions of higher education, through increased junior college expansion, and expanded scholarship, aid, and loan programs. The "credential," so necessary in the present and future economy, can only be obtained through some articulation with the higher education system. A fundamental challenge to new career programs is the establishment of these linkages.

---

[33]Grant Venn, *Man, Education and Work* (Washington, D.C.: American Council on Education, 1964), pp. 171–72.

*Local schools must develop means for generating and sustaining commit-
ment of youth to the education system and to community standards of
behavior.*

We contended at many points that lack of commitment to the legitimate
system is one of the individual experiences contributing to the delinquency
among some youth. We also argued that lack of commitment is partly produced by educational failure and a sense of meaninglessness of school
demands and rewards in relation to future payoff. Beyond that, however,
we contended that persistent subordination and exclusion of youth from
meaningful participation in the educational process is an independent condition generating a lack of commitment. We noted that a resulting need is to
create means for integrating youth into the educational planning, decision-
making, control, and instructional processes wherever possible.

EDUCATIONAL PLANNING AND DECISION MAKING. Earlier we mentioned that youth should be included in curriculum planning and in the
development of new teaching approaches. As we will discuss in greater
detail later, we also believe that students should be included in new units
within the schools for "monitoring" educational operations and outcomes;
for continually developing new plans for innovation and experimentation;
and for bringing the school and community closer together. Moreover, we
contend that there are many faculty committees dealing with routine operational matters as well as planning and decision making to which students
could very well belong and contribute.

Involvement of youth in educational planning and decision making,
which could extend into almost any areas we could think of, with the exception of finances, must be full and meaningful involvement. Students must
not be relegated to positions of second class citizenship, as at present, but
must be perceived, treated, and listened to with respect and openness.
Further, participation must not be restricted to "good," "smart," or college-
bound students, as is usually the case now, but must be opened to all students. As we will see later, those who are persistently excluded because they
are behavior problems or underachievers are the very ones most in need
of being integrated into such legitimate activities.

EXERCISE OF AUTHORITY. Most schools have some form of student
government which is intended to develop responsibility and to build in student opinion and influence in the formulation and enforcement of school
rules regarding conduct of student affairs and individual pupil behavior.
Usually, however, student governments are tools of the administration and
have little independent influence. Areas of responsibility are restricted and
minor. We believe that student government represents a potentially useful

mechanism for genuine—not superficial—involvement of students in educational decision making, and especially in the formulation and enforcement of rules of student behavior. While many schools have "student courts," they usually are given jurisdiction only over minor violations, and important decisions regarding school responses to student misbehavior are left to teachers, counselors, or administrators. We believe that students should be given a greater influence in these matters. This is especially true of students who have violated school rules in the past.

PARTICIPATION IN EXTRACURRICULAR ACTIVITIES. Another means by which potentially or currently uncommitted youth can become involved in legitimate activities and interests is through participation in extracurricular activities. Research by Schafer indicates that students who participate in extracurricular activities receive higher grades and drop out less often than those who do not participate, even after other factors are controlled.[34] More intensive study of the same sample by Schafer and Armer reveals that athletic participation by itself has a positive effect.[35] Even after father's occupation, intelligence test score, curriculum, and junior high school grades were held constant, athletes dropped out less often and received somewhat higher grades. Moreover, Rehberg and Schafer also found in a different sample that, even after other factors were controlled, athletes went to college more often than nonathletes.[36] Of even more significance in both studies is that the positive effect of athletic participation was especially marked among lower income, noncollege bound students—who are the very ones most susceptible to delinquency. It is not surprising, then, that Polk found that delinquents participated less often than nondelinquents.[37] We contend, therefore, that not only athletic but other extracurricular activities should be extended to broader numbers of youth. In part this means that current clubs and organizations—which are overwhelmingly middle-class oriented—should be diversified to include activities that have an appeal for lower income youth as well. It is our contention that involvement of potentially delinquent youth in such activities can be an important mechanism for increasing students' attraction to school.

---

[34]Walter E. Schafer, *Student Careers in Two Public High Schools: A Comparative Cohort Analysis* (Unpublished doctoral dissertation, University of Michigan, 1965), Chaps. 4, 6.

[35]Walter E. Schafer and J. Michael Armer, "Athletes are not Inferior Students," *Trans-action* 6 (November 1968): 21–26, 61–62.

[36]Richard A. Rehberg and Walter E. Schafer, "Participation in Interscholastic Athletics and College Expectations," *American Journal of Sociology* 63 (May 1968): 732–40.

[37]Kenneth Polk and F. Lynn Richmond, "Those Who Fail," Ch. 5 in this book. See also Chapter 7 by Schafer.

PARTICIPATION IN INSTRUCTIONAL PROCESS. As we pointed out earlier, students are generally forced to take a passive role in the teacher-learning process and are given little opportunity to become actively and meaningfully engaged. There are several ways in which a more active involvement might be fostered. One is use of older students as teachers of younger pupils, both during regular class sessions as aides, as suggested before; and after school as tutors. Mobilization for Youth in New York City recently released findings of their experiment in employment of tenth and eleventh grade students as after-school tutors of underachieving fourth and fifth grade students.[38] Tutors are recruited through a fairly extensive publicity campaign in the area served by Mobilization for Youth. A major emphasis of the program is on training, which occurs during a two-week period prior to the start of tutoring. Preservice training focuses on goals, organization of the program, duties of the tutor, and kinds of students and problems likely to be encountered. After tutors begin, they are supervised by regular teachers, through a weekly meeting.

The actual tutorial activities involve giving help to younger students in completing assignments and in improving their language skills. As the younger student improves in language skill, he progressively moves to more difficult materials. After the program has gotten underway at the beginning of the year, the typical tutoring session consists of 30 minutes of homework, 30 minutes of reading, 15–30 minutes of games and recreation, and 15 minutes of refreshments and roll-taking.

Fortunately, MFY built a research design into this experiment enabling fairly precise assessments of outcomes, both for the pupils and the tutors. Although no differences were found in reading improvement among pupils receiving two hours of tutoring a week, those receiving four hours per week did make significant gains. It is also reported that . . . "although these results in pupil improvement were gratifying, the impact on reading levels of tutors was astonishing, for the experimental tutors made more than 100 percent gains over the controlled tutors in reading achievement."

Clearly, then, involvement of students in the instructional process can have considerable effect on the achievement of tutors, and consequently on their interest and commitment to school. We suggest that this may be an important means for deterring tendencies toward delinquency and for generating or sustaining commitment to education and the wider legitimate system. As we will see later, special efforts must be made to channel delinquent or delinquency-prone youth into such programs.

The above recommendation is one of a number we are offering which are based on the general principle that one of the most effective ways to respond to marginal or deviant students is to actively engage them in the

---

[38]Cloward, "Studies in Tutoring."

educational process. This principle also underlies the proposal that public school instruction in general be modified to place a greater emphasis on active rather than passive participation in the learning process. Use of programmed learning; exploration of issues and problems that are immediately relevant to the student and the community, with greater use of newspapers; work-oriented study for part of the day—these are all examples of means for actively engaging students.

A recent development that can serve the same end is the use of games. In a recent report of the development and evaluation of games, Boocock and Coleman began by noting three defects in secondary education: . . . ."it teaches for a long distance future"; . . . ."the enforced, involuntary character of the curriculum"; and . . . ."the dual role of the teachers as both teacher and judge."[39] One way of dealing with these defects, they argue, is to conjoin . . . ."a very old form of activity, games, with a very new one, simulated environments."[40] They contend that there are several advantages of the use of games in simulated situations. First, it brings the future into the present; second, games are by nature a motivating device; and third, "games are self-judging, the outcome decides the winner, and the player knows that he has won or lost by his own actions."[41]

Three particular games were developed and evaluated: a life career game, a legislative game, and a community disaster game. Each simulates a realistic situation and enables the student to participate in roles and activities that become highly involving and at the same time enable him to learn specific pieces of information and skills that would be much more difficult for him to learn thoroughly from a textbook, lecture, or even discussion.

Boocock and Coleman evaluated the effects of each game with an experimental-control design. They report:

> Experimentation with three games indicates that they are powerful motivators and that students can learn from them. In addition to specific information acquired from playing a particular game there seems to be a general effect, in the nature of gaining a broader or more accurate image of the kinds of environment which students will face as adults. This can take the form of a realization of complexity of future social situations which players had thought little about previously, a greater sense of being able to cope with one's environment and a greater interest in trying to do so, or a greater ability to see a complex social situation as an organized whole.[42]

This device seems to us, as well as to Boocock and Coleman, to have particular merit as a means for involving students who are not achieving up to potential or are not highly motivated.

---

[39]Sarane S. Boocock and James S. Coleman, "Games With Simulated Environments in Learning," *Sociology of Education* (Summer 1966): pp. 216–217.
[40]Ibid., p. 218.
[41]Ibid., p. 219.
[42]Ibid., p. 235.

We have some evidence that these games may be particularly valuable with the kinds of students who are not performing well under present educational conditions, but this has not been studied systematically.[43]

INSTRUCTION ABOUT LAW AND ORDER. Earlier, we saw that a frequent argument is that delinquency results from lack of respect for law and order and that the way to reduce delinquency is to teach such respect. We further noted that while delinquents do exhibit lack of commitment in the form of disdain for community laws and law enforcement agencies, this attitude is in turn linked to certain other circumstances and experiences of such youth. Therefore, we contend that efforts to change attitudes will be unlikely to have very much effect by themselves unless simultaneous efforts are made to reduce pressures toward delinquency. The other side of the coin, however, is that while efforts are made to change wider social conditions that generate delinquent tendencies, efforts must be made to develop attitudes in the individual that are supportive of law and order and of conforming behavior. One means for attaining that end is effectively to instruct in the public schools about the legal and law enforcement systems. Such instruction, especially when accompanied by other changes proposed in this paper, might both deter the development of delinquent tendencies and reduce delinquent acts among youth who have been delinquent in the past.

The immediate objective of such instruction should be twofold: (1) development of an understanding of social and psychological sources of crime and delinquency; and (2) development of an understanding of the background; rationale and operation of the legal and law enforcement systems. The longer-term objectives should be the development of motivation toward conformity and of the ability to use legal means to realize one's own interests. Before suggesting specific outlines and content, it is imperative to call attention to several pitfalls that must be avoided. First, all efforts must be made to avoid moralizing to students with lecture methods about how sacred laws are and how evil it is to break them. Second, instructors must avoid trying to deceive students, especially in the urban slums, with glib portrayals of the benign character of the law and police, when in reality the law and the local policemen are often anything but allies. Third, teachers must steer away from dwelling on abstract statements of principles and ideals, without reference to meaningful and relevant problems, issues and events. Fourth, students must not be forced into a passive role; rather, the teaching-learning process must be so designed that students are given the chance to become actively engaged in the search for important questions and answers.

Having stated these caveats, let us move on to raise the positive question of how such instruction might be organized and what might be taught.

---

[43]Ibid., p. 236.

We suggest that instruction begin, though not end, in the eighth or ninth grade, since it is at about this age when students often begin to fall into trouble. Moreover, eventual dropouts are usually still in school during these years. Attention to law and order could either be included within existing civics or government courses as a separate unit for several weeks or as a continuing matter of concern; or it could constitute a separate course.

Two alternative approaches might be followed. One would begin with an examination of general and abstract issues and principles: Why do men have laws? Why do men commit crimes? What is the individual's responsibility to the state? How do laws originate? From these general concerns questions and answers about particular, concrete problems and events would derive. The other approach would be inductive rather than deductive, in that the class would generalize from immediate problems and events to larger principles and issues. We advocate the second approach, which in our estimation is more likely to engage students and to provide instruction that will influence their behavior.

This approach would rely primarily on newspaper reports or direct experiences of pupils or families in raising issues and pursuing answers. Below are several examples of incidents that might be used as levers for examining pertinent topics.

1. A student describes a series of grievances his parents have against their landlord. The class might then explore issues like the following: Is the landlord violating any laws? What is the rationale behind these laws? What legal alternatives are open to the parents? How might they contact a lawyer? What would he do and why? What sequence of legal steps would be taken? What alternative outcomes might they follow from their action? How would such outcomes compare with illegal or extralegal actions by the parents?

2. Two gangs in the school have had a series of "rumbles" in recent weeks. Why did the gangs form in the first place? What motivates the members? What laws are being violated? Why do the laws exist? What are alternative outcomes of continued conflict? What is the role of the police? Why have they taken such courses of action? What constraints and mandates do police operate under? Why? What alternatives are open to a particular policeman? What takes place behind the scenes in the police department? What might the students themselves do to prevent rumbles?

3. The community was rocked by a series of riots during the previous summer. What underlying conditions in the community produced the riots? What incidents precipitated them? How do these conditions and incidents compare with those in other riot-plagued cities? What social changes might lessen the chances of riots in the future? What sequence of events occur before, during, and after the riots? What about the racial overtones, if present? What laws were violated? How and why did these laws come into existence? What are the economic, social and political consequences of the riots? How are individual students affected? What was the role of the police? What rationale underlay their behavior? What alternatives were open to them?

4. The night before, vandals broke most of the windows in the school. What are possible explanations for such behavior? What laws were violated? What are the consequences for the school in terms of inconvenience and expense? How are the students themselves indirectly affected? How are the school and the police responding? Why? How might such behavior be prevented in the future?

5. A student saw a policeman arrest a suspected thief on the way to school. What rights did the man being arrested have? What actions did the policeman have the right to take? What constraints did he operate under? If the question of police brutality is raised, what foundation is there in fact? What about police brutality in general? What is the legal process through which the suspected criminal will be taken? What contingencies exist at each point? How and why did that legal process develop?

These, then, are several among many possible examples of incidents that might be used as means for exploring problems and principles in crime and delinquency, the legal system, and law enforcement practices and procedures. As in other courses, instruction is likely to be enriched and made more meaningful if, in exploring these issues, teachers utilize community expertise: policemen, judges, social workers, probation officers, lawyers, and even criminals or excriminals. Each of these should be used with the explicit understanding that they will be open to the probes and inquiries of students. In this way, chances are all the greater that students will be interested and engaged and that instruction will be related to current circumstances and experiences.

Another alternative that should be explored is the use of games for learning about these matters. Especially when supplemented with the above design, games are likely to result in realistic, useful, and interesting learning experiences.

Implementation of these proposals requires attention to curriculum development and to appropriate training of teachers for such courses. Local school districts, especially in the cities, should encourage and support efforts by administrators and teachers to plan and develop further such instruction and materials. At all points, community resources and students should be involved. In addition, advanced law students might be used. Funds proposed above for curriculum development and continuing reeducation to teachers might be used for these purposes.

Means must be developed for recapturing, reequipping, recommitting, and reintegrating students who fall behind or deviate from school or community standards of behavior.

ELIMINATION OF EXCLUSION-ORIENTED RESPONSES. We have contended that one of the ways the school inadvertently contributes to delinquency is through its responses to students in trouble. We have contended that students who misbehave often tend to be labeled and sanctioned in such a way that they develop private and public identities as deviants and are treated punitively or are excluded from future opportunities to become engaged in legitimate interests and activities. The first step toward making the school's responses more positive and effective is for teachers, schools, and groups of teachers and schools to closely reexamine their current assumptions about students' misbehavior and about existing procedures and practices for responding to them. Special ad hoc efforts should be made in every school, district, and state in this regard. Teachers and groups of teachers should closely scrutinize their own objectives and assumptions in sanctioning students inside the classroom, and administrators, teachers, and counselors should look at more serious sanctions imposed outside the classroom. It is imperative that both parents and students be included in such efforts.

Steps must then be taken to develop alternative labeling and sanctioning practices that will avoid unnecessary labeling and punitive sanctions; and that will reduce the chances that students will be pushed away and denied further legitimate opportunities. Specifically, we suggest that corporal punishment, public and degrading sanctioning rituals, permanent special classes for troublemakers, denial of chances to participate in extracurricular and other activities, and other punitive and exclusion-oriented responses be eliminated. At a more formal level, we believe truants should be made the responsibility of the school and should not be shunted off to juvenile courts. Truancy is, after all, an educational problem and should be made the responsibility of educators, who will then be forced to ask why the school is so unattractive to some youths.

DEVELOPMENT OF POSITIVE RESPONSES. At the same time that steps are taken to eliminate practices that are likely to aggravate rather than alleviate delinquent tendencies, simultaneous efforts must be made to channel these students back into the mainstream of the educational system and to reequip and recommit them for positive educational development. In moving toward specific proposals in this regard, we begin by urging that schools avoid "early identification" merely for the sake of early identification. Too often predelinquents, potential failures, or likely behavior problems are publicly identified, ostensibly for the purpose of mobilizing school resources toward heading off deviant or failing tendencies, when in reality such positive efforts are never forthcoming or are inadequate, with the result that those who have been "identified early" remain "identified" in the eyes of teachers and peers but never receive any benefits. We urge that students be "identified" only when they will receive remedial or "rehabilitative" services in the near future. In that way, the hazards of identification are likely to be offset by the gains from special attention.

If the school is to take seriously its charge to "rescue" students in trouble, attention must be given to the creation of new mechanisms for channeling such youth back into the educational process. In most schools, this is no one's responsibility, though it may be shared by interested teachers, counselors, or administrators. In some schools, social workers are assigned this responsibility, though too often they are narrowly "clinically-oriented," rather than educationally-oriented. There is a need, therefore, for new roles or units whose responsibility it is to guide deviant students into particular programs, classes, or channels; and to mobilize school and community resources in his interest.

One suggestion is an analogue of the ombudsman who would be relatively autonomous from administrators and who would essentially serve the interests of the student. He would not only help the student become re-engaged in education but would be his advocate in relating to teachers, counselors, or administrators. For example, if a student had special difficulties getting along with a particular teacher, the ombudsman would mediate in an attempt to develop insights and skills in both persons. At the same time, he would have the power to plan the student's program and educational goals for a subsequent period of time. Moreover, he would serve as a constant source of criticism and innovation in the school.

Attention should be given by teacher training institutions, professional groups, and local educators to the operational feasibility of such a proposal and to viable means for training such persons.

An alternative mechanism is the creation of a "student advice center" within each school, consisting of teachers, counselors, administrators, and other students which would be available not only to students in trouble but to all students for advice in dealing with educational or behavioral difficulties.[44] Such a unit might be empowered with the authority to direct students having difficulties into those programs or classes deemed beneficial. It is imperative, however, that the student himself be included in such decisions.

There are at least two ways in which deviant students should be reintegrated into the educational process. First, efforts must be made to channel students in trouble into programs proposed earlier in this chapter that are available but not compulsory to all students. That is, intensive efforts must be made to direct them into career-oriented work-study programs; curriculum planning and innovative activities; groups concerned with formulation of school rules; activities relating to the control of younger students; tutoring and aide programs; and so forth. When students have academic problems, special efforts must be made to get them into tutoring or aide programs. When they are frequent violators of school rules, special efforts should be

---

[44] We are indebted to Virginia Burns, Office of Juvenile Delinquency, United States Department of Health, Education, and Welfare for this proposal.

made to direct them into positions of responsibility and authority. These responses represent a form of expanded, rather than restricted, opportunities.

Second, these programs and efforts must be supplemented with additional classes or programs for reaching troublesome students, pulling them back, and reequipping them for achievement and conformity. That is, such pupils must not be entirely isolated and set apart, but added efforts must be made through small classes, group counseling, or whatever, to deal in a positive way with the motivational, interpersonal, or academic difficulties that lead such youth to underachievement or misbehavior. Such classes or groups, which might in part be handled by parental or student aides, would meet for, say, a single period per day to focus on such things as reading difficulties, how to get along with (or tolerate) a particular teacher, how to take tests, what to do when another student "eggs you on," and so forth. The teacher or aide in charge of each group might also mediate between particular members and particular teachers.

Bringing deviant students together in this way, which has been tried in various forms in Ohio, Michigan, California, and elsewhere, has the danger of publicly or privately confirming deviant identities. This danger can be offset, however, by mobilizing collective support around change efforts and by dealing in a positive way with students' problems.[45] Unless intensified, not weakened, efforts are made to "rescue" deviant students, this supplementary type program should be avoided. Too often such an effort deteriorates into another form of separation and custodialship.

The key to both kinds of responses is that students are pulled back, rather than pushed away, and opportunities are created for alternative educational experiences that will enable the student to develop and to become committed to learning and conformity. Another way in which the schools can make alternative experiences available is by allowing students, who either become intolerable to the school or "get fed up" with it, to leave school, although under close and continuing guidance, for a time to work, with the proviso that they remain in the school's charge and that they return after the specified period has elapsed. . . .

---

[45]For example, see Robert D. Vinter and Rosemary C. Sarri, "Malperformance in the Public School: A Group Work Approach," *Social Work* 10 (January, 1965): 3–13; Donald A. Davis, *Personnel and Guidance Journal* 40 (May, 1962): 799–802; Arthur Goldberg in Staten Webster (ed.), *The Disadvantaged Learner: Educating the Disadvantaged Learner* (San Francisco: Chandler Publishing Co., Inc., 1966), p. 626; Nason E. Hall, Jr., in Webster, Ibid., p. 631; Don T. Delmet and Harry Smallenburg, in John Curtis Gowan and George D. Demos (eds), *The Disadvantaged and Potential Dropouts, Comprehensive Educational Programs: A Book of Readings* (Springfield, Ill.: Charles C. Thomas, 1966), p. 462.

REINTEGRATION OF DROPOUTS. Special efforts to reintegrate dropouts have been tried in Orange County, California, Los Angeles, and elsewhere.[46] Both these efforts seem to have been effective in returning, retaining, and reeducating dropouts. We propose that schools assign a counselor or other staff person the job of actively keeping track of students and mobilizing the most appropriate means for facilitating their community adjustment while out of school and for eventually bringing them back into the educational system. While the school would incur added expenditures in the serious implementation of this proposal, it must be recognized that such expenditures would probably be no more than the costs to the school if such students had remained in school. On this basis, as well as on the even more defensible ground that it is the school's responsibility, we urge that new means be developed for "rescuing" dropouts.

COORDINATION OF PROFESSIONAL PERSPECTIVES. As noted in an earlier section, the effectiveness of both classroom teachers and ancillary personnel, such as counselors, social workers, and psychologists, is often severely impaired by fragmentation resulting from diverging rather than converging objectives, perspectives, and activities in relation to students in trouble. In order to minimize this difficulty, we propose that local schools and school districts do what is necessary to insure a coherent and integrated thrust in responding to failure and nonconformity.

A specific means is the widespread decentralization of special service programs, so that social workers, coaching teachers, and psychologists are based at local schools or at a set of adjacent schools.[47] This would insure an emphasis on local problems and would be likely to keep special service personnel closer to educationally relevant problems and goals. Another mechanism is the creation of a "Special Service Committee" in each school, made up of classroom teachers, administrators, counselors, special service personnel, and students. This group would be charged with assessing the difficulties of a classroom or category of youngsters and arriving at a collective and unified plan of action for the next term or year. It would also have the responsibility of reviewing and acting upon relevant information pro-

---

[46]For example see Ralph C. Hickman, *California Education* 2 (December 1964): 5–9; Betty W. Ellis, Isaac H. McClelland and Samuel W. Harper, *Journal of Secondary Education* (April, 1965). For collections of reports of other programs, see Gowan and Demos, *The Disadvantaged and Potential Dropouts . . . ,* and Webster, *The Disadvantaged Learner.*

[47]Eugene Litwak, Frank M. Maple, Henry J. Meyer, Jack Rothman, Rosemary C. Sarri, Walter E. Schafer and Robert D. Vinter, in "A Design for Utilization of Special Services in the Detroit Public Schools," (Ann Arbor, Michigan: University of Michigan School of Social Work [mimeo], 1965).

vided by the Department of Educational Assessment, a new unit to be discussed later in the chapter.

We submit that a closer linkage between noneducational and educational perspectives and activities through such means as these would be likely to result in a more effective response to students in trouble, and, therefore, in the reduction and control of delinquency.

EXPANSION OF CURRENT COUNSELING AND SPECIAL SERVICE RESOURCES AND PROGRAMS. Most of the changes we have proposed call for "structural" alterations rather than for a simple strengthening of existing staff and approaches. Moreover, our analysis underscores the importance of modifying basic educational conditions for delinquency prevention and control. At the same time, we recognize that effective counseling and special service programs can play a key part in the school's responses to students with academic or behavioral difficulty. Within our perspective, the role of the counselor is changed from the situation where his task is to seek to adjust youth to a hostile and meaningless educational experience. Instead, given the structural alterations that have been suggested elsewhere, the counselor becomes a vital agent in the process of phasing the student into the program. Even if all the changes we have called for were provided, many low income and other youth would experience problems in adapting themselves to the educational system, problems that lie in the domain of counseling services.

Means must be created for bringing about closer cooperation and coordination between the school and families and agencies in the community.

As we noted before, efforts of both the school and various community agencies in responding to youth in trouble are often hampered by lack of coordination and complementarity of various agencies and organizations. Too often the schools and juvenile courts, police, social service agencies, and mental health clinics are unaware and unconcerned about what each other is doing in relation to particular pupils or categories of pupils. Therefore, new mechanisms are needed for sharing of information and coordination of various activities. Creation of an overlapping unit with representatives of various organizations is one possible type of mechanism. Another is creation of a new school-based, community-school coordinating role which would have this responsibility assigned to it.

An aspect of school-community cooperation mentioned before is retention by the schools of many of the responsibilities which now go to other agencies. Of particular significance is that truancy should be handled by the school rather than juvenile courts. In addition, application of the principle of maximum responsibility by the schools for socialization and rehabilitation of youth call for greater mental health services within the schools for serious cases of emotional disturbance. Although the danger still exists that clinical services will be isolated from more central educational concerns, the chances of this are less if such services are offered within the school rather than by other community agencies.

IMPROVING SCHOOL-FAMILY COOPERATION. If one of the factors hampering effective instruction, especially in lower income areas, is school-family distance, then mechanisms must be created for decreasing that distance and for fostering better cooperation. This means that the school must develop a more effective "outreach" for changing family and neighborhood conditions that are antithetical to educational objectives and activities, at the same time that efforts must be made to draw parents closer to the school. We propose several specific means for increasing school-family cooperation.

SCHOOL-COMMUNITY ADVISORY PANEL. Attached to each school should be a School-Community Advisory Panel consisting of parents and students.[48] This panel would represent the interests of parents and students served by a local school and would essentially oversee and react to school conditions and practices. Members would be elected by local parents and students. The panel would be empowered to request the local Department of Educational Assessment for certain information about school practices and outcomes, and administrators and teachers would be expected to take seriously the reactions and recommendations of this group. Such recommendations would pertain to such things as curriculum change, relationships with parents, employment problems, community use of school facilities, and so forth.

Creation of such a panel in all schools has the merit of opening up avenues of communication and influence between school and parents and of giving parents a sense of accessibility and involvement in the educational system—accessibility and involvement which is now often lacking, especially in lower income areas, either objectively or in terms of parents' perception. In addition, it has the merit that the school would become more visible and open to community surveillance and hence there would be greater pressure on the school to make needed adaptations and changes. Thus, an added element of innovation would be developed. Both greater public accountability and greater emphasis on innovation will also be fostered by new quality control and innovating units which will be proposed later in the chapter.

THE COMMUNITY SCHOOL. Another means of drawing pupils and parents closer to the school is the community school which remains open from morning to night and through the entire week and year for various educational as well as noneducational activities for parents and students.

---

[48]Ibid.

This is especially likely to be a potent means for drawing parents in depressed areas closer to the schools, since they are most in need of educational and social programs that might be added to the traditional six hours per day program for pupils. Additional extracurricular and educational activities should also be extended to pupils as means for intensifying educational services and for drawing them closer to the schools. Finally, other social agencies might use school facilities during evening and weekend hours for extending services to an area. The intent of all such efforts is to cement the commitment of the community to the educational enterprise and process.

Federal funds should be appropriated for the development of quality control in education.

If it is true that current lags in education result from the failure of the schools to assess themselves and their "outputs," then a very important change to be made is the creation of a structure and machinery for the routine collection, processing, analysis, and use of information. We urge that the Federal government avoid becoming directly involved in "monitoring" at the local level in order to insure protection of the principles of pluralism and decentralization in education. But we do urge appropriation of Federal funds for the training and initial hiring of personnel, purchase of equipment, and establishment of facilities for the creation, at the local or district level of new units for monitoring the local educational program.

With such funds, each school district would create a new Department of Educational Assessment that would have access to all records of pupils and staff performance in each school. It would be responsible only to the superintendent and would be autonomous in authority from personnel in the schools from which it collected information. This department would be charged with routinely feeding information back to each school, to departments that cut across schools, and to higher level administrators and policy makers. In order to lessen the chances that information would simply be used to defend current practices or would be filed away without being built into the decision-making and planning process, each school might have a committee made up of teachers, special service personnel and administrators that would be charged by the superintendent with closely examining feedback information, and with submitting a regular report on its use of those data. In addition, legislation might require that relevant information be made public (in an aggregate fashion) so that the schools' performance would be under greater public surveillance. Moreover, the School-Community Advisory Panel might be given the authority to request certain information that is not regularly collected or made public, as long as such data referred to matters of ligitimate concern to the Panel.

While the actual collection and use of feedback or quality-control data would be anchored into the local schools or district, procedures might be created whereby the state department of education could collect information over the entire state. If this were done on a standardized basis, data on a national scale might be collected for certain purposes through the state department of education, although the political risks would be high.

Among the information collected in this way would be information referring specificallly to the performance and progress of groups of pre-delinquent and delinquent students. For that reason, this proposal has direct relevance for delinquency prevention and control. Of greater importance, however, is that the broader, underlying educational conditions that produce failure, irrelevancy, and exclusion would be subject to closer scrutiny and to greater change.

Local schools and school districts with the support of federal and state funds must develop means for fostering and supporting local innovation.

We pointed out earlier that a second factor producing rigidity, inflexibility, and lag in education is the failure of teacher training institutions and the local school district to encourage and reward innovation and inventiveness. We submit that change must not and cannot entirely begin and be carried out from above but must be initiated and implemented in part in local school districts and in local school buildings. Therefore, we propose that much more emphasis in rewarding and promoting school personnel be placed on innovativeness and experimentation. This criterion should be applied to groups of schools, single schools, and teams within schools as well as to individuals, in order to assume collective concern with change and a maximum of coherence in innovation.

In addition, we propose an allocation of funds by local districts for released time for individuals and groups of individuals to consider current patterns of operation and to propose new patterns. Feedback information from Departments of Educational Assessment would be highly valuable for this purpose. Funds might even be provided for the hiring of an entire or partial school staff for a summer period to develop a coherent and well-developed plan of change for the next year or years.

Finally, we propose the creation of a unit or position (perhaps within the Department of Educational Assessment) charged with the responsibility of keeping abreast of latest research and developments in other school systems and with the responsibility of proposing local application of such development and information. In addition, it would be responsible for development of plans for use of federal funds.

We again submit that juvenile delinquency has its roots in the fundamental failure of the school to adapt to outside changes and that so long as that failure persists, delinquency, as well as other school-related problems will persist. Therefore, we urge the development of effective means, such as those suggested here, for increasing the capability of school systems to change.

INDEX